TEACHING THE BIBLE

TEACHING THE BIBLE

ESPECIALLY IN
SECONDARY SCHOOLS

BY

A. VICTOR MURRAY

President of Cheshunt College, Cambridge
Emeritus Professor of Education,
University of Hull

CAMBRIDGE
AT THE UNIVERSITY PRESS
1955

CAMBRIDGE
UNIVERSITY PRESS

University Printing House, Cambridge CB2 8BS, United Kingdom

Cambridge University Press is part of the University of Cambridge.

It furthers the University's mission by disseminating knowledge in the pursuit of education, learning and research at the highest international levels of excellence.

www.cambridge.org
Information on this title: www.cambridge.org/9781107480377

© Cambridge University Press 1955

First published 1955
First paperback edition 2014

A catalogue record for this publication is available from the British Library

ISBN 978-1-107-48037-7 Paperback

To

WINIFRED

CHRISTINE, JOHN
RUTH AND DAVID

PREFACE

The aim of this book is to supply a practical answer to a very practical question, namely, in what ways does the teaching of Scripture differ from the teaching of history on the one hand and the teaching of English on the other? Differences cannot be stated without at the same time indicating similarities, and it is obvious that as the Bible is both history and literature its use as a text-book must involve both of these teaching techniques. It is, however, 'more than' history and literature, and it is just the definition of 'more than' which creates the practical problem. There are many excellent teachers of other school subjects, literature for instance, who when they come to teach the Bible interpret this 'more than' by tacking some moral of their own on to a Bible story—a method they would never employ with Milton or Burke. I have even heard teachers whose own point of view is that of the best historical scholarship drop it altogether when teaching the Bible and, on the ground that Scripture is 'more than' history, fall back on a method which presupposes an uncritical verbalism.

All this indicates a certain confusion in the teaching of the subject, a confusion which is also present in the minds of those teachers to whom Scripture is no more than history or literature even if as much. And the way out is not a matter of technique alone, at any rate not the technique of the individual lesson. It concerns this but it concerns still more the interrelation of lesson technique and a general attitude to the Bible itself.

The teaching of Scripture has this among other peculiarities, that it is entirely concerned with the exposition of one authoritative book. With no other subject is this the case. Biology teachers do not spend a year in weekly discussions chapter by chapter of Darwin's *Origin of Species*, nor are historians confined to the classroom exposition of, say, Gibbon's *Decline and Fall of the Roman Empire*. The canons of Biblical exposition therefore, both literary and historical, must be well understood, for they determine the attitude of the teacher as well as the conduct of every lesson. I do not see how it is possible to discuss the teaching of Scripture apart from this general reference. There is indeed good warrant for this in the Bible itself. To the Prophets every event had an eternal as well as a temporal significance and *both* were important. The principles that govern the action of God in human affairs are to be found in the concrete specific event, which, without this reference, may well appear completely meaningless. To many people, however, the teaching of the Bible seems easy because 'all you need to do' (so I have heard it stated) is to retell the Bible stories in your own words. To many others it is exceedingly difficult because they are conscious that more is expected of them than a history lesson, and yet they do not know *how much* more. I have had both of these groups in mind in Sections A and B of this book as well as the moralizers whom I have already mentioned. They each include many keen people, often constant attenders at summer schools for teachers, anxious to teach the subject well, without doing violence to modern scholarship on the one hand or the personal appeal to heart and conscience on the other.

Section C is concerned with strategy and Section D with tactics, or, to put it in other words, Section C deals with the Scripture syllabus and Section D with the lesson. The relation between these two is again as important as the relation of both of them to the first two sections. The earnest teacher is far too apt to make the lesson the unit and to feel that each lesson must have an 'application'. This straining after effect (for that is what it is, even though it be unconscious) breeds a certain uniformity of treatment which could be avoided if more attention were paid to the course as a whole. And for this purpose there must be a certain amount of architecture about the scheme. It must (to use a modern illustration) be three-dimensional and not a series of pictures observed in the flat wherein the succeeding picture blots out the one before it. One way of ensuring this I have discussed in Chapter x, where it is suggested that in the course itself there should be some re-interpretation at a later age of material learned earlier. This is fully in line with the practice of the Old Testament writers themselves.

PREFACE

In this book I have kept strictly to the teaching of the Bible itself and have not discussed the teaching of doctrine or Church history or morality. On these matters I have expressed some views in an earlier book *Education into Religion*. It is important, however, to realize that knowledge of the Bible is our chief aim, and that while 'lives of great men' or 'doctrines of the faith' have their proper place in religious education, they ought not to be allowed to replace the study of the primary documents of our religion.

The chapters of the book have arisen out of experience in teaching Scripture to boys, and in over twenty years of the training of teachers in Birmingham and in Hull. The first draft of the book had the benefit of the criticism of Miss Doris Bulley, B.D., Scripture Mistress at the Cambridge Central Secondary Modern Girls' School, for whose practical help I am very grateful. The final draft has been examined in close detail by the Headmaster of Rydal School, Colwyn Bay (Mr Donald Hughes), and his Chaplain (the Rev. Kenneth Underwood), who have made many suggestions which I have been glad to incorporate, and for which they have my sincere thanks.

A. V. M.

CAMBRIDGE
1 March 1955

CONTENTS

SECTION A

GENERAL PRINCIPLES

CHAPTER I

SOME PRELIMINARY CONSIDERATIONS

I THE SPECIAL NATURE OF SCRIPTURE TEACHING

It is an indication of how widely different the teaching of Scripture is from that of every other subject in the curriculum, that we needs must begin by presenting a case for teaching it at all. Even though it has been provided for in England by Act of Parliament and there are in use about two score 'agreed syllabuses of religious instruction', it is nevertheless far from being acceptable as a subject having a high educational value of its own, quite irrespective of its connexion with personal morality and the work of the Christian Church. And doubts arise in the minds of two quite different sets of people and for wholly opposite reasons. The first feel that it is a sacred subject, too sacred to be treated in the matter-of-fact way in which we tackle other subjects. Mathematics does not quicken the rate of the pulse, nor does History send up the temperature, but somehow it is assumed that Scripture does. There is an 'aura' about it which prevents the evolution of a sound method of teaching it, just because it is felt that it has so mystical a quality in itself that no method is needed.

The answer to this type of doubt is that, whatever may be the subjective disturbance in the teacher's own mind in handling this subject, the pupils' approach is not noticeably different from that towards any other subject. It is down in the syllabus to be taught, there is quite a considerable ground to be covered, and it is therefore just as well to work out a reasonably sound method of teaching it. And method, be it noticed, has two sides to it—tactics and strategy, in other words the technique of the individual lesson and the technique of planning the course. However much the contact with children in the Scripture lesson may excite the teacher and create in him an almost morbid fear of misusing his opportunity for influencing the child for his good, there can hardly be any such excitement about planning the term's work. Moreover, even if the teacher does feel like this, he cannot keep it up in every lesson unless he holds that in Scripture, as against other subjects, every lesson has to end with a 'moral'. He will be sore put to it to find a moral for some of the narrative passages of the Old Testament and he may do actual violence to the truth if he tries to wrest a moral from the stories of Jacob and David. He will be well advised to allow any 'moral' to take care of itself if it happens to be present at all.

The other type of doubter is the teacher to whom Scripture raises no personal problems at all. He is not expected to proselytize the ratepayers' children and therefore he can be completely 'objective'. Scripture is one subject among many. As a great deal of it is history, he can apply the technique of history teaching. Where the form of the subject-matter calls for it, he can use the technique of the 'appreciation' lesson in literature. History and literature cover all that need be taken notice of in the Scripture lesson, and no particular affirmation is required from the teacher himself.

This raises the whole question of whether there really is a separate technique for the teaching of Scripture. An earlier generation was content to believe that technique was in any case unnecessary, because all parts of the Bible were 'inspired', and the very words themselves had an effect on the soul of man no matter how they were presented. Today there are many who feel that with the coming of the historical method of studying the Bible the technique of teaching Scripture is in no way different from the teaching of history.

This is our problem, but it is the same kind of problem that earlier generations of teachers had to face when considering new subjects in the curriculum. The Clarendon Commission on the Public Schools (1861–4) considered the possibility of putting history into the curriculum. The Headmaster of Winchester, Dr Moberly, confessed: 'I wish we could teach more history, but as to teaching it in set lessons I should not know how to do it.' That is precisely how some people feel today about Scripture. The Commission reported:

> History, it is true, can never occupy as a distinct study, a large space in the course of instruction at a great classical school. To gain an elementary knowledge of history, little more is required than some sustained but not very laborious efforts of memory; it may therefore be acquired easily and without any mental exercise of much value,—which, however, is not a sufficient reason for not acquiring it.

History, however, has had to find its own specific justification and technique, and we have now had nearly a hundred years of experiment. Scripture will have to do the same, but at present there is a good deal of confusion concerning both method and aims. A quite competent teacher in a girl's grammar school in London with a B.D. to her credit, recently gave it as her considered opinion that the aim of Scripture teaching was to present a scheme of Christian theology, and so all her lessons were deliberately given a doctrinal twist. A not very intelligent view of Scripture teaching is that it inculcates moral standards and so may be relied upon to lessen juvenile delinquency. To some, church membership is the goal and therefore the Scripture classes must be linked in some way with a worshipping congregation—an aim which is not only clearly beyond the reach of the teacher in a county primary or secondary school, but also ignores the fact that the ratepayers' children are not sent to the day school to be attached to some particular church.

The educational case for Scripture and the qualifications for teaching it we shall consider in later chapters, but meanwhile we shall get light on the subject if we remember that, as the Bible requires for its understanding not only knowledge but also the appreciation of a way of life, Scripture teaching must have in it something akin to the teaching of art as well as of the teaching of literary and historical subjects. This necessarily involves a much closer relation of the teacher to the subject and to the pupil than is absolutely necessary in these other subjects. A teacher of art must be a practitioner in art, for he has to illustrate for the pupil what it means to him and not just how to do it. 'Worthwhileness' is something which somehow he has to get across to the pupil, and he cannot do that by mere insistence. He has somehow to demonstrate it.

At this point it is easy to be misunderstood, but it must not be forgotten that in the teaching of English also there is this necessary element of self-identification with the subject-matter. For instance, how could a man get across to a class the pathetic significance of Macbeth's outburst:

> Tomorrow, and tomorrow, and tomorrow,
> Creeps in this petty pace from day to day
> To the last syllable of recorded time,
> And all our yesterdays have lighted fools
> The way to dusty death....

if his only concern is with the bland comment of a school edition of the play: 'i.e. one morrow after another creeps on in this trivial daily progress till the last word is reached and the book of Time closed. While Time lasts a record of it is kept and the record will only cease when Time itself ceases'? *Macbeth* is a work of art and it requires artistic appreciation which in turn requires sympathy with the author and with the situation. Apart from this there is not a great deal of difference between 'learning *Macbeth*' and learning the multiplication table.

Similarly in history there is room for artistic appreciation. Motley had documentary justification for saying of William the Silent: 'As long as he lived, he was the guiding star of a whole brave nation, and when he died the little children cried in the streets'; but there is more in the statement than information—which over against the tremendous events of his reign might seem so trivial—there is a very powerful suggestion and to appreciate it requires an appropriate attitude of mind.

Now in the teaching of Scripture this need for self-identification is present all the while. It is not satisfied by drawing out a moral, nor by enforcing a doctrine, nor by the teacher himself being a professing Christian. It is satisfied only by an understanding of the author's meaning and an acceptance of its worthwhileness in the situation with which he deals. There is a *personal* demand made upon the teacher, and if he is unwilling to accept it he may teach the children the ancient Hebrew history, the life of Jeremiah and the travels of St Paul, but the real inwardness of the whole story as it appeared to the writer and to those who came after him, will be hid from him. The Bible is more than a book of history and literature, and it is more than a record of man's discovery of God and God's dealings with man. It is a book of religion and it is a book by which men have lived and died; and unless a teacher sees and appreciates the reason for this extraordinary fact, he will have missed the technique of teaching Scripture. What this means in terms of actual lessons we shall see later.

2 THE REVOLUTION IN BIBLE STUDY

The last hundred years have seen a revolution in Bible study. The old verbal inspiration theory has been discredited as being not only unscholarly but also as far too subjective. Let a reader take any modern commentary on the Bible, say Peake's or the S.P.C.K., and compare it with Matthew Henry or even Bishop Ellicott, and he will see how far we have come. Matthew Henry is often shrewd and stimulating—as when he notes the reason why God made woman out of the rib of man, not to be above him nor beneath him, but to be by his side, to be his equal—but his comments all accept the English version as it stands and they are of the nature of personal homiletic points. A good deal of Bible 'commentary' even today is of that nature. But with the coming of the historical method the primary task of the expositor is to find out what the author himself meant by what he says and what the people to whom it was addressed understood by it. This is indeed cardinal in any appreciation of the Bible. Apart from this it is simply a series of stories into which we can read any meaning of our own. And we may be sure that the author of the Garden of Eden story had no such view as that of Matthew Henry.

This position is of course taken for granted by any teacher who knows his subject. The historical method does not mean splitting up Genesis into fragments of different dates, insisting on three Isaiahs, casting doubt upon the Pastoral Epistles and refusing to identify the John of the Fourth Gospel with the John of the Apocalypse. Some of these may be the results of the method of approach but they are not that method itself. The historical method means putting the story back into its original setting and interpreting it in the light of that setting. In so doing we may find that its meaning *for us* is far more cogent than any subjective interpretation that we ourselves may read into it.

Nevertheless, between the Biblical scholar, and the ordinary citizen who sends his child to school, there is a very wide gap. It is due not merely to ignorance but to that kind of pseudo-knowledge which makes people content not to seek for further light. Distinguished scientists who in this regard are also 'ordinary citizens' persist in assuming that the Christian attitude to the Bible is precisely what it was in the eighteenth century. It has even happened that in the privacy of his own college room a physicist has been found writing an attack on views about the Bible which his next-door neighbour, a professor of Divinity, could have told him were no longer held by any theological faculty in a British university. If this is true of 'intellectuals' how much more is it true of the non-church-going public? 'God' and 'Christ' come into oaths, the word 'jeremiah' is taken as meaning a lugubrious person, jokes about Jonah in the whale's belly are not infrequent, and it is assumed that Christianity implies that the world was created in six days. Yet on the basis of such inaccurate and threadbare knowledge men will argue about the Bible with all the assurance of conviction. This is a fact for every teacher of Scripture to bear in mind. It is not that the children know nothing —it would be better if they did—but that they are told outside the school just enough to get it wrong. Much Scripture teaching fails

6

of its purpose because the teacher is unaware of the often vast distance that separates him from those whom he teaches. Questions which to the enlightened person are quite silly, such as the fatuous one 'Who was Cain's wife?' are by no means silly to other people. A great deal of elementary work needs to be done even with older children and many of the Agreed Syllabuses lay themselves open to criticism because they assume both a knowledge and a reasonableness which are often not present at all.

At the root of this is the fact that 'Scripture' is not just a school subject. It is the core of a complex of ideas, attitudes and social customs which all hang together. The most admirable work done in school may be completely neutralized by the sheer weight of opinion, or rather by the *mores*, of the home and neighbourhood. Father is often quite willing to accept what Johnny is told at school about shortened multiplication or the battle of Waterloo, but he thinks he knows better than Johnny about the Bible or the Church. More than ever, therefore, there is required of the teacher not only knowledge but a personal attitude as well. The teacher as a person is included in this neighbourhood group and in spite of himself his attitude to the group will affect his Scripture teaching and vice versa.

There is here an obvious diversity of aim between the Sunday school teacher and the day school teacher. The Sunday school teacher is a church member, that is to say, he belongs to a well-defined voluntary local group and wins his position by his status within that group. It is smaller—very much smaller—than the neighbourhood group and yet it is also larger because it is part of a denomination which covers the whole country. Moreover, in some denominations the local group itself has its position defined by the central authorities of the denomination. The Sunday school teacher's aim is to lead his pupils to become convinced Christians, accepting the Christian way of life as their own and becoming responsible members of the Church of Christ through the particular denomination represented by the Sunday school. The day school teacher has a miscellaneous class to deal with. They come from all kinds of homes and from many different denominations and from none. They are present under compulsion and the cost of their education is borne by the whole body of rate- and tax-payers. In England the voluntary schools established by denominations are able to have denominational teaching for children attached to their own church, but by reason of the fact that they receive grants-in-aid they have to make provision for others. This is usually done by teaching on the lines of the local Agreed Syllabus. The march of historical scholarship, however, and the greater understanding of the psychology of children have made it clear that the greater part of religious instruction need have no denominational slant at all, and many Church schools are content to use an Agreed Syllabus for *all* their children and to provide for denominational teaching along lines of worship rather than of doctrine. This is the easier to arrange since the Church of England is one of the parties to the Agreed Syllabus. Nevertheless, as the Church schools have a religious foundation they are able to equate their aims in religious teaching, at any rate for their own adherents, with those of the Sunday school. In the county schools, however, this obviously cannot be done. Yet for all children through the teaching of Scripture there is possible what Whitehead has called the vision of greatness[1] and the production of a sentiment of loyalty towards it. This in the last resort depends on persons and not on curricula, for it can be transmitted only from one person to another. Scripture, however, is an ideal means at the disposal of the school for such contacts to be established.

The historical method has thus made possible two things—the teaching of Scripture without denominational reference, and the formulation of Agreed Syllabuses. Scholarship knows no denominational or ideological barriers, and where they are imposed they discredit the scholars who impose them. When we look back on the bitter educational controversies in 1870 and 1902, it is astonishing to see how far the sober pursuit of truth on the one hand joined with a growing apathy on the other can produce results which quieten the religious passions of men. The Act of 1944, far more revolutionary in its proposals than the Acts of 1870 or

[1] *The Aims of Education*, a very wise book.

8

1902, went through Parliament with very little controversy on denominational lines. This position of course, is not taken up by Romanists to whom their own Church is the only valid interpreter of Scripture or by those Anglo-Catholics to whom Scripture is only ancillary to doctrine and tradition. There is, however, in all schools that receive grants from the State through the Local Education Authority a conscience clause providing for the withdrawal of children whose parents express their conscientious objection to the religious teaching of the school. Such a privilege is exercised mostly by Roman Catholics and by Jews. The existence of the privilege is, however, by most Englishmen viewed characteristically as a good reason for not exercising it.

The English Agreed Syllabuses are so called because they are the result of agreement among four parties—the Church of England, the Free Churches, the teachers and the Local Education Authority. We shall have to discuss them in some detail later. It is worthy of report that very rarely do decisions in the drafting committees go along party lines. Although the committees have been set up on a representative basis, they have in practice worked functionally and the voting, if any, has shown cross divisions of opinion.

The question is often asked whether Scripture ought to be an examined subject. The aura of sentiment that has surrounded the subject has often produced the feeling that to have examinations in this holy thing is somehow sacrilegious. This is surely a false reverence, and as far as the ordinary scholars are concerned, it is irrelevant. By the Act of 1944, Scripture is a statutory subject on a level with the rest of the curriculum. Moreover, the *content* of the Scripture syllabus is necessarily historical and literary, and it is possible to examine for knowledge and understanding of facts without anybody being required to register his personal religious convictions. To leave Scripture as the one subject that is never examined is to lower it in the estimation of the pupils, to prevent it being taken seriously, and to make for irresponsibility in the teaching of it. No doubt there is another side to the question. If appreciation of Scripture has about it an aesthetic quality, this appreciation can no more be tested by objective standards than can appreciation of art. Nevertheless this is often used as an excuse by both teachers and pupils to avoid the necessary hard study which not only is 'examinable' but also (and more important) provides the only sure basis for authentic appreciation. There is about Scripture teaching far too much contentment with *general* appreciation based on little or no acquaintance with the documents themselves. This is as noticeable in the writings of the late Professor Joad and Mr C. S. Lewis as it is in the sentimental teaching that is given in some Sunday schools. It is even to be found in some theological colleges and it was, at any rate until recently, characteristic of very much of the religious education of the United States. It cannot be too often stated that the historical approach to the Bible requires a level of knowledge as thorough as a student would require in history or in mathematics if he were entering upon the teaching of either of those subjects.

3 WHAT DO WE MEAN BY 'INSPIRATION' AND 'REVELATION'?

There are two questions which every teacher of Scripture must answer for himself before he enters upon his task. The first is 'What do we mean by the inspiration of the Bible?' The second is like it but goes far deeper. It is 'What do we mean by revelation?'

The popular view of inspiration is that God told the writers of the Biblical books what to say, and so their writings are the very words of God himself. The medieval view was that all Scripture, rightly understood, has God for its author. The phrase 'rightly understood' apparently left a loophole for private interpretation, but it was partially closed before the Reformation and entirely closed at the Council of Trent by the acceptance of the Church as the official and only valid interpreter of Scripture. God being the author of Scripture, it was necessarily inerrant and perfect. The voice of God was as certainly to be heard in the lists of names in the Book of Numbers as in the fifty-third chapter of Isaiah. The Bible itself was held to assert its own infallibility—although in other walks of life a book's statement about itself could hardly be accepted as evidence. Such an attitude would justify the verbal inspiration of the Book of Mormon and Mrs Eddy's *Science and Health*, for they are both held by their authors to be inspired writings.

In the Old Testament, however, there is a continual recurrence of the phrase 'Thus saith the Lord', and this is held to prove that what follows was dictated by God himself to the writer. We shall see later how the phrase arose, but we must admit that when the prophet said 'Thus saith the Lord' he meant what he said. It was to him not his own opinion but the very word of God to his soul. Nevertheless just as men's consciences tell them very contrary things and yet each man believes that his message is the word of God for him, so there were contrary views held, each with complete conscientiousness, by the prophets. The classic instance is the contradictory views held by Isaiah and Micah—contemporaries—concerning the future of Jerusalem. Isaiah could introduce his conviction that God would preserve Zion inviolate with the usual 'Thus saith the Lord'. Micah was equally convinced that God would cause Zion to be ploughed like a field.[1] The event showed that Micah and not Isaiah was right.

The New Testament ends with two verses which were supposed to be the last word on this matter:

I testify unto every man that heareth the words of the prophecy of this book, If any man shall add unto them God shall add unto him the plagues which are written in this book: and if any man shall take away from the words of the book of this prophecy, God shall take away his part from the tree of life and out of the holy city, even from the things which are written in this book.

These verses were clearly intended to cover the Book of Revelation alone and are not concerned with the rest of the Bible, but even as a matter of evidence concerning this one book, they can hardly be held to 'prove' its inspiration. The verse added by a later hand to St John's Gospel, 'This is the disciple which beareth witness of these things, and wrote these things: and we know that his witness is true', would appear to be much more of the nature of

[1] Isa. xxxi. 4, 5; Mic. iii. 8–12.

corroborative evidence, yet here again it can cover only the one book to which it is attached.

The identifying of inspiration with verbal inerrancy (with which it has really nothing to do) has led to all kinds of dishonest methods of treating Scripture. For instance the plain truth about Jacob and Isaac and David has been ignored in order to fit the text into a presumed scheme more consonant with the character of a truthful and righteous God. Verbalism has dogged New Testament interpretation also and men have been more concerned to safeguard the accuracy of the narrative (as Western and modern minds conceive accuracy) than to safeguard the moral consistency of Christ.

The Bible itself is the best argument against verbalism. Jesus in the wilderness sets texts of Deuteronomy against a text from the Psalms. In Matthew's account of the Sermon on the Mount (ch. v) Jesus takes five texts from the Pentateuch, expands four of them from a commandment into a principle and flatly contradicts the fifth. In the Old Testament the Books of Kings insist on the value of burnt offerings, whereas Jeremiah and certain psalms reject such sacrifices altogether. Mark's gospel mistakenly attributes a text in Malachi to Isaiah (Mark i. 2); Matthew in xxvii. 9 attributes a passage from Zachariah to Jeremiah; Paul says in I Cor. x. 4 that the Israelites in the wilderness drank of a rock that accompanied them, although there is no such statement in the Old Testament, and he goes on to say that 'that rock was Christ'. All these apparent contradictions are easily understood on the basis of historical interpretation: on the fundamentalist basis of the inerrancy of the whole of Scripture it is quite impossible to reconcile them.

Inspiration therefore has nothing to do with the narrative as such. It is not words that witness to inspiration by God, it is people. The only medium by which God makes himself known to men is men. Even what is called 'the testimony of Nature' is not something that Nature itself offers: it is an interpretation of Nature by the minds of men. There is much more reason to look on the Bible as the record of what inspired men have thought and done than to look on the actual words as mechanically given by God to men. Besides, we have to remember that we do not for certain possess any part of the Bible as originally written. The earliest manuscripts, even the small fragments of the Chester-Beatty collection, are dated many years, sometimes many centuries, after the original record was composed. A study of the Revised Version marginal readings of the Book of Hosea or an enumeration of the various manuscripts of the New Testament with the thousands of variant readings should convince any verbalist that we have today no means whatsoever of knowing which is the 'inspired' text and which is not. The theory therefore, even for this reason alone, falls to the ground.

The deeper question remains. What do we mean by revelation? Even among people who are not verbal inspirationists there is often a good deal of confusion concerning the nature of revelation. Among modern theologians—with whose controversies we are here not primarily concerned—there are schools of thought based on a revival of Thomist studies or of Reformation writers who give the impression that they believe in the old theory that

> God sends his teachers unto every age
> With revelation suited to their growth.

The divine initiative is stressed all the time and man is represented as a passive recipient of the revelation. Indeed Christians are so much used to this kind of language that they forget that it means absolutely nothing to those unfamiliar with it.

In the teaching of Scripture, therefore, we have to remember that revelation is the name given by men to a discovery that they themselves have made and which proves itself afterwards to be a more than usually powerful indication of what they themselves believe to be the activity of God. Without this human medium there is no revelation nor can there be. It is not external facts that are 'revealed'. It is God who is revealed. The confusion between these two positions is well illustrated by an astonishing remark of Newman in his third discourse on university education: 'In the science of history the preservation of our race in Noah's ark is a historical fact which history never would arrive at without

13

Revelation.' The air may be charged with messages, but without a receiving instrument they might as well not be there at all. Yet this metaphor from wireless may easily mislead us. For the mind of man is not a mere receiver to pick up any message that may come along. It is itself part of the divine activity and it translates its convictions into terms with which it is familiar.

When dealing with the idea of revelation in history there are two stages to be borne in mind. We can best illustrate this from the story of Hosea. We say that 'God revealed' himself to Hosea as a God of compassion and mercy. This, as we have seen, does not mean that God spoke something to Hosea, presumably in Hebrew, which he wrote down at God's dictation, an idea which is both mechanical and fantastic. The 'revelation' was something which was both the result and the cause of Hosea's own brooding upon the situation in which he found himself. He is unhappily married and yet he will not avail himself of the law which would destroy his unfaithful wife. Why not? There could be only one reason. He was still in love with her. Why then does God not destroy Israel for her own unfaithfulness to her God? Surely for the same reason. God loves Israel and will neither compel her to return nor destroy her for not doing so. This is a new idea in the religion of Israel, and where did it come from? From Hosea's own experience, and yet it was not just invented by Hosea. It was borne in upon him as a sensitive plate receives the light which reaches it from outside. Turned round in the other way, however, it was due to God's activity in Hosea, or, to use the classic term, it was God's 'revelation' of himself to Hosea. He comes upon it as the result of his brooding, but it is also the cause of his conviction. 'Revelation' means that the initiative is not only with man: it is also with God, and indeed it is with man only because it is God who causes him to have the initiative. In a sense 'revelation' is an unfortunate word because it disguises the twofold activity that is needed, that of man and that of God.

These theological considerations are naturally not such as can be put before children at any age and the teacher will find that the idea of revelation as the activity solely of God is one which is not in the least difficult for young children to grasp. Indeed it may be the one which comes most naturally to them. But older children will most certainly find a difficulty here which is not to be cleared up by any magical definition. The teacher need not be a theologian, but he does need to be clear in his own mind about these problems which arise in the teaching of Scripture and are indeed characteristic of it. The fact that many of them arise through mistaken conceptions in the past is not a sufficient ground for ignoring them. In Scripture far more than in any other subject there is often a good deal of *un*learning to be done before we can start fairly on our real task.

CHAPTER II

THE EDUCATIONAL CASE
FOR SCRIPTURE

1 AN EDUCATIONAL CASE AS OPPOSED
TO SPECIAL PLEADING

The discussions which were held in England before the passing of the Education Act of 1944 were most illuminating. Whatever may be the religious state of the English people themselves, there is no doubt that most people wish to have religion taught in the schools. The reasons, however, are often curious. The old fallacy of formal training still lingers on in this sphere when it has long been disproved everywhere else, even in the teaching of classics. Scripture is believed of itself, no matter how it is taught, to produce the good life. To some keen Christian workers, aware of the decline of the Sunday school, compulsory attendance at the day school provides an opportunity to compensate for this decline by having compulsory religious teaching. All these and many other reasons of the nature of special pleading were heard both in and out of Parliament.

There must, however, be for every subject an *educational* reason or reasons to justify its place in the curriculum. This is the only ground that can be common to all the various interests that are concerned with the schools. Apart therefore from the justifiably vested interest that the Church has in this subject, are there more general reasons which would justify its inclusion?

2 LITERARY VALUE OF THE BIBLE

There are a good many. And first there is the plain fact that Christianity has been the most powerful force in moulding Western civilization, and the Scriptures are the documents of Christianity. It is a commonplace that there are three roots of our

16

civilization—Rome, Greece and Judaea, and to understand it at all there must be a due appreciation of all three. The first two are freely accepted by everybody, but the third has so often been looked upon (from outside) as so much the private possession of a party that it has been assumed that the only contribution of Judaea was the founding of the Christian Church as one institution among many others. The historian, of course, knows better than this. Christian ideas softened the asperities of the barbarous tribes that overran Europe, the Church kept the lamp of learning alight, it pioneered the care of the sick, it humanized Roman law, it challenged the doctrine that might is right, it gave the impetus that founded schools and universities, and in every corner of human life it exercised its influence. The misdeeds and wickedness of Churchmen from time to time, or our own personal rejection of the Christian faith, ought not to blind us to the enormous share taken by Christianity in building up our common life and institutions.

A good deal of this in later years in England was due to the spread of the Scriptures. Both T. H. Huxley[1] and Sir Arthur Quiller-Couch have expounded in classic phrase the debt that English literature and the English way of life owe to the Authorized Version of the Bible. Every teacher of the Bible would do well to read and mark the three stimulating lectures in Quiller-Couch's *On the Art of Reading* and the earlier lecture on the *Capital Difficulty of Prose*. They were delivered in Cambridge forty years ago and they had no small influence on what can only be called the recovery of our appreciation of the Bible as an integral part of our English heritage. He gives a remarkable quotation from Newman:

How real a creation, how *sui generis*, is the style of Shakespeare, or of the Protestant Bible and Prayer Book, or of Swift, or of Pope, or of Gibbon, or of Johnson!... Whether we will or no, the phraseology... has become a portion of the vernacular tongue, the household words, of which perhaps we little guess the origin, and the very idioms of our familiar conversation.... So tyrannous is the literature of a nation: it is too much for us. We cannot destroy or reverse it....We cannot make

[1] 'Science and Education', *Collected Essays*, vol. III, pp. 397–8.

it over again. It is a great work of man, when it is no work of God's....
We cannot undo the past. English literature will ever have been
Protestant.

This admonition is all too often forgotten, for Scripture is often
read—and taught—for its content alone. But the form of it is part
of its very meaning, and lack of appreciation of its form leads
people to read books about the Bible, Biblical history and commentaries without actually reading the Bible itself. Quiller-Couch
gives wise counsel: 'Very well, then: my first piece of advice *on
reading the Bible* is that you do it.' And it is not only literary connoisseurs who will appreciate it: it is something which quite small
children can appreciate for the sound if not at the moment for the
sense. Herein is the case for learning passages by heart, not as a
task but unconsciously through having heard them read and re-
read again and again. Children take to it as they take to a musical
tune, and it is easy to catch and to retain. Then at a later stage when
it is well in their possession they can learn its meaning. The Bible
well read is as necessary a part of the learning of Scripture as the
studying of contexts and texts. It is the music of the Psalms and
not just their unexpected relevance to a later situation that has
retained them in the minds of all serious readers of the Bible.

3 MORAL TRAINING

One of the problems that every school has to tackle is that of moral
training. As we no longer believe in the power of words without
a context, responsibility for moral training is often laid upon those
school activities which have least to do with the curriculum—the
prefect system, a scout patrol, compulsory games and the like. It
often happens that the theory of formal training or of the transfer
of training is held to operate in these non-curricular activities even
though it is admitted that it no longer holds in the syllabus.
Training in the very necessary virtues of civic pride and common
loyalty is thought to be adequately provided for by football or
cricket because the team spirit is necessary in both of them.

Yet the fundamental error of formal training remains. It seeks to inculcate an attitude to life by purely mechanical means, and this is as true of football as a training in co-operation and of Latin as a training in reasoning, as of doctrine and Scripture as a training in morals. Personal qualities are transmitted only by persons, although we need to have knowledge of facts and principles as well.

The cardinal fact about both the Old Testament and the New is that they treat morality not as a mechanical process consequent on instruction but as an attitude to a total situation. The familiar phrase 'the application of Christian principles' contains an idea which is fundamentally fallacious. Neither Christian nor Hebrew principles were worked out in isolation and then, when classified and codified, 'applied' to the situation in hand. Moral questions always appear in a context of persons and not one of ideas. Their solution is to be found in action not in discussion. The Bible knows nothing of casuistry, which is the science of dealing with moral problems before they have arisen. That 'circumstances alter cases' is a dangerous doctrine if it means that our understanding of circumstances causes the problem to disappear—'tout comprendre c'est tout pardonner'—but if it means that every situation has to be taken in its context it is the characteristic attitude of the Hebrew and the Christian religion. It was a favourite maxim of Sir Henry Sumner Maine that English positive law has the appearance of having been 'secreted in the interstices of procedure'. Nothing could better describe the development of moral principles in the Bible. There is little abstract reasoning—that was not the Hebrew way of doing things—but there is a great deal of action. God is known by his acts, and men are most characteristic in their acts. Jesus gives different advice to the rich young ruler and to Nicodemus because their circumstances were different. He inveighs against the evil attitude of the Pharisees but he does not condemn the woman brought before him for her adultery. St Paul at times sits loosely to abstract principles either in ethics or in theology. The difficult problem of meat offered to idols is treated on the ground that if this worries other people you had better have nothing to do with it. This is a common-sense rather than an ethical judgement, but it is as relevant to drinking beer or doing football pools as ever it was to buying meat from the heathen temples. Even where there are divisions in the Church on matters of doctrine, Paul takes up what to some people is an astonishing position: 'Some indeed preach Christ even of envy and strife; and some also of goodwill.... What then? Only that in every way, whether in pretence or in truth, Christ is proclaimed: and therein I rejoice, yea, and will rejoice' (Phil. i. 15–18). Jesus himself treated many of the contemporary problems in the same apparently off-hand fashion by declaring that the Sabbath was made for man and not man for the Sabbath.

The Bible therefore exhibits a thoroughly healthy and sensible approach to moral training. There is a standard—the life and character of Jesus himself, but there are no abstract maxims which have to be 'applied'. If 'forgiveness' is a desirable attitude to have, it is taught not by discussion but by stories such as those of Jeremiah, the Prodigal Son and Christ on the Cross. That 'honesty is the best policy' appears in Elisha's treatment of Gehazi. It would, however, be quite a mistake to look on them simply as stories illustrating a principle. The stories, so to speak, *are* the principle. And in all of them regard is had to the persons themselves and to the situation itself, and every situation is dealt with on its merits.

4 CORRELATION

So far we have looked at the educational value of the context of Scripture. We come now to certain other considerations of a more technical character.

It is a good rule when making up a curriculum to choose certain subjects for the sake of their correlations. Outside school life 'subjects' as such do not exist, and it is well to remember that fact. Ordinary citizens in a bus do not discuss congruent triangles nor do they get excited about the causes of the Hundred Years War. Life is much more of a whole, and geometrical and historical considerations come in if and when they are needed. School subjects are abstractions and classifications artificially made for the purpose of connected study. This is, of course, a necessity of thought, but it is equally necessary that means should be taken to correlate them so that they can appear as what they are, namely aspects of life. In this regard subjects vary in their degree of affinity with other subjects, but among those that have a high degree of correlation is Scripture. It has correlation with history, English and geography as well as those links with life and civilization which we have already mentioned. In a later chapter we shall discuss the correlation of Scripture with these various subjects. There are, however, certain more general considerations which should be mentioned here.

In the first place, correlation is not merely a matter of sketching in the background of a particular situation—St Paul's travels with the background of Mediterranean life and culture, or the settlement of Canaan with that of the configuration of the land. It requires some collaboration in the staff room. The geography teacher is well aware of the importance of the contrast between the desert and the fertile land. He ought to be equally well aware that one of the best illustrations of this is Palestine in Old Testament times. The history teacher may feel that history really begins with Greece and Rome. It would be helpful, however, if he knew that Amos was contemporary with the earliest settlements on the banks of the Tiber, and that Nehemiah was probably living at the same time as Plato. What used to be called 'sacred' history has been so shut off from the rest of historical studies that these coincidences are often ignored even when they are not unknown. The growing interest in archaeology has brought the history of Israel into the picture along with Egypt, Babylon and the Minoan age in Crete (for did not the Philistines come from Crete?), but it is far more important that the pupils should realize that long before Greece and Rome were of any account on the world's stage, the villages of Judaea rang to the music of the psalms and listened to discourses that have not lost their freshness even at the present day. The Scripture teacher will emphasize this in any case, but if it is corroborated in the history lessons the effect will be all the greater.

It is in English, however, that the greatest opportunity arises. It has already been noticed how great was the influence of Quiller-Couch in putting the Bible into its rightful place as a great source of later English literature. George Sampson a little later, in that unconventional and inspiring book *English for the English*, also made a strong plea for the use of the Bible in the English syllabus:

> The Bible needs to be 'depolarized'....People too often read the Bible as if its persons and events belonged to another world. The men of the Middle Ages were much nearer the artistic truth of Biblical narrative when they saw in their pictures apostles and patriarchs and evangelists habited like themselves. We may be all the better for not reading the Bible fanatically and superstitiously; but we are much the worse for not reading the Bible at all.... What we want chiefly to do is to break down the tradition that still keeps our wonderful Bible as a book apart to be read only in some unnatural way at certain moments of a seventh of a week.[1]

It may be said that as far as the schools are concerned, this tradition is in a fair way to being broken down. No modern anthology of English literature is complete without extracts from the Authorized Version. The Agreed Syllabuses have made it familiar to every Local Education Authority, and publishers vie with one another in producing editions, modern translations, illustrations and commentaries. Nevertheless in schools the tradition that keeps 'Scripture' and 'English' as subjects apart is still to be broken down. Quiller-Couch and Sampson have helped to do this as far as the English lessons are concerned. But the Scripture lesson is still too much concerned solely with the Bible as 'content' or even as a guide to morality and not sufficiently with it as a great English treasure. Let us hear George Sampson again on this matter:

> Part of the initiation into literature should be a glimpse of the glory of language, a fostered sense and feeling that language is a form of beauty with its roots in the imagination.
>
> *Through the tender mercy of our God, whereby the day-spring from on high hath visited us, to give light to them that sit in darkness and in the shadow of death, and to guide our feet into the way of peace.*

[1] *English for the English*, pp. 88–9.

Do we ever stay to dwell on the loveliness of a passage like that, in which almost every word is a poem: or do we not just go passively through it as the hustled tourist goes through a foreign picture gallery, encompassed with beauty and seeing almost nothing?[1]

He points out however, that it is unreasonable to mix two different kinds of lesson. 'The explicatory lesson is one thing and the presentation of a poem something quite different.' The syllabuses tend to ignore this distinction, and by crowding so much detail into the scheme, to make it impossible at any time to stand and stare. For English people the Bible does not yield its full effect by simply getting back to the original language and the original thought. This is the scholarly approach and a very necessary one. But to make the word by word 'meaning' of a passage to depend on this would be like an attempt to begin chemistry by learning a table of the elements and their atomic weights. The expert has to know these but these alone are not 'chemistry'. Similarly in Scripture teaching some anthropological knowledge is needed to understand Genesis, and the document theory of the Pentateuch is most illuminating, but one can be familiar with all this and yet miss the real inwardness of the Bible. Hence it is that unlettered and unscholarly men all down the ages have often had revealed to them things that were hid from the wise and prudent. It is possible to be too clever in our Bible study and to be so much concerned with the Hebrew way of life and the Hellenistic way of life as to forget that the Bible speaks also to our English way of life and indeed has had a great deal to do with the forming of it.

5 TWO PRINCIPLES OF GRADING: THE HISTORICAL AND THE PSYCHOLOGICAL

A further educational reason for Scripture is that it inter-relates two types of grading. All subjects have to be graded and there are various principles to be noticed. A subject may be graded historically—that is to say in the way in which it gradually reached its present form. It was no doubt this consideration which for

[1] *Ibid.* pp. 81–2.

many years put 'Euclid' into the mathematics curriculum—a name which nowadays is quite unknown to the younger generation. Or it may be graded according to what are believed to be sound psychological principles. In mathematics this may lead to geometry being done before algebra and even (so advocated Sir Percy Nunn) solid geometry before plane geometry. The principle here is to start with concepts with which the child is already familiar and work from that point. In history this principle creates a dilemma, for 'familiarity' has different meanings. The spears, axeheads and woad of the ancient Britons may be more 'familiar' to a sturdy child of twelve than the dignified procedure of the local town council or the events of the World Wars. This dilemma is often treated in Scripture as easily solvable. The earlier parts of the Bible both Old and New Testaments are held to be suitable for young children and the Prophets and Epistles for older children, and the syllabus is graded accordingly. This, however, leaves out of account two important and indeed unique facts about Scripture teaching.

In the first place, what are called the 'earlier' parts of the two Testaments were as a matter of fact written last—at any rate in the form in which we have them today—and behind their writing there was a principle of selection, the understanding of which is very important for older children. Thus the delightful stories in Genesis and the historical books are admirable material for young children but they are equally admirable, although for a different reason, for the Sixth Form. Yet the syllabus is often so arranged that the pupils miss the experience which all the ancient writers had—of going back and reinterpreting what they had already understood at a lower level.

The other fact is that changes go on in the interpreting mind itself. The Bible has always 'spoken to men's condition' right down the centuries and this could have happened only if there was some quite intimate connexion between the mind of man in all its moods and the minds of men whose lives are recorded in the Bible. For it is not just a record. It is really an interpretation of the record, an assessment of it in the light of what were the highest spiritual values that men knew at the time. T. H. Huxley, in a famous passage speaks of the 'humanizing' influence of the Bible[1] and this is what he means. There is in this ancient record a revelation of man to himself which is as characteristic as its revelation of the ways of God. It may be doubted whether there is any experience that comes to modern man which, reduced to its simplest terms, has not come to men at all times and which is recognized and weighed up in the Bible and brought into relationship with God.

This does not mean that the teacher has to be a preacher. It does mean, however, that with a wise knowledge of his subject-matter he can gain as good (and some would say much better) guidance to the spiritual and mental development of his pupils as he would get in any psychology book. For there is a natural history of emotions as there is a natural history of human personality as a whole, and the clue to it all is not very easy to find. Adolescence, for example, is often considered to be the years between, say, fourteen and twenty-two. The truth is that the symptoms of adolescence are apt to recur at any age where men come up against situations with which they feel powerless to deal. The chief obstacles are human weakness, human ignorance and human sin. Even a cursory acquaintance with the Psalms will show how very much aware the authors are of this human situation, but they are not the only Biblical writers who show this awareness. It is one of the motifs of the Bible as a whole. The grading of the subject, therefore, depends not only on the development of the Biblical story itself, and not only on the psychological ability of the pupil to grasp its meaning, but also on factors of growth within the pupil's own personality.

This argument has never been better put than it was by Huxley in the passage just mentioned. Huxley in theological matters was an agnostic, but he had a very keen sense of spiritual values and of ways of attaining them. Accordingly at the first meeting of the London School Board in 1870 when it was proposed to solve the religious problem by cutting the Bible out of the schools, it was

[1] 'Science and Education', *Collected Essays*, vol. III, p. 398.

Huxley, the scientist and the agnostic, who secured its retention. His argument appears in a famous article in the *Contemporary Review* in 1870 on 'The School Boards: what they can do, and what they may do' from which the passage just mentioned is taken. After speaking of the 'moral grandeur' of the Bible, and the value of its historical setting—'it forbids the veriest hind who never left his native village to be ignorant of the existence of other countries and other civilizations, and of a great past stretching back to the furthest limits of the oldest nations in the world'. He continues:

By the study of what other book could children be so much humanized and made to feel that each figure in that vast historical procession fills, like themselves, but a momentary space in the interval between two eternities, and earns the blessings or the curses of all time, according to its effort to do good and hate evil, even as they also are earning their payment for their work.

Here is the case for more than a superficial acquaintance with the Bible as history or literature. It is a matter not perhaps so much of grading as of cross-referencing, so that a pupil's own development may influence both the choice of what is read and the interpretation of it. For let it be remembered that the Agreed Syllabuses are nowhere intended to be more than guides. They are not *prescribed* and the wise teacher will adapt them to his own purposes. Teachers in boarding schools have a better opportunity for getting to know their pupils and this knowledge will help them in their Scripture teaching.

CHAPTER III

THE TEACHER

I THE AMATEUR AND THE SPECIALIST

The teaching of Scripture in schools has several peculiarities as
against the teaching of other subjects. It is even yet, for the most
part, the concern of amateurs. In its modern form it is a new
subject (the earliest of the Agreed Syllabuses was put out only in
1924) and therefore lacks the benefit of generations of experiment
and discussion such as have established a technique among older
subjects. Then again not only is the technique still to be discovered but the subject-matter itself is under discussion. The old
fundamentalism, whether Protestant or Catholic, has not yet given
way to the proved results of modern scholarship. It is as though in
the teaching of biology we still had to make up our minds between
the cataclysmic theory of Cuvier and the evolutionary theory of
Darwin. Consequently the historical approach in schools is continually having to have regard to unhistorical theories passionately
held or ignorantly condoned by people outside school. Of no
other subject is this the case, or at any rate, so completely the case.
The position therefore of the teacher and his qualifications are far
more intimately concerned with the outside world than are those
of the teacher of arithmetic or history.

At the same time, a further difference is evident in that we lack
the middleman who can mediate to the school the results of expert
knowledge without himself being an expert. This is often very
noticeable at summer schools for the teaching of Scripture. The
authorities who lecture are so often the experts themselves and
their work helps to inform the minds of the teachers who attend.
But often this creates the greater confusion when it comes down to
teaching children in the class-room. In conferences for teachers of
history or science or any other subject, the researchers themselves
are unnecessary because there is a sufficient supply of middlemen

who know the work of the scholars but also know the needs of the children. In Scripture, however, there is still a good deal of very ill-digested and misunderstood knowledge put across to children under the impression that this is 'the modern point of view'. Worse still, the teacher may have quite a good grasp of historical scholarship and yet may revert to an old-fashioned unhistorical position in expounding 'What do we learn from this?'— whether the 'this' is a historical narrative, a prophetic utterance or a parable.

Let us deal first with the question of the amateur. He can be an amateur either in the original sense of a lover of his subject or in the derived sense of not being a professional or, of course, he may be both. In grammar schools (ages 11–18) teachers are expected to have a degree in their subject, and in secondary modern schools (11–15) it is also becoming increasingly desirable. In primary schools, there is already specialism in music, art and craft and physical education, which means intensive training in that subject during the two years in a training college with or without a third year given to that specialism alone. In Scripture, however, it is still very unusual for a teacher even in a grammar school to have so much as a diploma in the subject, to say nothing of a degree, although in secondary modern and primary schools there is a slowly growing number of teachers who have taken this subject as their specialism in a training college. Yet even in these last instances there is usually nothing like the background of solid knowledge such as most teachers in their own grammar school days acquired in other subjects. In all these ways therefore, the subject is still in the hands of amateurs.

One of the administrative provisions following the Act of 1944 has eased the situation for the English primary and secondary modern schools. By allowing Scripture to be taught at any period in the time-table it is now possible to eliminate the teacher who does not wish to teach it but who was compelled to do so as long as it was confined to the same time of day for everybody. Consequently no one now need teach Scripture unless he wishes and people who make this choice have usually had some preparation for it in their training college days. This is great gain. What has not yet been secured, however, is the elimination of that lover of the subject whose primary and often only aim is propaganda for a denomination or a school of thought. The lady mentioned on p. 3 was obviously labouring under a handicap in a school for all comers: she would have been much more at home in a purely denominational institution. On the other hand, the person who begins with a real unprejudiced love of the subject for its own sake has a great initial advantage, and provided he is willing to underpin his enthusiasm with knowledge and hard work, he is the best possible person to train for the teaching of this subject. Of course, enthusiasm for this or any other subject is no substitute for competence, although in the present state of things it often has to be. And in this subject, so controversial, so much linked up with people outside, with such an emotional appeal, it is more necessary than in any other subject that the teacher should know his job *as a teacher*.

One further characteristic feature shows itself with older children, particularly at the upper grammar school age. By the time a child is sixteen he has acquired sufficient familiarity with his school subjects to have some judgement of his own about them. He can find his own way round a library and pick and choose what he wants. In Scripture, however, this is the age which needs not less but more guidance. The reason is not because it requires more detailed knowledge—'it is not knowledge that we chiefly need'— but because the Bible is a book of religion and this is the difficult age for religion as for many other things. The Bible cannot be fully understood unless there is an appreciation of the appeal it makes to the personal commitment of the reader. This, in spite of themselves, naturally introduces a tension between teacher and pupil which is not to be solved either by dogmatism on the part of the one or by indifference on the part of the other. There is all the difference between proselytism and guidance, and in school the second is justified where the need for it arises, while the first is not, not even where the opportunity offers. There is a tension therefore in the teacher's own mind apart from that between himself and the pupil.

In no other subject does this arise, at any rate to the same degree, and an appreciation of its existence is a necessary qualification for the teacher of Scripture. It is just because of this that the technique of history teaching as of English teaching is not sufficient if applied to the teaching of this other subject. There is more to it than that, and the 'more' is something integral to the teaching of the subject and not something additional to it, neither a degree on the one hand nor a morbid interest in conversion or Church membership on the other. It is an attitude of mind.

This attitude of mind is shown not only in the Scripture lesson itself but also in the teacher's own relation to the school assembly. 'Religious education' in England includes both of these activities. Worship is the fusing of a number of elements—the recognition that God is the centre of all our study, the bringing together of a whole community at one time for this purpose, the reference to a historical community in the Old and New Testaments and down the ages, and so the sense of 'belonging', the appeal of music, order and corporate silence and the affirmation of a loyalty. It is here where the Bible is given its proper setting and it is in worship rather than in moral teaching that the foundations of Christian conduct are most truly laid. The classroom and the assembly hall thus supplement one another.

This attitude of mind is therefore one of wholeness. It is often urged as a complaint against specialists that they know all about their own subject and are not interested in any other. The specialism of the Scripture teacher, however, is of two kinds, one of which is quite the opposite of this. He needs to know his own subject— the Bible, its contents and its background, but he also needs a certain quality of co-ordination. *All* subjects in which men are interested should also be of interest to him for are they not all part of God's revelation of himself and his universe to man? The old poet said: *Homo sum: humani nihil a me alienum puto*—'I am human and nothing that is human will fail to interest me'. The Scripture teacher should also be able to say: *Christianus sum: divini nihil a me alienum puto*—'I am a Christian, nothing that has to do with God will fail to interest me'. The phrase 'to do with God' will be found on amplification to include everything. It means not only interest in the creative works of other men, but also appreciation of them when they are done. In a practical way in school this will no doubt work out as correlation with other subjects and other members of staff, but beyond this the teacher himself needs to have that vision of wholeness which it is a function of religious education to provide.

2 ACADEMIC QUALIFICATIONS

The academic qualifications open to a would-be teacher of Scripture are varied, even for the person who has not had the opportunity of studying the subject at college. A B.D. is naturally desirable and courses leading to this degree are provided at London, Manchester, Wales and other universities. The B.D. at Oxford and Cambridge is a post-graduate degree requiring in the case of Oxford an M.A., the passing of a qualifying examination and the presentation of a thesis. At Cambridge it is awarded on published work alone. London University also offers a B.D. externally. For honours both Hebrew and Greek are required but Greek alone for a pass, and there are two examinations, the intermediate and the final.

At Oxford and Cambridge every first degree is a B.A. and it can be taken in theology as in any other subject. At Cambridge, as an alternative to the Theological Tripos, there is a new course for a Certificate of Proficiency in Christian Theology which carries with it a B.A. degree. It is a three-year course with an examination at the end of each year, and the subjects are Theology, the Bible, the Christian doctrines of God and of the Church, and Church History including religious life and thought, particularly in Great Britain since 1830. Both Hebrew and Greek are optional. The London pass B.A. in three subjects, internal or external, may include Theology as one of them and the other two may be subjects akin to it.

At a lower level, but much more possible and perhaps even more practicable for teachers already in the profession, there are the external diplomas. London University offers a diploma in which Greek but not Hebrew is compulsory and the subjects are Old

Testament, New Testament, Biblical Theology, Philosophical Introduction to Theology, Church History, and *one* of the following options: Hebrew, Introduction to the Vulgate, Comparative Study of Religions, English Church History, Christian Ethics, Christian Worship. The examination can be taken once as a whole or in two parts and the necessary qualification is matriculation or exemption therefrom. Of a similar nature and standard is the Lambeth Diploma which is governed by a committee of the Church of England but which is open to members of any denomination provided they are baptized Christians, a curious regulation for an academic diploma.

At a lower level still there are the various Certificates of Proficiency in Religious Knowledge arranged externally by various universities of which the London syllabus is typical. It requires a general knowledge of the whole Bible with the special study of set books on the Old and New Testaments. There are also *two* optional subjects to be chosen from the list—Introduction to the Old Testament, Introduction to the Gospels and Pauline Epistles, Greek Testament, a period of Church History, Comparative Study of Religions, History of Christian Doctrine, Christian Worship. Hebrew is not required at all, nor Greek (except as an option). This examination also may be taken in two parts.

It is advisable that every teacher of Scripture should have one of these university (or Lambeth) qualifications. They all presuppose the historical method and they all require a good knowledge of the whole Bible. This, however, gives rise to a question which has been a moot point. Is it better for Scripture to be taught by a specialist or by an unspecialized class teacher?

The arguments for the class teacher are that he can correlate his Scripture with the rest of his subjects, that he has a more intimate knowledge of his pupils and can help them in their difficulties, that Scripture is not isolated as something special but is brought into contact with the rest of life. There is also with some people the feeling that specializing in this of all subjects means an intellectual approach and gets in the way of the devotional approach—whatever those question-begging terms may mean.

The arguments for the specialist are that he must know a good deal more than he can teach. The Bible is a big book (the Oxford and Cambridge Bourgeois 8vo editions run into well over a thousand double-column pages) and requires intensive study of a kind not applied to any other book except a classical text. The amount of knowledge needed even to teach it to children would certainly take as long to acquire as any subject for a pass degree. The proper technique is a matter of hard work and experiment and it by no means comes automatically to a person who is well-disposed to the subject. Furthermore, if in a grammar school every other subject is specialized, to hand this one over to the ordinary form master as an unspecialized subject, is to lower it in the estimation of the young.

These are all valid arguments. What is *not* a valid argument is that this subject requires such a rarefied atmosphere that the un-hallowed hands of the 'specialist' ought not to be allowed to touch it. It is clear, however, that on the balance of argument the specialist is needed, but we have to ask, 'What kind of specialist?' The possession of even a B.D. degree does not of itself constitute the right qualification. In Scripture *the way* you know the subject counts as much or even more than what you know. Consequently there are excellent teachers of Scripture whose knowledge may be elementary but who have it in a way that is far from elementary. They might not be able to answer such a question as 'explain the importance of the Septuagint for the textual criticism of the New Testament', but they would be sufficiently familiar with the work of Deissmann to be able to illustrate their lessons on the Gospels with references to the colloquial language of the period. Without being able to sort out J, P and E into their appropriate sections, they would know the significance of these documents to explain the contradictions that children find in Genesis. Above all, with-out being expert on New Testament criticism they would know why it is necessary to know that the Epistles were written before the Gospels and that the Fourth Gospel is the latest of all. The expert will of course know these things also, but in his case simplicity is not so easy to come by. T. H. Huxley used to say that a really wide expert knowledge was necessary in order to make a simple introduction to a subject because only in that way did the writer know what was of vital importance and what was not. In Scripture, however, the difficulty of simplicity is increased rather than diminished by further knowledge. Nevertheless, when it is ultimately achieved the effectiveness of the teacher is very greatly increased.

So far the qualifications indicated are those of the teacher as teacher. For some appointing bodies, however, these are not enough. Questions of a personal nature are often asked of the candidate for a Scripture teaching post which are not asked of any other type of teacher. It is well, therefore, to consider how far such questions are justified.

What are we to say, for instance, in reply to a requirement that a teacher of Scripture should be what is called a 'professing Christian'? The phrase itself is far from clear. It may mean membership of some church and nothing more, or it may mean exactly what it says, but in any case the question implies that some outward sign is required over and above professional competence and interest in the subject. The question may be relevant where there is no specialism required, but in these days it is so unlikely that anyone would offer to teach a subject in which he did not believe and for which he had taken no training that the mere fact of his applying to teach it should be a sufficient guarantee of his integrity. The question ought not to be asked at all, not even in a denominational school where a man's own membership of the particular denomination should be sufficient, apart from his professional competence. Unfortunately, however, those who ask such a question have often in their minds some particular orthodoxy such as verbal inspiration or frequent Communion which may or may not be understood by the candidate.

SECTION B
SUBJECT-MATTER

CHAPTER IV

LANGUAGE AND LITERATURE

I TERMINOLOGY

One of the first questions to be settled is that of terminology. What are we to make of the name 'Jehovah' by which God is usually known in the English Old Testament? It is, of course, due to a misunderstanding of the printing of the Hebrew 'Yaweh'. It was highly dangerous to pronounce the sacred name itself and so the consonants were vocalized with the vowels of the Hebrew for 'Lord'. This was not understood by the English translators who took the vocalized form to be the actual name itself and so the word 'Jehovah' passed into our language. It may be doubted, however, whether for school purposes much is gained by the by-passing of four centuries of usage and introducing the more correct form Yahweh. The only value of it is to emphasize the distinction between henotheism and monotheism. To the early Hebrews Yahweh was one God among many, not yet recognized even by them as the one God of the whole earth. But this distinction can be brought out better in other ways. The name appears in our versions as 'the Lord' or 'the Lord God' and this is really the most satisfactory rendering. Both Jehovah and Yahweh are open to the objection that in children's minds they appear to be the names of someone quite other than God and it ignores the fact that it is the appreciation of the character of God that develops in the Old Testament and the name is not really important. It may be objected that this causes confusion between the God of the Old Testament and the God who is 'Father of our Lord Jesus Christ'. But the use of 'Yahweh' equally confuses the God of the Book of Judges and the God of the Second Isaiah. The verse (Exod. vi. 3) 'I appeared unto Abraham, unto Isaac, and unto Jacob, as GOD ALMIGHTY but by my name JEHOVAH I was not known to them' might be made *mutatis mutandis* to refer equally to God of the New Testament. From the children's point of view the use of the word 'God' is all that is necessary.

The term 'the Second Isaiah' contains a confusion between the name of the book and the name of the man. If 'Isaiah' refers to the book, then Isa. xl-lv is properly 'the second part of Isaiah' and lvi-lxvi the third part. If it refers to the man, then xl-lv is the work of 'the unknown prophet of the Exile' and lvi-lxvi that of 'the unknown prophet after the Exile'.

The term 'John' or 'St John' is the traditional ascription of the Fourth Gospel, and while 'Fourth Gospel' may be a better, more scholarly designation there is no need to drop the traditional title when referring to the Gospel in class.

2 THE USE OF 'DOCUMENTS'

A further question arises with older children concerning the use of the names of the documents. The acceptance of the historical method naturally involves—for the teacher at any rate—acquaintance with the symbols for the various sources J, B, D, E, and Q (leaving out such jargon as Proto-Mark, Proto-Luke, etc.). To some teachers the use of these symbols is itself the historical method and they completely bemuse their older pupils by the use of this kind of shorthand. It is worth pointing out that nothing is gained by this technique and a great deal is lost. How many people are aware of the Synoptic problem in the *Lives* of St Francis, or of the literary problems that lie at the back of the books of Livy? It is possible both to be very knowledgeable about these authors and to enjoy them without knowing anything at all about their source criticism. But enthusiasm for the so-called 'modern' method of teaching Scripture has often led teachers into precisely this kind of esoteric study, far beyond the interests of the children. There is nothing which can kill interest so soon as an amateur handling of what are after all questions for the expert. The differences between the documents in the Pentateuch can be noted and their significance explained without the pupil being required to deal with 'J' or 'E' as, so to speak, a thing in itself. It is far more useful for them to be made aware of the literary conventions of the ancients than with the conjectural reconstruction of individual documents.

3 ANCIENT LITERARY CONVENTIONS

What then are these literary conventions? The teacher should be aware of them and be provided with plenty of illustrations.

First, there was no 'collation'. Later writers dealing with varying accounts of the same thing made no attempt to collate them, but put them all in, leaving their contradictions to be sorted out by the reader. This, of course, is illustrated throughout by the different documents in Genesis, but simple examples are Gen. vi. 19, 20 and vii. 2, 3; xxxvii. 25-8; I Sam. ix, x. 1-16 and x. 17-24; and the surprising one, the story of Goliath slain by David in I Sam. xvii but by Ethanan in II Sam. xxi. 19, by Jonathan in *v.* 21 and by David in *v.* 22.

Secondly, there was no 'copyright'. Writings were free for all to use just as they chose, and they could be added to at the end, expanded in the middle with new material or given prefaces. A writer's work would be respected in his lifetime, but later writers who felt that what they had to say was in line with the works of a well-known predecessor would expand the earlier book with writings of their own.

A very good illustration of this is the Book of Proverbs. The book begins: 'The proverbs of Solomon, the son of David King of Israel'. But ch. xxiv inserts a little collection of twelve verses entitled 'These also are the sayings of the wise'. In ch. xxx there is inserted a collection of proverbs of Agur and in ch. xxxi another of 'King Lemuel'. These later people are unknown but Solomon had good publicity value and they got circulation for their own proverbs by being attached to his. In this case we can see the process actually at work and the pupils can find it out for themselves. 'Isaiah' xl-lv and lvi-lxvi are examples which need rather more explaining. As later summaries added to earlier books there are Hos. xiv. 9; John xxi. 24–5; Rev. xxii. 18, 19. As an example of a happy ending a good example is Amos. ix. 11–15, which of course is quite out of keeping with the rest of the book. As an example of an insertion in the middle of a book we have the speeches of Elihu in Job xxxii-xxxvii which are easily seen to be alien to the main story.

This attitude of ancient writers has its parallel in our own day. An unknown writer wishing to have his book circulated will seek a well-known person to write a preface. On the strength of the preface people will buy the book and so be persuaded to read the book itself. It is very important for children to realize that the ancient method was not dishonest but that it made use of a technique not dissimilar from our own. Great names were important and even where he had written nothing the name of a famous person might be attached to a book because it was characteristic. Thus Moses is credited with the Books of the Pentateuch, although it is obviously impossible that he should have written them. There is in Exodus an account of his own death and the bland theory that he wrote it down in detail because it was 'revealed' to him raises more problems than those it attempts to solve.

Thirdly, the ancient writers preferred *oratio recta* to *oratio obliqua*. Instead of writing 'he said that he would go' they preferred: 'He said "I will go".' This is an idiom not only in Hebrew but also in Greek. This device, however, has often led to the view that what the man is credited with saying is the exact verbal account of what he did actually say. We use the *oratio recta* only for the speech itself and not for the report of it through another person. The ancients used it for both.

There are two extensions of this usage which are found in the Bible. The first is the continuous use by the Prophets of the phrase 'Thus saith the Lord'. That is exactly what they themselves meant: it is not a phrase due only to the absence of abstract nouns and the use of concrete imagery. It is true that it was their way of saying 'I am absolutely convinced' or 'I feel in my bones that such and such is so', and it is also a result of their continual reference to a first cause and not to any intermediate causes. But it also springs from this method of reporting speech. The prophet believed that his message was due to divine inspiration but the words in which that message was proclaimed were his own. The idiom, however, makes it appear that not only the message but also the words were dictated by God. It is through misunderstanding of this idiom that so many passages of the Bible have been saddled with the theory of verbal inspiration. If it is the words that matter it would follow that where there are numbers of variant readings (as in Hosea) we could not be sure of the word of God at all!

Another extension of this principle is to be found in the conveyance of ideas through speeches rather than through statement. This, of course, is a characteristically ancient attitude which was developed by Sophist teachers into dialogue. Thucydides, Livy, Matthew Paris all put into the mouths of their heroes speeches which if never actually delivered were *ben trovato*, and they were not aware of any deception in so doing. Their readers as well as themselves knew quite well that this was the historian's technique, and it was a much more vivid way of conveying a message than by a disquisition.

Thus Thucydides says what he has to say about Athens by putting a speech into the mouth of Pericles. The relations between Saul and Samuel are similarly exhibited in the Old Testament by speeches. The temptation of Jesus in Matthew and Luke appears in a pictorial and dialogue form instead of as a study of the struggle in his own mind. The Fourth Gospel is the most outstanding example of this ancient technique and when we allow for it there is no need for older children to be put off (as they undoubtedly are put off) by what appears to be the egotistical attitude of Jesus. The high-priestly prayer in John xvii is clearly not a verbatim account of an actual prayer written down in shorthand by some reporter on the spot—the whole idea is repulsive. But it, and the last speeches, are the author's way of describing the significance of

Jesus for the world. And, of course they were written at least sixty years after the death of Jesus himself. In the stories of Nicodemus, the Samaritan woman and the household at Bethany we have the development of the dialogue form.

Fourthly, their attitude to causation was very different from ours. Anything which was incapable of a plain straightforward explanation was put down to the direct action of God. And from this it followed that where two inexplicable events took place at the same time there must clearly be some connexion between them. The mysterious stampeding of a herd of swine at the same time as the equally mysterious curing of a lunatic showed that the two must be connected. Further than that the spectators could not go, but in so much as Jesus was clearly responsible for the second he must also have been responsible for the first (Mark v. 1–21 and parallels). Again the Hebrew prophets were so obviously right in their message that it was quite inexplicable that people should not heed them, unless it was that God had intended it (Isa. vi. 9–10). Similarly with the Jews' rejection of Jesus' teaching (Matt. xiii. 14–15, Acts xxviii. 26–7). It was so strange that Hosea's wife had turned against him into evil ways that it must have been the intention of God from the beginning that he should marry a prostitute (Hos. i. 2).

From this last idiom it was easy to account for all strange happenings by writing them down at once as 'miracles' and recording them as such. There is a most valuable text in II Kings iii. 21–23 in which we see the process in action. Moab is fighting against Israel and Judah, and the Moabites come up to battle early in the morning and they see the sun shining on the water in the trenches that Elisha had caused to be dug. It was only 'as red as blood' but the Moabites said 'This *is* blood, and the kings are surely destroyed'. Here is a myth in the making. The Moabites took this event literally but the chronicler saw that it was only an appearance.

The cycles of hero stories in the Old Testament such as those of Gideon, Samson, Elijah and Elisha are full of marvels and miracles. The very setting in which they have come down to us makes it certain that whatever the facts may have been the report of those facts, inexplicable in any other way, treats them as miracles. The New Testament miracles, however, are of a different order and will be discussed in detail in a later chapter.

4 THE REWRITING OF HISTORY; LEGEND AND MYTH

The literary form in which the Bible has come down to us clearly needs to be understood and appreciated. And one fundamental feature of this form is the writing or rewriting of the earlier history in the light of the later.

It is often noticed that the Bible shows a development of the idea of God from the bloodthirsty deity of Judges v to the God of mercy and grace to be found in Hosea, and the transformation of the idea of holiness from something physical to something moral. The prophets were the agents of this transformation. With this in mind many of the problems which arise in children's minds about the obvious immorality of God in the early stories cease to be problems at all. 'That is what people used to think about God but they came to know better' is a quite adequate answer.

This development, however, is crossed by another, namely the development of the narrative itself. The development of religion is not one uniform progress from crudity to refinement. There are in the earlier narratives sections which represent views held much later, but are found there because those narratives have been re-written. Historical sense emerges relatively late in the history of the race and even in our time it is only a minority of people who possess it. Many even quite eminent scientists are totally devoid of it and where science becomes a cult or a fetish, the appreciation of history is apt to be entirely missing. Ancient writers did not possess it at all. A writer such as the unknown person who put the books of Samuel into their present form lacked historical sense in attributing to Samuel (date about 1025 B.C.) a point of view about sacrifice which represents that of the eighth- and seventh-century prophets (I Sam. xv. 22–3). No one knows the origin of the Sabbath, but it is pretty certain that it was a Babylonian moon festival, but the compiler of Genesis dates it right back to the very beginning of the world. The compiler of Exod. xxv had before his eyes the glories of Solomon's temple and so he expands the earlier account of Moses' tabernacle or 'tent of meeting' by inserting details from Solomon's temple built four or five hundred years later. Gold, silver, precious stones, costly carpets and rugs and heavy brass furniture were hardly the likely appurtenances of a wandering race of tent-dwellers continually on the move.

The New Testament within a narrower compass illustrated the same point, but here we can have recourse to the manuscript for corroboration of this thesis. The present ending of Mark's Gospel, as we see from the Revised Version margin, was added later in the light of the experience of the Church. The Parable of the Sower is provided (unlike the other parables) with a detailed allegorical explanation containing a number of unusual Greek terms, and is thought to be a later homiletical commentary on the words of Jesus (see C. H. Dodd's *The Parables of the Kingdom*). The saying about Peter and the keys in Matthew's Gospel (xvi. 17-19), which appears nowhere else, is so completely at variance with the parallel passages which record the incident in Mark and Luke that it must be a later writer's own comment on the story.

This process is not peculiar to the Bible. It is indeed partly inevitable in the writing of history. The further we are removed from an event the longer the vista becomes and as the perspective alters so there is need for revision. Certain events which seemed important at the time are now seen to have no consequences worth mentioning while later important events have been seen to trace their origin back to something that at the time was not noticed at all. Revision therefore is constantly required. But there is often more involved than this. It was said of E. A. Freeman that in his great *History of the Norman Conquest* he drew the character of Earl Godwin from what he knew of the character of Mr Gladstone. This is more akin to the attitude of the writers of the Old Testament who credited both their heroes and their villains with ideas belonging to later times, and to the habit of medieval artists who clothed the ancient Romans in doublet and hose.

How far is all this suitable to be retailed to children? The answer is: Not at all, at any rate not to younger ones. It is most important, however, that the teacher should himself be aware of these characteristics of his subject-matter. There is no subject so much as Scripture in which the set of a teacher's own mind is of even greater importance than the material and technique of the lesson.

One point at which it may be necessary to put these considerations before the children concerns the moral lapses of the Old Testament heroes. What are we to make of Noah drunk or Jacob deceiving his father and everybody else, or Jael's treachery or David's rape of Bathsheba? There is no problem at all if we adopt the historical method. These stories represent a lower idea of morality out of which Israel developed a purer religion. What is not permissible is to try to justify these people on the ground that as they were all 'heroes of faith' anything they did must ultimately have been right. On the basis of verbal inspiration we cannot evade the conclusions that God approved of Jacob and of Jael and this brings up a far greater problem than the critical attitude to the text as we now have it.

It is well, however, to note that the Bible itself makes its own criticism of such conduct. David is rebuked by Nathan, and the child that he has by Bathsheba dies. But the most notable example of this judgement upon wrongdoing is the story of the bloodthirsty ruffian Jehu. He was the instrument chosen for the destruction of the house of Ahab and he entered into the task with gusto (II Kings ix, x). 'Come with me and see my zeal for the Lord' (x. 16). He is apparently approved for all this, and the later writer inserts his comment at x. 30, although it is neutralized by the next verse. To Hosea, however, no good at all could come of all this orgy of blood even when done in the name of the Lord. Jehu's scandalous conduct at Jezreel (II Kings x. 1–11) weighs so heavily upon Hosea that he calls his eldest child Jezreel 'for yet a little while and I will avenge the blood of Jezreel upon the house of Jehu and will cause the kingdom of the house of Israel to cease' (Hos. i. 4).

This attitude of the Prophets to wrongdoing, whether done in the name of the Lord or not, is well illustrated in Amos i. 11 and ii. 1. Edom is here condemned for his merciless conduct towards Judah, but Moab is equally condemned for his brutality to Edom. The Prophets were concerned with sins against common humanity no matter how or why they were committed. Two blacks do not make a white, and vices do not become virtues by being practised in the name of God.

This use of the Bible to interpret itself and the use of one part as a comment on another requires in the teacher a pretty full knowledge of the whole Bible and of the relevance of the different passages. We cannot deal with 'periods' as we can in English history, for the records of the early period may reflect later ideas. The fact, for instance, that the prophecy of Micah is contemporary with the J document of Genesis requires that the story of Abraham's sacrifice of Isaac should be held together in the teacher's mind with Mic. vi. 7 even though for younger children it is taken simply as an illustration of obedience to the command of God. At the same time there is needed a very clear perception of the distinctions between myth, legend and history, as the canons of interpretation are of course different and the handling of them in class must likewise be different. The situation is complicated by the fact that there are both mythological and legendary elements in the history and they are recorded in the same objective spirit as the historical sections themselves.

A legend is a story which has become attached to a person or place of importance and has a basis of fact. There were historical personages named Alexander the Great and Charlemagne but the stories about them that we find in that medieval collection called the *Gesta Romanorum* are purely legendary. Historians are now prepared to admit that there was a historical King Arthur, but the stories of the Round Table and the Holy Grail are again legendary. In America lived a woman named Betsy Ross, but that she invented the Stars and Stripes flag is pure legend. The stars and stripes were the coat of arms of the Washington family and an eagle was their crest. That King Alfred burned the cakes is legend. In the Bible we have as historical characters Moses, Elijah and Elisha but the marvels that have grown up round their names are part of the legend. In their case it is fairly easy to sort out historical fact from legend. The stories of Abraham and the patriarchs are more difficult because there is no corroboration of the legend from history, but to dismiss the whole of those stories as legendary is to go beyond what is reasonable. It is as unreasonable as to treat the whole as history.

Myth is of quite a different order. Here there is no basis of historical fact at all, although this does not mean that there is no fact enshrined in the myth. The story of the Creation is myth but the compiler of Genesis had a very definite object in retaining that myth for it was a way of attributing the origin of all things to God. It is not so easy to understand the reason for the retention in Gen. vi of the myth of the sons of the gods marrying the daughters of men. There is, however, very little mythological element in the Bible for a myth is a way of explaining natural phenomena before the rise of science, and the Hebrews were very little concerned with speculation about these things.

With history, however, they were greatly concerned, for history demonstrated God's ways with men. Yet it must always be kept in mind that they wrote history in the ancient not in the modern way. The clue is to be found in the Hebrew Bible wherein Joshua, Judges, I and II Samuel and I and II Kings are called 'the Book of the Former Prophets', Isaiah and the others being 'the Later Prophets'. Both the basis of selection from the history and the comments upon what is selected were governed by the desire for spiritual edification. The mere chronological records were to be found elsewhere in books that are now lost—'Now the rest of the acts of Rehoboam are they not written in the book of the chronicles of the kings of Judah?'[1] From all this the writers of the Book of the Former Prophets made selections and allotted praise or blame according to the standard set by the writers themselves. The 'sin of Jeroboam the son of Nebat' was a standing reproach to any of the kings who followed in his wake and yet that 'sin' was the inevitable result of the separation of the kingdoms of

---

[1] See the list on p. 159.

45

Israel and Judah. To the prophetic writers of I and II Kings, Jerusalem was the only place where sacrifices could lawfully be offered, but as Jerusalem was now in a foreign country it was natural that Jeroboam should sacrifice to the Lord in his own country. The Prophets, however, clearly thought otherwise and this habit of the kings of Israel was held against them no matter how distinguished they were in other ways.

The titles of the books of the Bible are sometimes held to be as verbally inspired as the Bible itself. The books of the Pentateuch are called the Books of Moses and consideration of this one fact is often held to outweigh all evidence to the contrary. The chief difficulty arises with Deuteronomy. Even those scholars who do not hold the generally accepted opinion that this was the book discovered in the Temple in 621 B.C. (II Kings xxii. 8) cannot accept the view that it was 'written by Moses'. The evidence against it is all laid out in detail by Driver in the *International Critical Commentary*. But this is not the way in which to tackle the question with school children, not even older ones. In this particular case it is sufficient to point out that the Canaanitish worship of Baal did not affect Israel till the time of Gideon (to which one young objector once replied by saying that Moses 'foresaw' that it would!), that Jerusalem was not in the possession of Israel until the time of David (to which the same objector replied that Deuteronomy does not mention Jerusalem, but only 'the place which the Lord shall choose') and that, for instance, Deut. xxiv. 16 is obviously later and more advanced in its religious position than Joshua vii. 24–6.

Behind such problems is the youthful and adolescent difficulty in understanding history. The phrase 'unto this day' which is the constant comment of writers of the historical books is taken as meaning the present day. To the adult the right attitude seems to be so obvious but to the pupils it is often very far from obvious. The difficulty is a general one and not confined to Biblical history. A young undergraduate who had been reading the reign of William the Conqueror was once discovered at Bayeux inquiring earnestly if anyone could tell him anything about Odo of Bayeux! He went on to Avranches and was genuinely puzzled at the ignorance of the people concerning Hugh of Avranches, one of the Conqueror's notables! And with younger children even the use of a time chart does not always solve the difficulty. This is a psychological problem and is intensified in our generation by the domination of science. The science man is not concerned about the past and his evaluation of the position today does not depend on an appreciation of what was done yesterday. In history the opposite is true and as the Bible is a historical book it presents a genuine difficulty to children brought up under other disciplines. While all children are 'fundamentalists' up to a certain age, believing in an infallible parent or teacher if not in an infallible book, the influence of certain groups such as Crusaders prolongs fundamentalism far beyond the appropriate age. The method of history is discounted and everything appears to be contemporaneous with ourselves. The drawing of 'lessons' from the stories of Sarah and Joseph and Elijah is often done with this assumption. The eleventh century B.C., the eighth B.C., and the first A.D., are held to be all on the same level as the twentieth A.D. This is one of the explanations of the apparent paradox of the appeal of fundamentalism to science men. It is not *in spite* of their science, but *because* of it. It is thus quite easy to accept the lay-out of the English Bible as that of the original and to believe that it was so from the very beginning.

The question is then often asked, 'What does it matter whether we believe Moses or Isaiah's friends to have been the author of Deuteronomy?' The question is not always disingenuous, for as so framed, it is often an assumption that 'Moses' is a legitimate alternative to the eighth-century prophets, and that it is a mere matter of opinion which it is. It cannot be too strongly stressed that this is a completely mistaken suspense of judgement. An unexamined prejudice is not at all a permissible alternative to a considered judgement based on evidence, nor is fundamentalism a permissible alternative to historical scholarship.

The real answer to the question 'Does it matter?' is 'Yes it does matter'. Our concern is to find out when, by whom, for whom and why the various passages in the Bible were written, and only in this way do we arrive at its original meaning. The alternative is to take the text as it stands, with no context, and to read into it anything that happens to be in our own minds and that is relevant to ourselves. This may be interesting and indeed helpful, but it is not and must not be supposed to be 'Bible study'.

5 THE VARIETY OF BIBLICAL LITERATURE

It is well to emphasize the different literary forms that appear in the Bible and the fact that the form is important. There are law books (e.g. Deuteronomy and the various codes), narrative history (e.g. Samuel, Kings, Nehemiah, the Gospels and Acts), folk-lore (passages in Genesis and later historical books), the dramatic narrative (chapters in Daniel, the story of Susannah and the Elders), poetry (Psalms, Proverbs, Job and various other passages), short story (Esther, Tobit), popular philosophy (Ecclesiastes), the pamphlet (chapters in Daniel, Jonah, Ruth, Revelation), sermon literature (the Prophets), worldly wisdom (Ecclesiasticus), speculative theology (Job, the Wisdom of Solomon), letters (the Epistles of Paul). Each type of literature has its own particular standard of appreciation, and we shall not judge poetry as prose and popular philosophy as if it were history. It is justifiable, however, to find all these types enclosed in one book because there is the same motif running throughout. They are all concerned with the building up of the believer in the faith. Out of all the vast quantity that might have been written about the history of Israel, the Life of Christ and the apostolic Church, only a selection has been made and the basis of that selection was edification. The Bible is a book about God and his relations with man. It is not a book of science *at all* and it is only incidentally a book of history or a classic of literature.

CHAPTER V

THE BOOK OF GENESIS

I SPECIAL DIFFICULTIES

There is no part of the Bible which causes greater controversy than the Book of Genesis. It is the first book in the Bible and with a large number of people it represents as far as they have ever read. Consequently, their idea not only of the Old Testament but even of Christianity itself is derived from this book alone. This to constant and intelligent readers of the Bible may sound like an exaggeration, but it is far from it. The witness of many army chaplains is to this effect.[1] I have found a good deal of this type of ignorance even among graduate students preparing for the teaching profession.

Then again the Book of Genesis deals with origins, and this has always a fascination for the uninstructed as well as for the scientist. In a region where much of the evidence must always be conjectural there is plenty of scope for speculation. Conclusions of a sort can easily and quickly be drawn, and the honest, scholarly historian tries in vain to overtake the errors that arise. The situation is made worse when scientific men like the late Dr Rendle Short undertake to 'square' with modern science with its categories of measurement and experiment, a great literary work the appreciation of which lies quite outside those categories. It is as absurd a task as would be the correlation of, say, Shakespeare's *As You Like It* with a text-book on botany on the ground that they both refer to trees and forests.

Unfortunately, those who are well aware of this and who recognize Genesis as the early folk-tales of a highly religious people, themselves often provide the wrong answer to the claims

[1] During World War I a book was published called *The Army and Religion* which gave the testimony of a large number of chaplains to the astonishing ignorance of the citizen army concerning these matters. There was little improvement to be noticedi n World War II.

49

of the fundamentalists. The dividing up of Genesis into its Jahvistic, Eloistic and Priestly documents is very interesting and no doubt true, but this in itself is almost as far away from appreciation of the book as the pseudo-science of the fundamentalists. It must be kept in mind throughout that Genesis is a book of religion and not of science nor of literature. Its writers were concerned first and last about God and his relations to men. They expressed their knowledge of God in the way that was best known to them, and the important thing was not their manner of telling a story but the significance of the story itself. They had not the least idea that their stories would be read 2500 years later by men who spoke English, wore trousers and discussed the atomic bomb.

It is a frequent source of difficulty to young minds that there are so many stories of other countries that resemble those in the early books of the Bible. There is a Babylonian epic of creation which has certain similarities with the Hebrew. Noah was not the only person concerned with a world flood. Greek mythology also has its flood story and Deucalion was the Greek Noah who built an ark. This ark came to rest not on Mount Ararat but on Mount Parnassus. Babylonian mythology also has a story of a great flood. The same theme is found in Maori folk-lore and indeed all over the world. Clearly the flood and the ark motifs are common to many countries. When the Code of Hammurabi was discovered in 1901 the Rationalist Press Association rather gleefully published a small book called *The Oldest Laws in the World* one purpose of which was to discredit Moses as an original lawgiver. Professor Breasted's *The Dawn of Conscience* claims for Egypt many of the ideas which occur in the Old Testament, with the implication that the Old Testament writers copied from the Egyptians.

These are arguments that have to be met, but a wordy battle about origins is not the way to meet them. It is as if it were held to discredit Shakespeare's genius that he lifted plots from North's *Plutarch* and Boccaccio. Besides it is not known whether the Hebrews did so borrow their ideas from other people. What is certain is that they made quite a different use of these ideas from that which is found elsewhere. To them the universe was rational because it was the work of the one God whose character was righteous and consistent. They took the folk-lore of their country, the early and divergent stories of the Creation, for instance, and related them all to this God. The stories remain with all their *naïveté* but the moral is different and it is the moral that matters.

Furthermore, it is essential to remember the approximate dates of the documents that make up the Pentateuch, and the fact that the stories were written and rewritten and rewritten again. And with each rewriting the vista of history had lengthened and early stories and events were seen in a new light, and later events were seen to have had an unsuspected ancestry. The old story of Abraham and Isaac, for instance, in the form in which we now have it, was contemporary with the days of Micah and Isaiah. By that time a more spiritual religion was on the way in Israel and the crudity of sacrifice, particularly of human sacrifice, was seen to be displeasing to God. Therefore Micah writes: 'Shall I give my firstborn for my transgression, the fruit of my body for the sin of my soul?' The story of Abraham's sacrifice therefore appears not as a sin-offering but as a test of his faith, for God had no intention of allowing Isaac to be killed.

2 HEBREW COSMOGONY

The Creation story in Genesis requires first of all an understanding of the Hebrew view of the earth. The diagram on p. 52 therefore is a necessity. The earth is a circular island surrounded by the sea. Beyond the sea is a rim of mountains which uphold the firmament or the vault of heaven. The firmament has holes in it called the 'windows of heaven' through which comes the rain. Above the firmament are the waters and beyond them is the abode of God who 'sitteth above the waterflood'. Below the earth and the sea is the great deep which communicates with the sea through channels called 'the fountains of the great deep' (see Gen. vii. 11). In the centre of the earth is a vast cavern called Sheol to which the spirits of men go at death. The sun, moon and stars are suspended in space below the firmament of heaven. It is all very naïve and interesting and to try to turn it into a modern scientific account is complete foolishness.

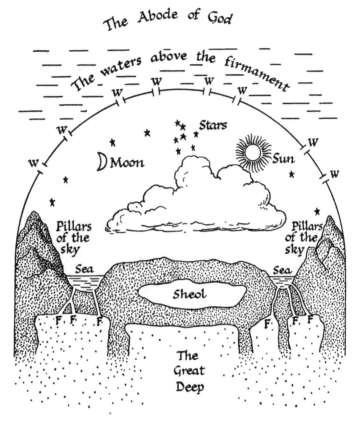

F = "Fountains of the Great Deep"
W = "Windows of Heaven"

Fig. 1

Nevertheless, the writers believed what they wrote and they took literally these items of folk-lore. But it is interesting to notice that they never personified the power of nature as did the Greeks and other ancient peoples. There was but the one God. He is a person, conceived anthropomorphically if you will, but still a real person and there was no need for a theological community centre such as Olympus was in Greek mythology. It is this very feature which creates difficulties and has led people to seek in Genesis a factual description of the origin of the world which they would never seek in other mythologies. Even in their folk-lore the Hebrews were monotheistic.

This unwillingness to accept poetry as poetry and to judge it by literary not mathematical standards has led to deliberate misinterpretations of the text. It is said, for instance, that the 'day' in Genesis stands for 100,000,000 *years*, a purely gratuitous falsifying of the writer's words. When he said 'day' he meant what we mean, namely twenty-four hours. On the story of the origin of woman Dr Rendle Short was too sound a scientist to feel happy about woman being made out of the rib of man and so he coolly declared that there is some doubt whether 'rib' in Gen. ii. 21, 22 really means a rib![1] But no Hebrew scholar has ever expressed a doubt about it. The word *tsela* means a rib.

It will further be clear from all this that the mathematical ingenuity that has been set to work on the years of the posterity of Adam has been as misplaced as the attempt to use the Egyptian pyramids as indexes to subsequent history. It is due not merely to Biblical literalism but also to a fatal absence of historical sense and to a Philistine attitude to literature. The modern teacher ought resolutely to refuse to be drawn into argument on ground chosen by the fundamentalists. Given the premises, the conclusions can be made to follow. But the premises ought not to be given. The Book of Genesis is far too wonderful a book to be used simply as a cockpit between ignorance and knowledge.

3   DIFFERENCE OF AIM IN TEACHING GENESIS
TO DIFFERENT AGE GROUPS

What then should be the aims of teaching the Book of Genesis? In the first place it contains excellent material for the very young. The stories of the early days of the world as the Hebrews

[1] A. Rendle Short, *Modern Discovery and the Bible* (3rd ed. 1952), p. 116.

conceived them are of course very popular. They are also very
well told, with an economy of words that is not usual in ancient
literature. The book falls easily into four parts:

(1) The origin stories: The Creation, Cain and Abel,
the Flood and the Tower of Babel.
(2) The Abraham cycle.
(3) The Jacob cycle.
(4) The Joseph cycle.

For young children it is sufficient to tell these tales as 'Stories
which Jesus would hear from his mother'. This not only by-passes
the embarrassing question 'Is it true?' but it puts also these Old
Testament stories from the beginning into the very setting which
accounts for their preservation for the use of Christians. Some
selection among the stories would need to be made, but even in
those which create problems, e.g. the rejection of Cain's sacrifice,
Abraham's sacrifice of Isaac, Hagar and Ishmael, Jacob's deceit,
lose some of their awkwardness when the child recognizes them
as 'just stories'. That indeed is what they are for young children
and the imposition upon them of a moral is neither necessary nor
relevant.

For older children the Jacob and Joseph cycles are excellent
connected narratives. The Joseph cycle, in particular, has the
coherence of a drama. There is an easily recognizable plot and it
has a happy ending, which is what all children like to have.

It is with yet older children that it is important to make a careful
study of Genesis for it is at this stage (ages round about fifteen)
that more serious questions begin to arise. It will be obvious to
any thoughtful reader that there are contradictions in the narrative.
One account (P) of the creation begins with a watery chaos and
records life beginning with vegetation and moving up to man.
Another account (J–E) begins with a dry waste and man is created
first, then plants, then animals, and last of all woman. There is no
reconciliation possible between these two accounts nor is it
necessary to make one. They are *two* accounts and in accordance
with what we already know of the habits of ancient writers *both*

THE BOOK OF GENESIS

are put in. There is no collation attempted by the compiler and we need not attempt one.

It is sufficient to indicate this in our teaching without going into any elaborate detail or underlining with different coloured inks the separate narratives. Over-elaboration tends to distract attention from the real aim of the stories and to fasten it upon the literary conventions of a bygone age. This may be interesting and indeed fascinating, but it is not Scripture teaching.

Apart from so-called contradictions in the narratives there are other questions which arise. What are we to make of the obviously mythological passages—such as that in vi. 1–4 about angel marriages? There is very little of this in the Old Testament but it is there. The story of the serpent in the garden again is clearly mythological, but how are we to explain it to children?

It is a help if we remember that in the first instance these stories arose, like all folk-lore, to answer the questions of the primitive mind, and that these are often the very questions that children themselves ask. We can group these questions under three headings—aetiological, etymological and ethnological. Under the first heading come such questions as 'What is a rainbow?', 'Why have snakes no legs?', 'How did different languages arise?', 'Why do women suffer pains at childbirth when animals do not?', 'Why are people ashamed of sex?' These and other simple questions are given simple answers quite satisfactory to primitive people and quite satisfactory to young children. They are not very different from 'How did the camel get its hump?' and other *Just So* stories. It is to be noted, however, that in Hebrew folk-lore all of these are related in connexion with some action of God.

Etymological questions arise in connexion with place-names. 'Why has such and such a place the strange name of "the house of God" (Bethel)?', 'How came the people to be called "Israel" (He who strives with God)?', 'Why has their great ancestor the discreditable name "Jacob" (the crafty one)?', 'How was Jacob's father called "Isaac" (laughter)?', Sometimes the answer is rough and ready and incorrect as when in Gen. xi. 9 the word Babel is derived from the Hebrew *balal*, to confuse, 'because the Lord did there confound the language of all the earth'. Babel is really Babylon, and the word Babylon means 'the gate of God'. But we ourselves are not unfamiliar with popular etymologies of this kind. Sweetheart is falsely derived from 'sweet' and 'heart'. The word 'helpmeet' which is not a word at all, is nevertheless given a suitable popular derivation, although it comes from a misunderstanding of the English of Gen. ii. 18.

Ethnological questions are such as concern the origin or characteristics of races. Why, for instance, was there a perpetual feud between Edom and Israel? The Esau and Jacob story gives its popular origin. Why were the Midianites wanderers while the Hebrews lived in settled habitations? Why are agriculturalists constantly opposed to town-dwellers? The story of Cain and Abel is given as the reason—and therefore there is no need for the writer to give any explanation of why Cain's offering was rejected. (The Old Testament is very suspicious of town life—see Amos ch. i and ii, for instance.) How did the tribes of Israel come by their curious names—Reuben (looked upon my affliction), Simeon (the Lord hath heard), Levi (joined), Judah (praise), Dan (he judged), and so forth? Gen. xxix. 31-xxx. 24 gives the traditional origin of these names.

The original readers of Genesis found answers to other questions which greatly concerned them and which depended upon a knowledge of history. Whence came the Hebrew race in the first instance? The migration of peoples as given in Genesis must have had a historical justification. The origins given for the institution of the Passover, the Sabbath and circumcision, however, are again the popular ones and are due to the desire of the writers to date all such things as far back as possible. We shall naturally not look for history in these accounts. Apart from what we know from other sources of the origin of these things, there are clear anachronisms in the narrative itself. Abimelech, for instance, the story of whom is usually left out of a teaching syllabus, is stated as being a king of the Philistines, but the Philistines are known not to have been in Palestine until long after the Patriarchal period.

4 CHARACTERIZATION

The Book of Genesis, however, for teaching purposes is far from being simply a museum of antiquities. The character-drawing in the cycles of stories is very well done. It is nearly always done by contrast. Cain is contrasted with Abel, Jacob with Esau, Sarah with Hagar, Isaac with Ishmael, Joseph with his brethren.

In the Abraham cycle there are a number of passages of high literary quality. The children will have been introduced to Abraham either direct from ch. xii (which raises the question of Abraham's deliberate lying) or by the retelling of the story. But four episodes which follow should on no account be missed either by young children or older ones. Abraham's intercession for Sodom (xviii. 16–33), his relations with Lot (xix. 1–28), his offering of Isaac (xxii), and the story of Isaac and Rebekah (xxiv), are told in superb narrative and should all of them be read aloud. With older children the questions which arise from the first three could also be dealt with. Abraham's intercession for Sodom bears all the marks of a later age when the question of the innocent suffering with the guilty had sprung into prominence. 'That be far from thee' says Abraham. 'Shall not the Judge of all the earth do right?' 'Right' here refers to something of far wider import than concern for a particular people. We are here concerned with 'human rights'. Abraham's relations with Lot is explained in xix. 37, as accounting for the origin of the Moabites. The story of his offering of Isaac is given partly to explain the phrase Jehovah-jireh (the Lord will provide), and partly as a pictorial illustration of the later prophetic objection to human sacrifice (see pp. 44, 51). The story of Isaac and Rebekah is a perfect idyll.

There are two notable passages in this part of Genesis which are of importance for the New Testament, namely the story of Melchizedek (xiv. 18–24) which is made use of by the author of Hebrews (ch. vii) and the striking interpolation of a later idea into the more ancient story of Abraham's call in ch. xv. It comes in *v*. 6, 'And he believed in the Lord and he counted it to him for righteousness' and is referred to not only in Heb. xi, but also via the reference in Hab. ii. 4, by Paul in Rom. i, 17 and Gal. iii. 11. These references to Genesis are best left until the relevant passages in the New Testament come to be studied. It is the use made of them rather than the passages themselves which is important.

Throughout the Abraham saga Abraham appears as the ideal Israelite, faithful, righteous, just the person to be the founder of a faithful and righteous nation even though it did not take over his name. The character of Jacob, however, is different. He is more like the real Israel as the prophets found it—crafty, deceitful, persistent and sinful, yet meaning well all the time, very much the kind of person to give his name to that kind of nation.

Jacob is first of all contrasted with Esau. There is first the story of their birth and upbringing. (It will be necessary to explain just what is meant by 'birthright'.) Secondly, in ch. xxvii, is the story of how Jacob stole Isaac's blessing—a most graphic account. It is followed by the complicated story of Jacob's relations with Laban who was almost as crafty as Jacob himself (xxix. 1–30). Inserted in this is the notable interlude of Jacob's dream of Bethel (xviii. 10–20). Finally Jacob is reconciled to Esau (xxxiii. 1–17) a narrative which is preceded by the story of Jacob wrestling at Penuel (xxxii. 22–32) which accounts for the origin both of the name 'Israel' and also for that of a Jewish food taboo. In v. 30 the place is called Peniel, and in v. 31 Penuel, a simple example of two accounts woven into one.

The older children may be invited to notice how the story of Jacob and Esau parallels the history of Israel and Edom. The references are to Edom barring Israel's approach to Canaan (Num. xx. 14–21, and Judges xi. 17); David's conquest of Edom (II Sam. viii. 14); Edom's recovery of independence (II Kings viii. 22); the hatred of Edom for Israel (Amos i. 11–12); and Edom's rejoicing at the capture of Jerusalem (Ps. cxxxvii. 7), and the bitter oracle against Edom, the book of Obadiah.

The story of Joseph is of a quite different character from the preceding sagas. It is a well-constructed whole and as we shall see (p. 95) it lends itself easily to dramatic representation. It also has much more in it of the historical element although exact dating is impossible. It explains how Jacob's descendants found their way to Egypt and so it connects with the Moses story in the Book of Exodus. (There are, however, two sections which do not belong to the story, namely the story of Judah and Tamar, ch. xxxviii, and the Blessing of Jacob, ch. xlix.) It also represents a later stage of development in religious thought. God is an over-ruling Providence and not an actor intervening directly in the personal affairs of the people concerned.

5 THE PLACE OF GENESIS IN THE SYLLABUS

How far should the background of these stories form part of a school curriculum in Scripture? The identification of various Old Testament kings with historical characters such as Amraphel with Hammurabi, or of place-names with historical places such as Shinar with Babylonia, can be a fascinating and indeed an endless quest. It is the proper concern of scholars, but it has also been a popular pastime for fundamentalists for a different purpose. It should be clear, however, to the teacher that the quantity of historical or topographical accuracy to be found in Genesis does not affect the spiritual purpose of this book any more than it would in the case of Bunyan's *Pilgrim's Progress*.

Nevertheless, some acquaintance with archaeological discoveries is useful for the teacher as a contribution towards the better understanding of the book. But archaeology is a subject that needs careful handling. It is so often used as a stick with which to beat the scholars. Many men who have done good work in archaeology have discredited themselves by trying to discredit the equally good work of others who have a different angle of approach. Books therefore, such as *Biblical Archaeology: its Use and Abuse* by Dr G. H. Richardson and Millar-Burrows' *What Mean These Stones?* are valuable guides which ought to be in the teacher's hand. The first was written as a sober examination of such books as *The Bible is True* and *The Bible Comes Alive* by Sir Charles Marston, in both of which really good accounts of archaeological work are spoiled by two major defects—an over-anxiety to substantiate the fundamentalist point of view, and a complete misunderstanding of what constitutes 'proof'. Someone picks up in the Jericho excavations a charred bit of rope and immediately this is used to 'prove' that the story of Rahab as given in the Bible is true. Is not this a bit of the very rope with which she let down the spies from the wall? This type of credulity would be looked on as ridiculous in any other field of knowledge. Why is it not ridiculous in connexion with the Bible? Professor Garstang gives as frontispiece to his *Joshua-Judges* a picture of a hornet which is said to be the badge of Thothmes III of Egypt, and *therefore* as Exod. xxiii. 28, Deut. vii. 20 and Joshua xxiv. 12 all refer to the hornet, Thothmes III must have been the Pharoah of the oppression and *therefore* the Exodus took place in 1447 B.C. What is omitted here is that the hornet was the symbol of *all* Egyptian kings from the first dynasty onwards, and so this reference really tells us nothing. It is not surprising when front-rank scholars become the victims of their own wishful thinking that popular writers like Dr Rendle Short should be even more credulous. The truth is that the Bible is a literary work and literary standards are therefore right and proper to use in examining it. It also deals with historical places and peoples and events and therefore historical methods are also rightly used. Many of the early sections of the Bible deal with periods for which there is no literary or historical corroboration and therefore archaeological methods are also in place. It requires all these approaches and not merely one alone in order to give us a real understanding of the Bible. Who were the writers? Where did they live? For whom did they write? Why did they write? To set one of these methods over against the others and, for instance, to hail archaeology because it establishes the truth of verbal inspiration (which it does not and cannot do, for these belong to two different categories) is to prevent one ever discovering the truth.

CHAPTER VI

SOME NEW TESTAMENT DIFFICULTIES

I THE USE OF A SYNOPSIS

The problems that arise in the teaching of the Old Testament are largely historical or literary and can be solved on these considerations alone. New Testament problems while often again historical or literary also raise issues of a different kind.

The New Testament is concerned with the central figure of the Christian faith and therefore questions of personal loyalty and adoration are involved. It is not easy to keep to the middle line between two extremes—treating the story as no more than a historical narrative, or refusing to apply our minds to it at all because such treatment is 'irreverent'. We can see at once the absurdity of the position that Christianity depends upon the literal acceptance of Genesis: but there is a certain reasonableness in the position that it depends on a tomb being found empty, as there is also, whether we accept the literalness of the fact or not, in seeking to make it depend on a virgin birth of Jesus.

There is, however, one great similarity between the two testaments. They were both written for edification and the historical parts (as we now have them) were written last. The Old Testament histories were based on a principle of selection made by the prophets. The Gospels were written after the Epistles of Paul and the principle of selection of their material was that it illustrated 'the way' as preached by Paul. Had there been no 'prophecy' there would have been no Old Testament. Had there been no 'Church' there would have been no Gospels. The Gospel created the Church, and the Church published the Gospels.

This is a principle of exegesis in both Testaments, but the importance of it in the New Testament is crucial. A quite false antithesis is often drawn between what is called 'the simple faith' of the

Gospels and the apparently laborious theological treatises of St Paul. The fact is that the Christian communities were established by Paul through his preaching and the contagion of his example and by the miraculous working of the spirit of Christ within the new community, and then, *after that*, the need arose for historical accounts of the life of Jesus. Accordingly all the Gospels, and not the Fourth Gospel only, are interpretations of the life of Christ in the light of the experience of later Christians, at any rate in so far as they are selections from the material available. The Fourth Gospel says so much: 'Many other signs did Jesus in the presence of the disciples which are not written in this book: but these are written that ye may believe' (xx. 30, 31).

The stories, therefore, that have come down to us from that early period owe their importance to the fact that they were held to be most characteristic of Jesus himself. We can even see the process at work in the Fourth Gospel where a characteristic story which in the first instance had been left out was later put in. This is the 'pericope de adulteria' of John vii. 53–viii. 11, R.V.

It is most essential in teaching the New Testament to have at hand a good synopsis of the Gospels. A good one for English readers is that by J. M. Thompson (Oxford Press). It has broad quarto pages and prints the parallel passages in the same line across the double pages, differing versions being shown in italics, and passages not found in one Gospel which are found in another are paralleled with a blank space. It is therefore easy to see at a glance the whole Synoptic layout. The text is the R.V. and the marginal readings are given. This edition has the advantage over Huck's Greek synopsis both in its line by line synopsis and also because it is worked out on a basis of Mark and not of Matthew. The study of all the synoptists *together* is one way by which the older children can come to understand the 'Synoptic problem' not as a 'problem' (of which far too much has been made in many books for schools) but as a most interesting example of the different impressions made by Christ upon different people who had the same loyalty. The human element in 'inspiration' becomes obvious without having to stress it or getting the whole question out of proportion. It is always much better for children to find out these matters in the ordinary course of study than by having them treated in isolation. The one difficulty in the case of Thompson's book is that it is far too expensive for class use, but the teacher should have a copy for reference, and even when the Gospels are studied singly, the parallel passages should be noted.

This use of a synopsis raises a general question. Teaching ought always to be positive, not in the sense of being dogmatic but rather as a presentation of assured results. Accordingly we shall find that most problems will arise of themselves, and the teacher can then give guidance in solving them. And even here it is more important to set before the child the standards that he is to apply rather than a dogmatic statement of a position. Many problems for instance, arise which challenge the moral character and consistency of Jesus. Here it is essential that our chief concern should be to preserve the moral excellence of Jesus rather than the inerrancy of the narrative as we now have it. Ingenuity the aim of which is to preserve both will not carry us very far and will often land us into still greater problems.

A warning should be given concerning the use of pictorial illustrations. These can often be used in such a way as to do violence to history. It is questionable, for instance, whether the Clarendon Bible, an edition often used in schools, is wise in the use of such illustrations as 'the reputed site of the feeding of the five thousand' or 'the site of the tomb of our Lord in the Church of the Holy Sepulchre' (*St Matthew*, pp. 59 and 97), both of which are, to say the least, very highly problematical if not untrue. The 'traditional site of the inn of the Good Samaritan' (*St Luke*, p. 67) has the same measure of historicity as the White Swan at Ipswich 'where Mr Pickwick stayed'. Palestine is full of so-called sacred sites, most of which have to be accepted with suspicion, and some of which are patently bogus.

2 SPECIFIC PROBLEMS

With these principles and cautions in mind we may now turn to consider a number of specific problems that arise in the teaching of the New Testament.

(a) *The Gospel prologues.* The prologues of Matthew, Luke and John create a difficulty, particularly those of the first two. John's prologue is obviously what it is, an introduction to the whole Gospel. It gives the setting of the life of Christ within the eternal purposes of God, and the technical term 'the Word' needs to be understood in the context of contemporary thought. The story proper begins, as in all the Gospels, with the mission of John the Baptist. Mark alone starts there without a preface of any kind.

Matthew and Luke, however, begin with the childhood stories, and while these are delightful story material in the religious education of young children, they certainly create difficulties with older ones. How could a star move along as a guide to a caravan, and how could it rest 'over a stable'? What exactly was it that the shepherds saw? If they were 'angels' had they any clothes on and if so where did they get them? (I mention questions that children have actually asked.) Is it a historical fact that once upon a time all the little male children in Bethlehem were slaughtered by order of the king?[1] And finally, if it was known from the beginning who Jesus was, why is it that in the Gospel history it is clear that the neighbours thought he was just 'the carpenter', and his own relations believed in him so little that on one occasion they came to take him home because they thought he was mad? (Mark iii. 21.)

The last question in particular presents us with so flat a contradiction that no rationalizing can possibly save the literal accuracy of *both* stories. It must be one or the other. If, however, we recognize that every Gospel begins with John the Baptist and that it is clear that Jesus was quite unremarkable until he suddenly appeared at the river Jordan and joined himself to this new move-

---

[1] There is no reference at all in Josephus who usually loses no opportunity of blackening Herod's character (see, for example, *Antiquities* XVI and XVII).

ment, the childhood stories fall into place as the *authors'* prologues to their Gospels. They bring together as in an overture all the themes that we are going to hear more fully in the Gospels themselves. The shepherds are the common people who heard Jesus gladly, Herod is the usurper, neither good Jew nor good Roman, who represents the evil powers of this world, the wise men in the stable are a picturesque elaboration of the homage that the truly wise render to God as seen in a little child, the relation of Jesus' infancy with that of John the Baptist makes evident the New Testament's relation to the Old. Simeon and Anna were of those pious folk whose numbers had never died out since the great Exile, who were looking for the consolation of Israel and to whom Jesus was the fulfilment of prophecy. Matthew's constant efforts to find an Old Testament text to fit every event, and sometimes to find an event to fit every likely text, at one point lands the commentator into a problem. Jesus lived in Nazareth, says Matthew (ii. 23) 'that it might be fulfilled which was spoken by the prophets "He shall be called a Nazarene"'. But nowhere in the Old Testament is any such text discoverable.

The Christmas and childhood stories therefore, are admirable teaching material for small children and are no less admirable for older children who can appreciate their symbolic nature. The question 'Are they true?' admits of the answer both yes and no. The writer's purpose was clear, especially if we notice from the apocryphal gospels the kind of stories of Jesus' childhood that were rejected. Why were some rejected and these retained? At this point we recall the principle of selection of the Gospel stories. These made for edification and the others did not.

(*b*) *The temptation in the wilderness* is merely alluded to by Mark. The incident shows Jesus' concern at the real meaning of John's ministry and his own relation to it. How was the kingdom of God to come? There were three possible lines of action. He might appeal to the worldly and material desires of men as did the Sadducees. He might, like the Pharisees, by meticulous observance of the law build up so great a 'treasury of merits' that God for his own honour would have to intervene in human affairs. Or lastly, like the Herodians, he might make terms with the 'powers that be' and by achieving influence with men on other grounds persuade them to accept as their own his attitude towards God. The Gospels of Matthew and Luke cast this dilemma into a pictorial form and the stones, the pinnacle and the mountain indicate these three possible contemporary choices. The mountain in particular was a symbolic mountain. Matthew says it was 'exceeding high'. Luke does not mention it at all but says that Satan showed Jesus all the kingdoms of the world in a moment of time. This is familiar apocalyptic imagery. All these choices represented what had come to be characteristic of different schools of post-exilic Judaism and it is notable that in rejecting them all Jesus goes back to Deuteronomy and to the purer belief in God to be found therein. The temptation overcome in the wilderness returns to Jesus again when Peter, before there is any crucifixion or resurrection, recognizes Jesus as the Christ (Mark viii. 27–35 and parallels). But Jesus sees this as a temptation, for the devils also recognized him to be the Christ (Matt. viii. 29) and mere recognition of this fact is not enough. Some more radical acceptance of his way of life is needed and this is only possible through some unwonted supernatural grace in the human heart made available by a more radical action on Jesus' own part. In other words death itself must be risked and even endured before life can come into the world. This thought occurs again on the occasion of the visit of the Greeks (John xii. 20–5) when for the third and last time the temptation comes to him to escape the Cross. (The fact that in all three Synoptists this recognition by Jesus of Peter's so-called 'confession' is recorded as in reality a temptation makes it clearer than ever that the words 'Thou art Peter and upon this rock will I build my church, etc.' which occur in Matthew's account alone, were not in the original text. They do not appear in the parallel passages.)

(c) *The money-changers.* The story of the money-changers in the Temple has been used again and again to justify the use of force and even of war and so it is worth while reconstructing the incident itself. The plausible theory that Jesus used force only on the

SOME NEW TESTAMENT DIFFICULTIES

animals will not help us much and is an attempted rationalization. In the first place the money-changers had every right to be there. The Temple tax could not be paid in money bearing a man's head for that was idolatry and so the Roman silver coins had to be changed into the Jewish copper coins. But this legitimate business of exchange had become a racket from which the high priest, Annas, was the chief gainer, and for this to be carried on at the very doors of the House of God was a first-class scandal. And so Jesus' wrath boiled over and he drove them out. But with what? Neither with whips nor with any physical force whatsoever. What could one man do even with a whip in a place thronged with thousands of people coming and going? It is nonsense even to think that it was by physical force. It was, however, a clear example of the tremendous power of moral authority. It was this same kind of power which enabled Ambrose of Milan single-handed to bar the entrance of the victorious emperor Theodosius and his troops into the Cathedral. Hot anger by a resolute man in a righteous cause has a strength far beyond anything that any physical agency could provide. The story of the money-changers, far from being a justification of the use of physical force, is a clear argument against it.

(d) *Jesus' own use of the Old Testament* often creates a difficulty. The favourite example is the reference to Jonah (Matt. xii. 39–41, Luke xi. 29–32). If, as we now realize, the Book of Jonah is a story written to enforce a lesson, how is it that Jesus appears to treat it as literal history? 'The men of Nineveh shall stand up in the judgment with this generation, and shall condemn it: for they repented at the preaching of Jonah; and behold a greater than Jonah is here.' The references to Jonah occur in Matthew and Luke where Jesus refuses to give a sign to 'an evil and adulterous generation'. They are additions to the parallel passages in Mark, while Matthew further adds a reference to 'the Queen of the South'. They may of course be Matthew's and Luke's own expansion and illustration of the remark of Jesus, in which case no problem arises at all. Or it may be that Jesus quotes Jonah as we quote Shakespeare's Hamlet or Milton's Satan to drive home a message, the value of which does not depend at all upon whether Hamlet or Satan ever lived and said the words attributed to them. Or it may be that we have to take our Lord's attitude to Jonah as being exactly the same as that of his contemporaries and that this apparent ignorance of the real nature of the book was part of the human limitation which Jesus accepted. To deny omnipotence to Jesus because his humanity was a real humanity, and at the same time to postulate omniscience, is an inconsistency which makes nonsense of what we believe to be the Incarnation. The words of Christ in the New Testament cannot be used to guarantee the authorship of passages in the Old. Jesus also appears to believe that devils were beings that could take up their abode in a man's soul quite independently of the man. That is not our modern view of madness, and yet it is no reflection on the character of our Lord. If we accept Paul's statement that Jesus 'emptied himself' of divinity and took the form of a servant (Phil. ii. 7) this is simply one of the indications of it.

(e) *The miracles*. This is the most controversial question of all and it is well to make a careful study of the miracles (i) in their contexts; (ii) in the parallel passages in the other Gospels (this is where Thompson's synopsis will be found most useful), with a clear understanding of one's own attitude towards them. To take the line that 'miracles do not happen' and therefore they never did happen, is as unwarranted as to assume that to explain a miracle is to explain it away. We have also to remember the literary characteristics of ancient authors (see above, pp. 38–40) and the attitude of simple people towards anything that they do not understand. A considerable lapse of time separates the life of Christ from even the earliest written account, and stories grew in the telling in those days even as they do now. Nevertheless, such a unique and powerful personality as that of Jesus must have had an influence such as we cannot today estimate. This must be allowed for, but it is a good canon of procedure to consider first the literary transmission of the stories then the historical setting and not till then the psychological and moral questions involved. It is very profitable to consult a book such as M. R. James' *The Apocryphal New Testament* and see from the apocryphal gospels the sort of miracles that were *left out* of the canon as compared with those that were left in. The legends of mere wonder-working for the fun of it, so to speak, are left out, and only those are retained which—whether correctly reported or not, are concerned with some human need. In this regard the attitude of the Fourth Gospel to miracles as deliberate 'signs' is much nearer to the Old Testament attitude than that of the Synoptic Gospels. In the Synoptists the miracles are incidental and their importance is minimized at any rate by Jesus himself if not by his followers. It is the story itself that is important and the mind of the person involved. 'Thy faith'—and not, so to speak, 'my supernatural power'—'hath made thee whole.'

Above all we have to hold fast to the principle that what matters is the character of Jesus and not the inerrancy of the narrative as we now find it in our English Bibles. In many cases we can never know the actual facts—they have become confused in the memories of different people and have been transmitted through various literary media and oral tradition. The Resurrection appearances are a case in point. But the character of Our Lord stands out quite clear amid all the variant readings of the Gospels, and it is that which in all things must be our standard of interpretation. A simple instance of this is in the story of the Gadarene swine where the incident as reported makes Jesus do an unheard of thing—namely taking away the livelihood of the owners of a herd of swine. This is so completely alien to what we know of his character that it is clear that the report is at fault. An understanding of the primitive mind and its ignoring of secondary causes (see p. 40) indicates where the confusion lies.

We must also accept Jesus' own attitude as we find it in the Synoptic Gospels. To him the 'miracles' appeared to be not only of secondary importance but also a very possible hindrance to the Gospel itself. He steadfastly refused to work 'signs' to order, and would not base his authority on any external manifestations of his power. And if he did not use them as a guarantee of his own power, neither would he encourage the disciples to use them as a guarantee of theirs. There can be no more authentic word of Jesus to be found anywhere in the Gospels than his word to the 'seventy' when they returned with joy and said 'Lord, even the devils are subject unto us in thy name'. He was glad of it, but he continued 'Howbeit in this rejoice not that the spirits are subject unto you, but rejoice that your names are written in heaven' (Luke x. 20). He bids people who were healed to go away and say nothing about it publicly. It is not until he has established his position on other grounds that he sends word to John the Baptist about the sick being healed and the dead being raised up, and—in the same category—'the poor have the Gospel preached to them'—a remark which might make it appear that the lame, blind and dead are those who hitherto have been so spiritually. And if we look closely into the miracles reported in the Synoptists we shall see that they were all done to help someone in need and never for his own glory.

We can therefore take John's treatment of the miracles as edification rather than history. This is in harmony with the rest of the Fourth Gospel. From the point of view of late Christian apologetic they were treated as signs and yet the Synoptists throughout treat them otherwise. But if we approach these stories as the Synoptists indicate that Jesus himself approached them, it will not appear to us that the whole Christian faith is jeopardized if we treat them as of minor importance. To rest the 'divinity' of Jesus on the fact that he did miracles is to go quite against the first three Evangelists and is indeed at variance with the essential inwardness of the Gospel. If they are clearly capable of interpretation along what are often called 'natural' lines, this does not take away from the significance of the situation within which they are reported as having taken place. There are those who say that to speak of Jesus being seen in the dim light walking along the sea-shore is less impressive than to think of him right out in the middle of the sea. This, however, magnifies the importance of the physical details far beyond the point of the story. The incident was not a demonstration of how clever it was to be able to walk upon the sea. That part of it is merely incidental. Similarly if we take into account the *whole* situation of the stilling of the storm it becomes clear that the point of it was the effect of a calm, fearless, confident attitude to danger upon the minds of other men who had none of these qualities. 'And immediately there was a great calm' in the minds of the disciples whatever continued to go on outside. The old evangelical hymn comes right to the point of that story:

> With Christ in the vessel
> I smile at the storm.

Explaining a story is not the same thing as explaining it away, and to draw attention to the way in which men's minds worked in those early days, both spectators of events and their later reporters, is not to destroy the stories but to attempt to see them as they appeared to Jesus himself. We must always ask 'What was this miracle done *for*?'

From this standpoint, therefore, we may now look at the miracles themselves. They fall into two classes—the miracles of healing and the others. The miracles of healing do not raise the problems with us that they raised in our grandfathers' time. The tremendous psychic influence of our Lord over the minds of men would extend to their bodies also, and faith in his power could, as we say, 'work miracles'. And it was always in the first place to the minds of men and to their faith that Jesus made his appeal. This in itself would cut out the miracles of healing from the category of 'signs'. His power was seen particularly in the case of the mentally afflicted and it is interesting that no case of this type of healing is recorded in the Fourth Gospel. The author clearly had his own opinion as to what constituted a 'sign'. But over leprosy, and haemorrhage and catalepsy (Jesus himself said that the 'dead' damsel only slept) his power was equally manifest.

The nature miracles, however, are of a different order, and here we must apply our canons of interpretation and come to the literary question first. The story of the stilling of the storm is perhaps the simplest of this type. There are some incidents recorded as miracles which are clearly parables. The coin in the fish's mouth (Matt. xvii. 24–7) bears on the question of the means whereby Jesus and the disciples were to pay their taxes. It was to be by their physical labour, the fishermen from their fishing. The cursing of the fig tree (Mark xi; Matt. xxi) taken as it stands seems pointless until we notice that in Luke the story is stated to be a parable (Luke xiii), and also that the fig tree was the characteristic prophetic symbol of the Jewish nation (Jer. xxiv).

Nevertheless, there is a hard core of three difficult cases. The fact that they all occur in the Fourth Gospel may furnish us with a clue to their interpretation. These are the raising of Lazarus, the turning of water into wine and the feeding of the five thousand. And, of course, beyond these there is the greatest story of all: the Resurrection. The teacher will have to look at them, as at all the miracles, not in the attitude 'let us get rid of the supernatural elements'—but rather from an acceptance of the *situation* as it stands, and with an attempt to understand how the story came to us in its present form.

It is imperative to remember the didactic character of the Fourth Gospel. To take the incidents in it exactly as they are given in the text is to avoid the very necessary labour of interpreting them in the light of the author's intention. He had the technique of the Greek moralists and he uses his characters as exponents of his own message. Nevertheless, he was a Hebrew and he has the fondness of the Hebrew for the use of a story to enforce a lesson. If we look carefully at the stories of Lazarus and of the turning of water into wine we shall see how different they are from the Synoptic miracles. In the Synoptists there are accounts of the raising of the dead, but usually the term 'dead' represents what the neighbours themselves thought about it. Jesus himself says of Jairus' daughter 'She is *not* dead, but sleepeth' and of course they laughed him to scorn. This was not said in the case of the widow's son at Nain but there is no reason why this should not have been a similar case. But of Lazarus it is explicitly stated otherwise (ch. xi). Verses 4 and 11–16 are very important because they indicate that the incident is set in the middle of a discussion, and *vv.* 17 and 19 enhance the story by stating that Lazarus has been dead four days. The discussion continues in the house at Bethany and its real text is in *v.* 25, 'I am the resurrection and the life: he that believeth in me shall never die'. It is not unreasonable to think that here is another of the writer's discourses about Jesus—written long years after the Crucifixion—and recalling the discussion which arose through the report of Lazarus' illness. The improving of the occasion with a discourse is all in the Johannine manner, and the fact that Jesus wept, surely an authentic touch, is strangely inconsistent with the physical raising up of Lazarus' body. 'He that believeth in me shall never die' says Jesus, and adds 'believest thou this?' The story is an interpretation of the difference that Christ makes to the death of loved ones and it misses its point if the physical details are stressed as a 'miracle'.

The turning of the water into wine, if it stood by itself, would be of the same class as the apocryphal miracles and we should wonder how it got into the canon, but again it is the author's picturesque illustration of the difference made by the presence of Jesus in any situation. It is set right at the beginning of the Gospel and is, as it were, its signature tune. The old wine of Judaism was all right in its way but the water that comes with Christ is better than any wine. The running short of refreshments at a party is a very tiresome occurrence but what does it matter? The people are still there, there is still good fellowship and above all there is the wonderful Guest who makes all the difference to any company. Here again the stressing of the physical detail of an illustration misses the point of which it is an illustration.

The story of the Feeding of the Five Thousand occurs in all the four Gospels and is the only miracle common to all. It is clearly, therefore, a very important part of the New Testament narrative. Told as it is, it raises many difficult questions. It is clear on the surface that without a quite extraordinary display of supernatural power it was impossible that this small amount of food could have satisfied five thousand hungry people and that they could leave twelve basketfuls. And in the light of the Synoptic attitude to miracles and of Jesus' own rejection of the temptation to turn stones into bread, what was the point of it? Literary considerations here do not help us, and so we must look to the second canon of exegesis (p. 68)—What is the historical situation behind this story? If we remember the small size of Galilee and the short time it takes to walk along one side of the lake we may well ask ourselves, could not these people have gone home? They were not far from home in any case, not more than an hour or two at the very most. Why, therefore, was it necessary to feed them at all? The necessity was not indicated in any other incident in the life of Jesus, and moreover from the story it would appear that the people after being fed stayed there all night—within easy reach of home. The fact that of all that vast crowd there was to be found only one person with any food, in itself indicates that some comparison is intended to be drawn between the immense number of hungry people and the apparent smallness of provision. It would have been just as big a 'miracle' had there been a hundred people, but five thousand makes it all the more startling. Then we have to notice that there is a 'doublet' to the story. There is an account of another crowd, but this time it is four thousand. All these accounts should then be compared with the story of the Last Supper, particularly in Mark xiv. 22, Matt. xxvi. 26, and Luke xxii. 19. We should also note that the story of the Last Supper does not occur in the Fourth Gospel at all. We have, there, a discourse which follows this story of the five thousand and is concerned with Jesus as the bread of life and the water of life. It is this passage in John's Gospel which seems to be the key to the whole story. It contains the teaching of the early Church on the Eucharist. Christ is the spiritual food for an infinite number of people—four thousand, five thousand, the whole world, and it comes to them through his disciples, 'Give ye them to eat'. It is a New Testament application of a story in the Old Testament where Elisha performs the same kind of miracle, a story which would be familiar to all the Evangelists (II Kings iv. 42–4). Granted, however, that this may be the origin of this story, it is still a matter of conjecture, for the incident is given with all the wealth of detail of an eyewitness's description. In Mark, for instance, the crowd sit on the 'green grass'. With younger children it will have to be told as it stands and the difficulty of it simply accepted.

We must, however, remember the inwardness of the teaching of Jesus. The story, about the leaven of the Pharisees (Matt. xvi. 6–12) indicates how much in his mind was the comparison of physical bread and spiritual bread. It seems most likely, therefore, that this incident, recorded as a physical miracle, had to do with some teaching of Jesus of a metaphorical kind. Only then would there be any real point in the story, if we adopt, as I assume we are adopting, the total life and character of Jesus as our standard of interpretation. Moreover, there are frequent references to the lesson that this story was expected to teach the disciples. What, for instance, is the meaning of Mark's comment after the story of Jesus walking on the sea—'They understood not concerning the loaves, but their heart was hardened'? (vi. 52).

If we look carefully at the three Synoptic accounts of this incident we shall see that in every case Jesus takes the bread, looks up to heaven, blesses the bread, gives to the disciples who in their turn give it to the multitude. John's Gospel says that Jesus gave thanks and then distributed the bread himself. In other words this was no mere giving of bread to hungry people; it was a ritual act, and those cannot be far wrong who hold that this is an account of an early Eucharist in which the exhortation and the illustration have combined to form a picturesque and highly symbolical story.

How to teach this to older children or to answer their questions about it is not easy. One truthful way out is to tell the story exactly as it is and if questioned to say that this is the way the story has come down to us. *How* exactly it all happened we have no means of knowing. It is not necessary to go into any theories of the Eucharistic significance of the narrative, not even to point out that in the Fourth Gospel this story takes the place of the story of the Last Supper.

Belief in the Resurrection is cardinal to the New Testament. Everything is possible if this is possible. But the dilemma is this: If Jesus' body rose from the tomb, where did it go to? We no longer hold the pre-Copernican view of the universe which is necessary if we would say 'Up into the sky'—although that is what the narrative in Acts actually says. On the other hand if the body did not arise, how was the tomb found empty and how was it that the disciples were quite certain that Jesus did arise? One thing is certain and that is that we shall never know just what happened. The disciples' own recollections conflicted and there were many stories which were passed down along different channels of tradition. It is noticeable that in Matthew's account even the Resurrection itself did not convince *all* the disciples. 'And when they saw him they worshipped; *but some doubted*' (xxviii. 17). Thus even the Resurrection, the greatest miracle of all, is not 'a sign'. It is important to notice that Jesus did not appear to Pilate or Caiaphas or any of those who disbelieved in him. He was known only *within the circle of faith.*

There is no answer possible to all the questions that arise and it is useless to try to manufacture one. There are, however, certain facts which have to be granted:

1. Every account insists that Jesus was known to be alive. The very variations in the story are a guarantee of its authenticity.

2. The disciples were changed men, and in so far as we can know of the existence of Jesus only through his followers, their own account of the cause of the change has to be accepted.

3. The Resurrection was an integral part of the preaching of Paul. He was a late arrival in the apostolic band, but he has no doubt at all about this fact.

The fact that Christians all down the ages have borne witness to the same experience is not itself a proof of the Resurrection, for it might be held that the coming of the Spirit at Pentecost was the real beginning of the new life. Nevertheless all that can be said is that the Resurrection of Jesus happened, but how it happened or with what manner of body he came out of the tomb, or what happened to that body afterwards are insoluble questions. One general position might be established, namely that we ourselves cannot tell how a completely unique person like Jesus Christ would affect the physical world. Clearly in this case the attempt of a merely literary solution of the problem, as in the case of other recorded miracles, is quite inadequate.

(*f*) *The Crucifixion.* The right way to teach the Crucifixion is perhaps the hardest of all the problems in Christian education. There is no doubt that the morbid elaboration of the physical details has been the root of a great deal of the anti-Semitism on the Continent, while what Dr John Mackay calls 'the patronage of the dead Christ'[1] has led in Roman Catholic countries to a very unhealthy type of piety. Indeed the very word *pieta* is the technical term for a picture of the dead body of Jesus. The cosmic and the ethical significance of the Crucifixion are not really subjects for children's contemplation at all, although with the adult it is here where his Christian experience can be said to begin. We are concerned, therefore, only with the story itself, and it must be taught in such a way as to honour the Master's own prayer: 'Father forgive them, for they know not what they do.' All kinds of facts come together at the Crucifixion—the deadly sin of worldly religious leaders, the culpable timidity of administrative officers, the fickleness of the Jerusalem mob, the cowardice of Jesus' own friends, the cruelty of common soldiers, the soulless insipidity of politicians. It is most important to give each factor its due weight and not to give the impression that Jesus was put to death simply 'by the Jews'. In what sense could it be said of any of these groups that 'they know not what they do'? This is the question to be kept in mind if we are to follow our usual standard and see this terrible event as Jesus himself saw it. Pity for the evildoer rather than for the victim is the right attitude. It does not diminish the individual's responsibility but it does give point to the belief that it was human sin that brought Jesus to the cross. And he came that men might be delivered from the power of sin, even the men who put him there.

3 ACTS AND THE EPISTLES

The teaching of Acts is sometimes a completely time-wasting exercise in geography, accompanied by a great deal of map-drawing. When, however, the narrative in Acts is studied in its context of life and politics in the Roman Empire it takes on colour

[1] *The Other Spanish Christ*, p. 111.

and movement. In addition to its need for contexts there is no book in the Bible which so much requires imaginative handling in order to bring out the full historical and religious significance. As an example of the opposite take the lugubrious hymn of S. J. Stone, especially if set to the funeral dirge, *Macedon*:

> Through midnight gloom from Macedon
> The cry of myriads as of one,
> The voiceful silence of despair
> Is eloquent in awful prayer,
> The soul's exceeding bitter cry
> 'Come o'er and help us, (*dim*) or we die.'

The passage in Acts to which this miserable verse refers is that notable section in ch. xvi when at *v.* 10 the narrative suddenly breaks into the first person plural and we realize we are reading an eyewitness's account: 'And a vision appeared to Paul in the night. There came a man of Macedonia standing, beseeching him, and saying "Come over into Macedonia and help us". And when he had seen the vision straightway we sought to go forth into Macedonia.' Anything less funereal than this can scarcely be imagined, and if, as seems likely, 'the man' was Luke we have here the original account of how the Gospel crossed over from Asia into Europe.

The book of Acts gives the historical framework into which the Epistles are to be fitted. The controversial question such as whether Philippians comes late or early need not worry the teacher for it makes no real difference either way. Still less does it matter whether he accepts the North or the South Galatia theory. These are interesting points but they do not raise the kind of historical problems that affect the text in any way. It is important, however, to bring out the fact that these Epistles were not theological treatises composed in the study but were written on the road and deal with very practical questions that had arisen. From the point of view of teaching children, and even adults, the position of Deissmann is more relevant than that of, say, Peake, who believed that there was a corpus of doctrine called 'Paulinism' which it was Paul's concern to expound. Deissmann's view is that the Epistles were written *ad hoc* and the situations with which they deal have to be understood if the Epistle is to have any meaning. The fact that two important Epistles were lost indicates that if Paulinism is a body of doctrine developed apart from local situations we lack two very important 'sources' for it, and it would not be easy to reconstruct them. But to see, for instance, the early chapter of I Corinthians in the light of what we know from Acts of Paul's visit not only to Corinth but also to Athens is to see how very much on the spot Paul is in all his writings. This historical method also prevents us wasting time over those sections of Paul's writings which were purely *ad hominem* and of no more than local interest, such as Gal. iv. 25–31.

4 REVELATION

The Book of Revelation has always had a strange fascination for untutored minds. If it is looked at historically it is no more difficult than any other book, unless we are dealing with the original Greek, which is exceedingly difficult. Revelation should be compared with Acts and the change of attitude to the Roman Empire noted. Moreover, there is this perpetual comparison with ancient Babylon —the Christians like the Jews of olden time are in exile and the bitterness of Ps. cxxxvii is repeated with greater depth in the whole Book of Revelation. For it was not only exile that the Christians were suffering but also cruel persecution, and the book reeks with un-Christian hate and fury. Yet while this is so, and the future doom of Rome is looked for with savage anticipation by her helpless victims, it is still more notable that over against the figure of the brutal Roman Empire there is exalted the strangest symbol that ever took hold of the imagination of men—a lamb with its throat cut! The resounding music of Handel 'Worthy is the lamb that was slain' clothes the metaphor with decent re-spectability and makes us forget how incredible it is. But the opposite of the physical might of the kingdoms of this world is not another still mightier kingdom—not even 'the ghost of the deceased Roman empire' by which Hobbes meant the Papacy— but a realm of humility, gentleness and love, where suffering rather than self-assertion is the law of life. This is the kingdom of 'the lamb as it had been slain' and the crude, savage symbolism of this despairing cry of the persecuted saints should not hide from us the fact that its real significance is to be found not in the interpretation of the number 666 nor of 'time, times and half a time', but in the central pathetic figure to whom alone universal dominion has been committed by God.

CHAPTER VII

POETRY AND DRAMA

I POETRY OF THE OLD TESTAMENT

It is a weakness of the Authorized Version that it is printed throughout in prose. The Revised Version gives a better view of Hebrew literature for Job, Psalms and other acknowledged 'poetical' books are printed as poetry. But for the English reader even this gives no idea of the quantity of poetry that the Bible—and particularly the Old Testament—contains. For this we must go to a modern version such as Moffatt's or the American Revised Standard Version.

From these it is clear that almost the whole of the Book of Isaiah and a great part of Jeremiah are poetry, and that there are nearly fifty poetical passages in the historical books. Psalms are not confined to the Old Testament hymn-book, but they are to be found in Jonah, Nahum, Habakkuk, Deuteronomy, II Samuel and II Kings, while the same psalm appears sometimes in two different places. Pss. xviii and cv, and parts of Pss. xcvi and cvi, appear twice, as a reference to the R.V. margin will show. Similarly proverbs are found elsewhere than in the Book of Proverbs. There are a number of such sayings to be found in the historical books, of which Samson's riddle and proverb in Judges xiv. 14, 18, and the first verses in II Sam. xx, may stand as examples. The Hebrew word for these is *Meshalim*, the plural form of *meshal* which means a comparison or a metaphorical saying.

The characteristic medium of prophecy was the oracular utterance which was delivered in rhythmical speech like the Welsh *hwyl*. The earlier Prophets seem to have relied on music to stimulate their inspiration. Elisha when asked for his advice on one occasion sends for a minstrel (II Kings iii. 15). In the Books of the Prophets these oracles are embedded in narrative, the amount of which is variable. There is scarcely any in Hosea and Isaiah, more in Jeremiah, but a large amount in Ezekiel. The *form* of prophecy is therefore important and to treat the poetical passages as plain matter-of-fact prose narrative is to show a failure to appreciate the nature of poetry.

The psalms of the Old Testament here and there show a striking similarity—and also *dis*similarity—to Babylonian penitential psalms and some of the hymns of the period of the New Kingdom of Egypt. This will be of interest to older children especially to those who have come up against the sophisticated argument that the Bible has 'copied' from the Egyptians and Babylonians. Freud's book on Moses touches on this theme and it is also part of the argument of J. H. Breasted's *The Dawn of Conscience*. It is well to recognize such similarities, for they indicate something that is common to the human mind everywhere.[1]

2 FORMS OF HEBREW POETRY: PARALLELISM

The form of Hebrew poetry is 'parallelism' and it is sometimes difficult to bring home to children that this is poetry at all. It corresponds to nothing with which they are familiar in English verse. There are, however, two aspects of it which are unexpected. The first is that it still retains its poetic qualities in translation. Concerned as it is with the *idea* more than with the words the idea can be got over even though the words are altered. It does not require the Hebrew words in order to convey to the English reader the full flavour of the distich

> Pride goeth before destruction
> And a haughty spirit before a fall.

The qualities which make these lines poetry in Hebrew are retained in the English version. The same is true of prophecy as in Isa. xl. 9:

> O thou that tellest good tidings to Jerusalem
> Lift up thy voice with strength;
> Lift it up, be not afraid;
> Say unto the cities of Judah, Behold your God.

[1] At the same time the dissimilarities also need stressing. The Babylonian Penitential Psalms are published by the S.P.C.K. in a little booklet costing sixpence, and the Egyptian parallels will be found quoted in T. H. Robinson's *Poetry of the Old Testament*, and in full in A. Erman's *Literature of the Ancient Egyptians*, p. 288.

Secondly, although the Hebrew verse form is of a different character from any English verse form, it is not altogether different from English *musical* form in folk-songs and hymns. In his little book *Melody Making* Sir Walford Davies takes several simple songs and shows how songs are built up on a basis of parallelism. If we indicate each movement by a letter we shall find, for instance, that the structure of the tune *The Vicar of Bray* or of the tune *The Bluebells of Scotland*, runs like this, A A B A. The hymn-tune *St Deinio* or *Joanna*—'Immortal, invisible, God only wise'—has the same structure. The tune *The Lincolnshire Poacher* is as follows: A B B A or in old notation:

Now compare this with Ps. li. 1:

> Have mercy upon me O God
>> According to thy loving kindness
>> According to the multitude of thy tender mercies
> Blot out my transgressions.

The structure of the first tune, A A B A, corresponds roughly to the structure of the concluding verses of Ps. i. 5, 6:

> Therefore the wicked shall not stand in the judgment
>> Nor sinners in the congregation of the righteous
>> For the Lord knoweth the way of the righteous
> But the way of the wicked shall perish.

All forms of parallelism do not exhibit this kind of correspondence, but it is sufficient to indicate that parallelism is not something quite alien to English experience.

There are of course different kinds of parallelism. There is the synonymous,

> The heavens declare the glory of God
> And the firmament sheweth his handiwork...;

6-2

the antithetical,

> A soft answer turneth away wrath
> but grievous words stir up anger...;

the comparison or emblematic,

> Better is a dinner of herbs where love is
> than a stalled ox and hatred therewith...;

or,

> As cold waters to a thirsty soul
> So is good news from a far country...;

the climax,

> I will sing
> Yea I will sing
> Praises unto the Lord...;

the quatrain,

> Except the Lord build the house
>   They labour in vain that build it.
> Except the Lord keep the city
>   The watchman waketh but in vain...;

the giving of a reason,

> Tell it not in Gath
> Publish it not in the streets of Ashkelon
>   Lest the daughters of the Philistines rejoice
>   Lest the daughters of the uncircumcised triumph.

The structure of the first Psalm is particularly interesting, for it sums up nearly every kind of Hebrew verse form. It is almost what we should call a sonnet form. The first and longer part deals with the blessedness of the good man, and it falls naturally into two parts of similar structure.

> Blessed is the man
>   that walketh not in the counsel of the wicked
>   nor standeth in the way of sinners
>   nor sitteth in the seat of the scornful
> But
>   his delight is in the law of the Lord
>   And in his law doth he meditate day and night.

And
He shall be like a tree
  planted by the rivers of water
  that bringeth forth its fruit in its season
  Whose leaf also doth not wither
And whatsoever he doeth shall prosper.

The second part is of six lines arranged in three lots of two and deals with the position of the wicked. The third pair sums up the whole story in a final contrast between the good man and the wicked man.

It is a useful exercise to get pupils to find for themselves examples of these types, or to be given a passage in prose, such as the Balaam story in the Authorized Version (Num. xxii-xxiv) and from a study of the language to discover the poetical sections.

3 OTHER POETIC DEVICES

There are other poetic devices to be found in the Old Testament. There is the stanza form. In Amos, for example, the verses from ch. i. 3 to the end of ch. ii, fall easily into eight stanzas each introduced by the words

  Thus saith the Lord
  For three transgressions yea for four
  I will not turn away the punishment thereof.

Sometimes it is the end of the stanza that contains the characteristic words. Isa. ix. 8–x. 4, is one prophecy in four stanzas, each of which ends with the refrain—

  For all this his anger is not turned away
  But his hand is stretched out still.

If we look at Isa. v. 25 we shall notice the same refrain.

Pss. xlii and xliii are really a single psalm of three stanzas, each ending with a refrain of four lines at xlii. 5, 11 and xliii. 5. Ps. xlvi has also three stanzas marked at the end by the unknown rubric 'Selah'. Ps. cvii is divided up by the refrain

  O that men would praise the Lord for his goodness
  And for his wonderful works to the children of men.

The five psalms that comprise the collection known as *Lamentations* show the stanza form very clearly. This is most true of ch. iii which is arranged in twenty-two stanzas of three 'verses' each. They are an excellent example of synonymous parallelism.

With the stanza form goes a certain rhythmical quality which cannot always be noticed in an English translation. Perhaps the greatest single psalm in the Old Testament is that found in Isa. lii. 13 to the end of ch. liii. In the English Revised Version it has five stanzas of three verses each. In the Hebrew these stanzas increase gradually in length as the poem goes on and there is an assonance which almost amounts to rhyme. For the full appreciation of the form of this great poem and its effectiveness as a medium for its meaning, we must necessarily turn to George Adam Smith's *The Book of Isaiah* (vol. II, ch. 20). There is no writing anywhere which so completely makes for an understanding of the Hebrew prophetic technique as this famous chapter. To give us the flavour of the Hebrew itself he transliterates one of the stanzas and even the English reader can catch something of the effect it must have had on its first hearers. Then he translates into the rhythm of the Hebrew the whole five stanzas with all the original emphases (p. 343):

> Surely our ailments he bore
> And our pains he did take for his burden
> But we—we accounted him stricken
> Smitten of God and degraded.
> Yet he—he was pierced for crimes that were ours,
> He was crushed for guilt that was ours
> The chastisement of our peace was upon him
> By his stripes healing is ours.
> Of us all like to sheep went astray,
> Every man to his way we did turn,
> And Jehovah made light upon him
> The guilt of us all.

The construction at the beginning of lines 3 and 5—'but we'—'Yet he'—is an 'anacrusis', namely a word which is outside the metrical scheme and emphasizes the statement about to be made.

The Hebrew mind worked in concrete images rather than in abstract forms and consequently even in prose the Hebrew could not avoid imagery and similes. The metaphors are always graphic and apposite. The wicked 'grind the faces of the poor', they 'draw iniquity with cords of vanity and sin as it were with a cart rope'. The good man will be 'as a nail fastened in a sure place'. God will make for his people 'a feast of fat things'. Men have 'made a covenant with death, and with hell are we in agreement'. The nations of the earth are 'as a drop of a bucket, and are counted as the small dust of the balance'. When the servant of the Lord comes he will be characterized by gentleness: 'a bruised reed shall he not break and the smoking flax shall he not quench.' The people of God have been chosen 'in the furnace of affliction'. (Here the metaphor of the refining fire of the furnace corresponds to the familiar one in the New Testament of the 'tribulation'—the threshing of the wheat with a flail (tribulum)—to drive away the chaff.) The promise to the faithful is that

> When thou passest through the waters
> I will be with thee
> and through the rivers
> they shall not overflow thee.
> When thou walkest through the fire
> thou shall not be burned
> neither shall the flame kindle upon thee.

The nemesis of the ungodly is that 'they sow the wind and they shall reap the whirlwind'.

These are but a few samples of prophetic imagery, and every one of them is a most apposite metaphor.

It is the same with similes. What more wonderful simile of the peace of Messiah's reign could there be than is found in Isa. xxxii where every ordinary man 'shall be as an hiding place from the wind and a covert from the tempest'. In ch. xxxv 'the wilderness and the solitary place shall be glad for them and the desert shall rejoice and blossom as the rose'. Both Micah and the writer of I Maccabees depict the land of peace as a place in which 'they shall sit every man under his vine and under his fig tree, and none shall make them afraid'. In Isa. v is the long simile of the vineyard which was used by Jesus in more than one parable.

To notice these metaphors and similes and to remember that they are not 'flowers of speech' but apt illustrations of the situations with which they deal is to have an appreciation of poetic diction even in our own language.

<h4>4   PROVERBIAL SAYINGS</h4>

The material of Biblical poetry can be divided into two classes. First, there are proverbial sayings, local or tribal slogans and songs, and spells. Secondly, there are the longer poems, poems of praise and victory, dirges and psalms.

Num. xxi includes three local songs of particular interest. The first, in *vv.* 14 and 15, is almost meaningless except that it is quoted from 'the Book of the Wars of the Lord'. These seem to have been collections of songs made at different times to celebrate

> Old unhappy far off things
> And battles long ago.

Verses 17 and 18 are the Song of the Well invoking a blessing on a well that has just been dug. The last verse of the well-known hymn 'Holy Spirit, truth divine' refers to this passage

> In the desert ways I sing
> Spring, O Well, for ever spring.

Verses 27–30 celebrate a victory over Sihon King of the Amorites and perpetuate Israel's claim to land which had belonged to Sihon. In days before there were written records, history and even legal history was remembered in song.

Songs of blessing and of cursing were a common form of poetry. There are many of these but for school purposes we need notice only three. First, Gen. xlix. 5–27. This is in the form of Jacob's blessing on his sons, but is a collection of pieces concerning each of the tribes in turn. It is interesting as illustrating the different reputation that the tribes held, just as among ourselves there are proverbial sayings and jingles concerning Yorkshiremen, the

Scots, or Taffy the Welshman. Secondly, the exciting story of Balaam in Num. xxii-xxiv. It is a painful thought that this graphic story should have become the target of ignorant objectors to the Bible because it records that an ass spoke. Balaam was sent for by Balak, a Moabite chief, to curse his enemies the Israelites but he finds that he cannot do it. The story is admirably told and included in the narrative are four oracles representing Hebrew poetry at its best. Thirdly, Deut. xxxiii. This is the Blessing of Moses and has certain similarities to the Blessing of Jacob. The differences between the two should be noted, and if the position of the tribes is compared with what we know from the historical books we shall be able to come to a rough conclusion as to the date of the later poems. It is a magnificent poem, all in one piece and of the same metre throughout. It contains at least two passages that are well-known out of their context in *vv.* 25 and 27.

The chief source for isolated proverbial sayings is of course the Book of Proverbs itself. (It should be noticed that the phrase 'proverbs of Solomon' does not cover the whole book.) They are concerned with good common-sense and worldly wisdom although it is all related to a man's attitude to God. The right relation to God is described as 'fear', meaning by that not terror but respect. It is an Old Testament version of the New Testament aphorism: 'Seek first the kingdom of God and his righteousness and all other things shall be added.'

Of the same kind is the Apocryphal book Ecclesiasticus. It is chiefly and sometimes only remembered by ch. xliv ('Let us now praise famous men') but it deserves much more notice than this, especially if the scholarly translation by W. O. E. Oesterley is used.[1] Beside ch. xliv we may note particularly: xxxviii. 23–34, on Craftsmen; xxxix. 1–11, on the Scribe; xxxvii. 27–31, discretion in eating; xxx. 1–13, the training of children; xxv. 1–11, things beautiful and things hateful. Indeed, the whole book is worth knowing and is very 'quotable' both for its poetry and for its illustrations of Jewish social life in the second century before Christ.

---

[1] *The Wisdom of Ben Sira*, S.P.C.K. In this edition the sections are given headings which make clear the reference.

5 POEMS OF VICTORY

There are three great paeans of victory in the Old Testament all of which are magnificent poetry.

In Exod. xv there is the 'Song of Moses' in celebration of the crossing of the Red Sea. The 'Song of Miriam' which follows it in *v.* 21 repeats *v.* 1 and seems to have been a refrain. Sir Walter Scott in Rebecca's song in *Ivanhoe* (ch. xxxix) has caught the spirit of it:

> There rose the choral hymn of praise
> And trump and timbrel answered keen
> And Zion's daughters poured their lays
> With priests' and warriors' voice between.

In Judges v we have one of the oldest pieces of poetry in the Old Testament, the Song of Deborah. It has a genuine Homeric ring to it and it tells of a society in which any kind of ruthlessness was justified against the enemy. It ought to be read aloud and properly declaimed, for the English here catches the full thrill of the Hebrew. It contains magnificent examples of climactic parallelism:

> The kings came and fought;
> Then fought the kings of Canaan....
> They fought from heaven,
> The stars in their courses fought against Sisera.
> The river Kishon swept them away,
> That ancient river, the river Kishon.
> O my soul, march on with strength.

Notice the atmosphere of breathless excitement created by the deliberate gaps in the narrative as we pass from one theme to another. In *v.* 24 Jael comes in, without any previous introduction and in the next verse Sisera is introduced without his name being given. At the end of *v.* 27 we are switched without warning away from the battlefield to Sisera's own home with the subject of the sentence again coming later:

> Through the window she looked forth and cried,
> The mother of Sisera cried through the lattice
> Why is his chariot so long in coming?

And then after the confident suggestions of her maids of honour, there is another gap in the story followed by the crashing climax—

> So let all thine enemies perish, O Lord!

This is as fine a poem as anything in Homer, and is indeed one of the world's great odes. The teacher of course will not need to be reminded that it cannot by any effort be made into a Christian poem whether by allegorizing or in any other way!

The third poem of this type is the so-called Song of Hannah in I Sam. ii. It has little to do with Hannah, but seems to be a triumphal ode for some unknown victory and has been inserted here because of the one reference in *v.* 5 to the barren woman who became the mother of children. The theme is also to be found in Ps. cxiii and in the Magnificat (Luke i).

6 DIRGES

Just as we have paeans for victory so we have dirges for defeat and sorrow. There seem to have been mourning women whose duty it was to lament for the dead (Jer. ix. 17–20). The best known of these poems is to be found in II Sam. i. 19–27 where it is taken from the Book of Jasher. This is David's lament for Saul and Jonathan, who

> Were lovely and pleasant in their lives
> And in their death they were not divided.

All the enmity between David and Saul is here forgotten and the father shares with the son the affection of the son's friend. Compared with this, the other dirge in the historical books—David's lament for Abner (II Sam. iii. 33–4) is clearly a fragment of a longer poem.

The most notable dirge, however, is the Book of Lamentations chs. i, ii and iv (chs. iii and v are psalms). They are concerned with the destruction of Jerusalem by Nebuchadnezzar and the word 'How' which occurs three times in the first verse should be translated 'Alas' for it is a groan and not a question. The verses were

written in the time of the Exile and the painful description of the
city's sorrows turns in i. 11 to a personal lament by Jerusalem herself:

Is it nothing to you, all ye that pass by
Behold and see if there be any sorrow like unto my sorrow which is
   done unto me.

She confesses her sins and still hopes for restoration. The second
chapter recalls the horrors of the siege itself, the smashing of the
gates, the famine, the corpses, the cannibalism. God has allowed
all this to happen and he has become as their enemy. Chapter iii
is a meditation upon all this and a suggestion as to its meaning.
It is a psalm rather than a dirge and is concerned with the relation
of God to his people. Chapter iv has a two-verse instead of a three-
verse stanza and it returns to the theme of ch. ii with further
description of the horrors of the siege and the capture of the king
(*v.* 20). All this was due to the sins of the leaders, the prophets and
the priests (*v.* 13). Chapter v again is a psalm somewhat after the
manner of ch. iii and concludes a book which shows the break up
of the old order that came to an end with the Exile. There are
certain passages in these chapters that are worthy of learning by
heart, such as the great section in iii. 27–36 concerning the faith-
fulness of God.

A passage which is often referred to as a dirge is Amos v. It is
a lament over the moral decline of Israel as the prophet saw it. It
is in the stanza form but it is an oracle rather than a dirge. It anti-
cipates rather than recollects, but it is akin to Lam. iii and v.

7 THE BOOK OF PSALMS

The greater part of Old Testament poetry is to be found in the
Book of Psalms and it is well to remember that these were intended to be sung. It is the hymn-book of the second Temple.
Like all hymn-books it is a compilation from various sources
written at various times, and it also expresses various moods of
religious experience.

In the English Revised Version and the American Revised
Standard Version, what we call the 'Book' of Psalms is seen to

consist of five books. They are arranged as follows: Book I,
Pss. i–xli; Book II, Pss. xlii–lxxii; Book III, Pss. lxxiii–lxxxix;
Book IV, Pss. xc–cvi; Book V, Pss. cvii–cl. These are separate
collections and each ends with a benediction such as:

> Blessed be the Lord the God of Israel,
> From everlasting and to everlasting.
> Amen and Amen.

The titles of the psalms are worth noting if only to show that they
were not all attributed to David. Book I are called psalms of
David. In Book II, Pss. xlii–xlix are psalms of the sons of Korah,
Ps. l of Asaph, and Pss. li–lxxii again of David. In Book III,
Pss. lxxiii–lxxxiii are psalms of Asaph, Pss. lxxxiv, lxxxv, lxxxvii
and lxxxviii of the sons of Korah, and Ps. lxxxix is a psalm of
Ethan the Ezrahite who is mentioned in I Kings iv. 31. Book IV
is a miscellaneous collection including the Hallelujah psalms,
Pss. civ–cvi, which are also continued in Book V, Pss. cxi, cxiii,
cxv–cxvii, cxxxv and cxlvi–cl. Book V is largely anonymous and
liturgical and includes the Pilgrim psalms, Pss. cxx–cxxiv.

The psalms were set to music and many of the puzzling instructions at the beginning of psalms, as for instance at the head of
Ps. lxxxviii, as well as signs such as 'Selah', were instructions to
the musicians. They had percussion, strings and wind instruments,
and the people had very little part in the Temple service except
to say 'Amen' or 'Hallelujah'.[1] There appear to have been several
guilds of musicians—some such as Asaph, mentioned by name.
Many of the psalms go back to pre-Exile times, but it was after
the Exile that they were collected first into five books and then
into one. Some are as late as the Maccabean revolt. The point of
view is that of the prophets and many of them express themselves
strongly against the sacrificial system. Many also are expressions
of private devotion which have later been set to music and used
in the services. The chief themes are the lovingkindness of God
and his righteousness.

As the psalms for the most part cannot be fitted into any
chronological scheme they tend to be left out in Scripture

[1] See II Chron. xxix. 26–8.

syllabuses. This is unfortunate for they represent yet one more factor in the religious development of Israel. Even in times when prophecy had ceased and religion had become stereotyped there were these warm personal expressions of experience to which the people could turn. It is a useful exercise to go through the book and classify the psalms under such headings as nature psalms, historical allusions, the Law, and the Temple.

There are two 'correlations' here which must not be missed. First, there is the connexion between reading the psalms in the Scripture lesson and singing them in assembly. Secondly, there is the place of the psalms in history. Rowland Prothero's (Lord Ernle) famous book *The Psalms in Human Life* sheds no light on the Book of Psalms itself, but it is a wonderful portrait gallery gathered from every nation, tribe and people and tongue of those to whom the psalms have brought inspiration and consolation. It is a necessary book for the school library.

8 DRAMA: SUGGESTIONS FOR DRAMATIZATION

Drama was not a literary form among the Hebrews or the early Christians. Yet they had a fine dramatic sense in narrative, for not only were they fond of character contrast but they had a keen sense of irony, and an appreciation of climax. Not all their dramatic narratives, however, are capable of dramatization. It would be difficult, for instance, to dramatize for school purposes the stories of Samson, Gideon, Balaam or Elijah, dramatic though they are in themselves. They depend too much on action of a kind that cannot very well be represented on a stage although it lends itself admirably to a film. Milton has seized on a particular aspect of Samson's career which is suitable for drama after the classical Greek pattern, but this again is not very well suited to representation on a school stage. The Book of Job again is a drama but after the Greek pattern. It is akin to Aeschylus' *Prometheus Bound* where the hero, rendered helpless, carries on a dialogue with various people who are all concerned to blame him for his own misfortunes. Milton's *Samson Agonistes* ought certainly to be read in school, if not acted, for Milton's ending is very much the kind of thing which the ancient writer would have approved.

There are several dramatic incidents which would be suitable for dramatizing and acting and there is one story which is almost a complete drama just as it stands. This is the story of Joseph in Gen. xxxvii, xxxix, xl–xliv. Joseph son of Jacob becomes unpopular with his brethren who thereupon wish to slay him. They are dissuaded by Reuben who nevertheless joins in a plan to get rid of him and pretend to Jacob that his son has been killed. (All these factors have their corresponding incidents in the later part of the play, and their appearance should be noticed.) Joseph then goes down into Egypt and falls into the toils of Potiphar's wife. (This from the dramatic point of view is an artistic device to enable his skill in dream interpretation to come to the notice of the authorities.) He flies from her, leaving a damning bit of evidence in her hand. (Here we have the handkerchief motif as we find it in *Othello*.) He is unjustly cast into prison but there his interpretation of his fellow-prisoner's dream ultimately releases him. Thus the very thing which got him into trouble with his brethren got him into favour with Pharaoh. Then comes the famine and this is the connecting link between Joseph in Egypt and his brethren in Canaan. They send to Egypt for corn, but they do not recognize the official with whom they deal. Nevertheless, he recognizes them and in spite of the fact that he continues to play upon their ignorance, we are told 'he turned himself about from them and wept'. This touch is really the key of the whole drama. Joseph is not revengeful, but wishes to ensure that his brethren have changed their hearts. This proves to be the case and we are shown the anguish which they suffer in order not to hurt their father whom at the beginning they only too willingly deceived. The withholding of Simeon and the sending for Benjamin as well as the manipulation of their sacks, while all the time the men fail to recognize their brother, are like incidents straight out of Boccaccio or Shakespeare, so cleverly are they worked into the story. Reuben comes in again, this time as his father's comforter. At the close everybody recognizes everybody else and it all ends happily.

Other Old Testament dramatic incidents will need a good deal of adaptation for dramatization. As has already been noticed the Old Testament writers are fond of characterization by contrast. In the story of David, for instance, there is first of all his relationship with Absalom—the fond father always believing the best and so completely paralysed by the conflict between his affection for his unworthy son and his duty to put down rebellion, that finally other people have to act for him. When finally he laments for his son, ignoring the dangers through which his faithful servants have passed in order to deliver him, Joab has had enough and tells the king that he ought to be ashamed of himself (II Sam. xix. 5–7).

The story of David and Saul is again a dramatic character study of the two men, heightened by the fact—on which the drama really turns—that David's greatest friend is Saul's son. Here is certainly a piquant situation, and it is recognized in the story itself as told in the Bible. Our interest is now with David and Saul and then switches to David and Jonathan until finally both Saul and Jonathan perish together at Gilboa. David's victory is turned (this time) into a worthy and beautiful lamentation both for his friend and also for his friend's father. The story may be given a fitting end with the account of Mephibosheth who is honoured by David as the son of Jonathan and grandson of Saul (II Sam. ix).

The history of Jehu has all the elements of a dramatic tragedy but it is Ahab who is the tragic figure (I Kings xxi; II Kings ix. 10; Hosea i. 4). It is a play upon the theme of the right thing being done in the wrong way and consequently turning into the wrong thing. Ahab has some good in him although he had to die, and there was much evil in Jehu although he had to kill him. There are six possible scenes which we might allot as follows:

(1) Ahab and Jezebel discussing the case of Naboth. Jezebel is a foreigner and has no understanding of how the Israelite felt about social justice. Ahab represents a different tradition and has qualms about taking strong action. Jezebel after the manner of Lady Macbeth in a similar situation ('Infirm of purpose: give me the daggers!') forces Ahab's hand and the deed is done.

(2) Elijah's interview with Ahab and Ahab's penitence.

(3) Elisha is told to anoint Jehu King of Israel for the house of Ahab is doomed. Jehu takes up with alacrity this work of destruction.

(4) Jehu at Jezreel. The murder of Jezebel.

(5) In the middle of further slaughter Jehu says to Jehonadab, 'Come with me and see my zeal for the Lord', and just before his treachery to the prophets of Baal he says sarcastically, 'Ahab served Baal a little, but Jehu shall serve him much'. We have then at the end two judgements passed upon him by the writer. 'Thus Jehu destroyed Baal out of Israel' and 'But Jehu took no heed to walk in the law of the Lord God of Israel with all his heart.'

(6) Hosea passes sentence on the whole grim story. 'Call his name (his son) Jezreel, for yet a little while and I will avenge the blood of Jezreel upon the house of Jehu.' To this Matt. vii. 21–3 is a fitting conclusion.

The Elisha and Naaman story is an excellent play upon contrasted characters, with the dealings of Gehazi with both of them as a kind of sub-plot. (See 'Specimen Lessons', p. 200.)

The graphic story in Isa. xxxvi, xxxvii and II Kings xviii, xix is a dramatic dialogue, and the contrast between the type of confidence shown by the envoy of Assyria and the other type of confidence shown by Isaiah is the real theme of the story. We have first of all the two parties in the state—the pro-Assyrian and the pro-Egyptian. Isaiah will have nothing to do with either—'through the voice of the Lord shall the Assyrian be beaten down' (Isa. xxx. 31)—and ch. xxxi condemns both parties. Then the Assyrian danger becomes threatening, and Assyria sends an envoy. The envoy is aware of this hope in Egypt and he warns the people against it—'this broken reed'. At the same time, despite the frenzied pleading of Eliakim and the others to him to be quiet, he calls in a loud voice to the people in Hebrew and over the head of Hezekiah, not to believe their king when he tells them to trust in God. Have the gods of the other nations been of any use? Isaiah, however, has already told Hezekiah that in quietness and confidence will be his strength. Hezekiah is puzzled to know what to do, but Isaiah tells him what to say. It is a glorious message of defiance rather like David's challenge to Goliath—'who is this uncircumcised Philistine, that he should defy the armies of the living God?' (I Sam. xvii. 26 and 45-7)—and it is this rather than the flight of Sennacherib which gives the really dramatic touch to the story. It is so unexpected and is indeed such a reversal of what one would expect, and yet there is more reason for it than there is for the Assyrian's boastfulness. And, of course, in the sequel it is completely vindicated.

The story of Nebuchadnezzar has in it the same element which is so common in Greek tragedy—in the *Persae* for example—that judgement upon *hubris* or the overweening pride which arrogates to itself credit which belongs only to God. Nebuchadnezzar was no tyrant but was a strong king and could afford to be reasonable. The story begins with the first siege of Jerusalem by Nebuchadnezzar at the close of the reign of Jehoiakim and during the short reign of his son Jehoiakin. All the 'best people' were taken to Babylon, and Zedekiah left as king in Jerusalem. Pss. xlii and xliii (originally one psalm) express the feelings of the captives who were called by Jeremiah the 'good figs' (Jer. xxiv). The 'bad figs' (should we say the 'bad eggs'?) who were left behind ignored Jeremiah's advice and plotted against Babylon. So Nebuchadnezzar comes a second time and puts an end to the kingdom of Judah. Lam. ii and iii is a sad comment on this. We now turn to the story in Dan. iv. 28, where Nebuchadnezzar, having made his conquests and settled in Babylon, walks in his palace and glows with self-satisfaction (Dan. iv. 30). But 'while the word was in the king's mouth there fell a voice from heaven' pronouncing his doom. He goes mad and only recovers when he repents of his sin. But nevertheless his doom is writ.

The Book of Esther is not particularly religious but it is an excellent drama. The good man here is persecuted by the bad man, but the fate which the evildoer intends for the righteous descends upon himself.

Nehemiah has certain dramatic elements. The work of building up Jerusalem goes on in spite of Samaritan opposition. But here again there is no dramatic *action*, although one can imagine a good film being made of the story.

The Book of Tobit has already been dramatized in *Tobias and the Angel*.

Jonah is a story that is easily dramatized, for while it depends on action the necessary dialogue is also given. The great fish is introduced into the story to account for Jonah's second chance to go and do the will of God, but it need not be introduced into the play. The psalm in ch. ii is not part of the story.

Scene 1. Jonah argues with the Almighty concerning Nineveh. He is bidden to go and prophesy there but he does not wish to do it because he does not want the Ninevites to be converted and he is shrewdly afraid that this may happen and that God will spare them. Jonah has no use for the heathen.

Scene 2. He has run away and finds himself on a ship manned by heathen sailors (note the irony of this fact). The storm comes on. He is discovered to be the cause of it, but the heathen, for their part, do all that they can to spare him. However, he has to be thrown overboard.

Scene 3. He is again told to go to Nineveh, and this time he goes and what he feared happens. The Ninevites repent and are spared.

Scene 4. His final argument with the Almighty. Why has He done it? Jonah's attitude to the withered gourd is contrasted by God with his attitude to the poor Ninevites, 60,000 of them 'and much cattle'.

The New Testament does not lend itself very much to dramatic treatment although, of course, many of the incidents have been made the basis of drama, and in the Middle Ages the Gospel stories were an integral part of the miracle plays. The New Testament material, however, needs paraphrasing in order to make it suitable for this purpose. The Book of Acts, especially the career of St Paul is full of stirring scenes but without that unity of action which is necessary for good drama.

Nevertheless, it should be remembered that school acting need not necessarily be dramatic in the technical use of the word. Some of the parables of Jesus lend themselves to simple representation by young children, especially in miming. The Christmas stories are also favourites for this purpose. For the rest, however, the incidents have to be selected and grouped and written out more fully. Henri Ghéon's play, for example, on the stations of the Cross is simply an expansion of the traditional story in the form of dialogue among a number of witnesses. This is not strictly drama although it requires acting. Dorothy Sayers' *The Man Born to be King* is an excellent series of dramatic incidents.

The teacher should be clear about the purpose of dramatic representation. It may be only a change from the chalk and talk type of lesson, or it may be the exact and most suitable medium for conveying the significance of a story. The Joseph story, for instance, is infinitely better dealt with by drama than by discussion, although this last might have to come first. Where characterization is concerned more than climax or movement, drama is the obvious means for conveying it. Younger children no doubt love dressing up and the interest will be in the incidentals, but for older children expression and interpretation are the things to look for in the production of a play. Selection of what to dramatize will depend on the amount of scope given by the play for such interpretation.

SECTION C

THE SYLLABUS

CHAPTER VIII

PRINCIPLES OF SELECTION

I CHARACTERISTICS OF SCRIPTURE TEACHING

If we compare the principles of selection for a Scripture syllabus with those that govern selection of an English or an History syllabus—two subjects very much allied to Scripture—we shall see certain important differences.

The History teacher—say of English history—has before him roughly eighteen hundred years of history as his subject-matter. In the case of younger children his selection will be based on the capacity of the child to understand and his principle will be mainly biographical. After this he has three choices, the consecutive method, the concentric, or the topical. In the case of the first he again has alternatives—shall he begin with the earlier period in the belief that the ages of warfare, romance and chivalry correspond more to the young adolescent's interests, or shall he begin with the twentieth century and work backwards, since the twentieth century is where the child is at present? On the concentric method the same ground is covered several times but with differing interests—say, first, political history, then social, then economic, or on the second occasion it may be covered in more detail than the first. The topical method explains itself—the topics can be biographies or movements or institutions or customs. And for all this the teacher has scores or even hundreds of books at his disposal and can select any particular author that he fancies.

The Scripture teacher has one book only and all his teaching is in a sense a commentary on that one book. The modern historians of the period—Oesterley, T. H. Robinson, Wheeler Robinson, Deissmann, Glover and others—have used the same source-book which he himself uses, and so, even in spite of himself, he is put in the position of a researcher from the original documents. He must know how to handle material of that kind and he must know what the history teacher need not know, how his text-book has come to be what it is now. The history teacher is not so concerned with the antecedents of G. M. Trevelyan or 'Warner and Martin'.

Moreover the record of these centuries of ancient history is concerned with one theme only—namely religion. Political and economic history cannot be separated here as they can elsewhere because the whole story is written for edification and for no other purpose.

The dilemma therefore, of the Scripture teacher is that he necessarily has to have a quite mature position about his material even in order to teach young children who may never need to know the grounds of that position. Added to this is the emotional quality which is attached to the words of Scripture (though not necessarily by the teacher himself) in a way in which no emotional quality at all is attached to the words of the English historian. The outside world does not have its withers wrung nowadays about the War of the Spanish Succession nor even about Henry II and Becket. In Scripture teaching on the other hand the teacher is vitally *concerned* and cannot teach it properly unless he really is concerned.

The teacher of English literature again has a large range of choice, but here the chronological sequence matters little if at all, save that the earlier period has less affinity with the child's interests (except in ballad literature) than the more modern period. Choice, therefore, is guided by the child's power of comprehension and not by the position of a certain author in some assumed scheme of development.

In a sense the Scripture teacher has no such choice. He has a whole literature before him and he cannot stop at any point half-way in its development. If the length of a child's school life determines the division of the material into so many 'years' the teacher is nevertheless dealing with the whole of it. This he does not only in the sense that the whole ground has to be covered in sequence, but also in the more difficult sense that an understanding of the whole of it is necessary to the understanding of any single part. Clearly therefore some of the later parts of the story have to be studied before some of the earlier. We have already seen the importance of a firm grasp of the character of Christ as the standard by which to judge, say, the end verses of Ps. cxxxvii. This is a judgement passed by the Bible on the Bible and is the complete answer to those who are repulsed or who pretend to be repulsed by the more bloodthirsty passages in the Old Testament. The use of this standard, therefore, is necessary if we are to make the early passages in the Bible mean anything *to us*. But *at the same time* such passages have to be understood in the context of their own origin and this alone would give us sympathy with the writer of that particular psalm. The twofold duty of applying the standard of contemporary life and *also* the standard by which the whole Bible is to be judged, makes the selection of suitable material far from easy. The difficulty is often avoided in the New Testament by cutting out the Epistles altogether and making the life of Jesus and the narrative of Acts do duty for the whole of the New Testament. This, of course, does violence to the circumstances in which the Gospels themselves came to be written.

The difficulty of selection is again increased by the fact, already noted, that the earlier parts of the Bible were revised many times in the light of later events, so that a passage which appears to be earlier may actually be later. In order, however, to get this puzzle straightened out it is not necessary to burden the child with the documentary hypothesis and it certainly would be a mistake to do what is sometimes done by some so-called 'progressive' teachers of the Bible, and attempt to sort out all the various strands of the early narrative. This might be a fascinating game, but if it stood alone it might go far to destroy any respect that a pupil may have for the ancient writers. It would be much better to follow a consecutive scheme of the history from a modern book such as is given at the elementary stage by Miss Allen, later by Miss Rattey and A. W. F. Blunt, and at the advanced stage by Wheeler Robinson[1] and use the Biblical narrative in the form of excerpts from the original texts to illustrate the story as given in the text-book.

2 SUGGESTED PRINCIPLES OF SELECTION

We may therefore suggest a few principles of selection to be observed in framing a syllabus:

(1) The Bible is to be kept together as far as possible in every year of the syllabus. In the case of the youngest children the Old Testament would come in as it does in the Cambridge *Little Children's Bible* as 'Stories that Jesus would hear from his mother'. Thereby we save ourselves from the mistake of leaving out the Old Testament altogether and also from the embarrassment of having to give a short answer to the question 'Is it true?' With older children it is essential to keep the prophets in close connexion with the histories, and the Epistles in close connexion with Acts and to show how in both Old Testament and New the narrative sections owe their survival to that same process of edification which is to be found in the prophets and St Paul.

(2) At *each* stage provision should be made for history, prophecy (including in this, in the New Testament, the Epistles) and poetry. The Psalms are of course very difficult to fit into any chronological context but they can at least be associated with the worship of the first and second Temples and even the third Temple, while the psalms of the Exile can roughly be dated. The study of the history of Israel involves the historian, the priest, the prophet and the poet and their interactions.

(3) It is more important to preserve a coherent picture of the life of Israel than to cover the whole of the literature. This inevitably means that some parts will be touched only as selections. Thus it is better that Genesis should be done twice—say at age 9

[1] *A Short Introduction to the Old Testament* by Irene Allen (Oxford Univ. Press); *A Short History of the Hebrews* by B. L. Rattey (Oxford Univ. Press); *Israel: Social and Religious Development* by A. W. F. Blunt (Oxford Univ. Press); *History of Israel* by H. Wheeler Robinson (Duckworth).

and again at age 15—than that we should attempt the whole of, say, Ezekiel at any stage. Amos should be done as a whole with selections from Hosea, Isa. i-xxxix (excluding the isolated prophecies listed in George Adam Smith's table of contents) with selections from Micah, I and II Kings with selections from Chronicles. The Gospels should of course be covered several times—the Synoptic material in the early stages, then one Gospel treated more systematically, then still later, the synopsis of the three Gospels together with selections from the Fourth Gospel. This may involve missing out some of the later New Testament material but the principle of cohesion is more important than that of comprehensiveness. The aim of the selector should be to keep before the pupil at every stage that the Bible is a book of religion. If he gets this firmly fixed in his mind it will not matter if he covers no more than half the Biblical material while he is at school. The test of the effectiveness of Scripture teaching is to be found say ten years after the pupil leaves school. What has he done with it in the meantime? To go slowly at school and to see that what is done is done well is far more necessary than superficially to cover the whole ground.

(4) A close attention should be paid to the *form* of the story as well as to the story itself. There is again difference here between the teaching of Scripture and the teaching of history. Why, for example, must we still read Gibbon and Motley? They are not originals; they are secondary authorities who use the originals. Out of State papers and documents and memoranda they reconstruct a situation in such a way as to bring it vividly to life. How they say it is as important as what they say. But the average history text-book is not like this at all, and it relies on the teacher to bring it to life either in his teaching or by reference to these master historians. But in Scripture this aesthetic quality is in the English *original* itself and the pupil must be put into the way of appreciating it. A good deal of scorn has been poured on the unintelligent use of the 'Kings of Israel and Judah' as Scripture material, but for anyone who has a sense of style the narratives as narratives are most effective. The story of the battle of Mount Gilboa, for instance, at the end of I Samuel, is admirable terse and vivid reporting and

the method of telling the story enhances the story. It might be compared with the story of the death of Brutus in *Julius Caesar*. In the story of the four lepers at the siege of Samaria in II Kings vii, the narrative is more important than the incident. These stories ought not to be rushed through as if it was the history only that mattered. The form also matters. It is this which gives educational value to the otherwise not very important prophecy of Nahum and adds interest to the undated prophecy concerning Babylon in Isa. xiv and to the similar chapter in Revelation. Where selection has to be made this factor must be kept in mind. There is a value in 'purple passages'.

(5) Following upon this, provision should be made, at any rate at the younger end of the school, for learning by heart. This will not be suitable in every lesson for every passage, nor should it be made into a task. But to hear passages well read and often read is a way to appreciate them and so to 'learn' them. It is here where the school assembly can be very helpful, for the unhurried reading of a passage of Scripture, without note or comment, can of itself be impressive and make the words easy to be retained.

(6) Ought the syllabus to include the Bible alone? As the Agreed Syllabuses are concerned with 'religious instruction' they often include a considerable amount of Church history, some include doctrine as such, and some give instruction in prayer and worship. These subjects do not strictly come into a scheme of Scripture teaching but they cannot entirely be ignored. As the Bible is concerned with edification the question of personal religion is bound from time to time to arise, but for purposes of this syllabus it should be allowed to arise in connexion with the *lessons*. The Scripture syllabus gives a Biblical setting to all such questions and it is part of its aim to show how closely related the Bible is to human life and need. To make these matters a separate subject is both to formalize something which ought to be a relationship between a teacher and a pupil and also to make the Bible a mere matter of antiquarian interest.

Church history, of course, comes in, at any rate to the end of the New Testament period, but if we are to get in nearly two millenia of later history, it cannot come under the heading of 'Scripture'. There is an opportunity here for some co-operation with the history teacher. Medieval history is largely Church history, the Reformation period is not only of political interest, the seventeenth century in England is the century of religious controversy, and the eighteenth century, often considered dull at home and exciting abroad, witnessed the growth of evangelicalism in all its forms. The Scripture teacher should not be expected to do the work of the history teacher, and the Biblical material by itself is sufficient for a whole school life in that subject alone without trespassing into other fields.

There is, however, a wealth of extra-Biblical material which is strictly relevant to the Scripture course.

The educational value of the 'pseudepigrapha' is that they supply just that colourful background of thought and action which is so characteristic of the Old Testament and which many people miss in the New. Here is the Messianic hope expressed not in the quiet contemplation of Simeon and Anna but as a call to battle and to endurance. For instance, whatever may be the date of the Book of Enoch, it provides a very cogent commentary on Matt. xxv which also deals with the final judgement of the world. The Old Testament, the Rabbinic Law, the books of worldly wisdom like Ecclesiasticus and the popular apocalypses—these represent the background of the New Testament, and they also represent the aspirations of different strata of the population of Palestine. We read of Simon the Zealot. Who was he? Who were the Zealots? In the popular apocalypses we read the literature which fed the flame of zealotry and which must have been known to many to whom Jesus spoke. These writings can now be obtained in English in a series published by the S.P.C.K., and the teacher should be furnished at least with the *Book of Enoch*, the *Testaments of the Twelve Patriarchs* and the *Assumption of Moses*. In the same series there is a very excellent translation of the *Wisdom of Ben Sira* or *Ecclesiasticus* which is well worth using. The book, of course, is to be found in our Apocrypha, together with the Wisdom of Solomon, the story of Susannah and the Elders (a story with which the compilers of the *Concise Oxford Dictionary* seem to be un-familiar (see the entry under 'Daniel'), but which Shakespeare uses in *The Merchant of Venice*), the story of Tobit, and the book which gives us the background to Daniel, namely, the First book of the Maccabees. These apocryphal books were as well known to the Jews of the first century A.D. as the Old Testament, and should therefore be included in the syllabus.

(7) The teacher should use a Bible with the Apocrypha and with the marginal references and readings. It is safe to say that many of the superstitions of verbal inspirationists would not have occurred if there had been habitual use of such an edition. It is clear at once, for instance, from the margin, that there is no means whatever of knowing what exactly Hosea said and what therefore were the words (not the 'word') of God to him. With over 150 variant readings it is open to the reader himself to make what choice he will, and, if he likes, to endow that choice with the qualities of an inerrant text. Where all manuscript authority is not only very late but also very varied, it is difficult to see how such a verbalist theory could ever have taken hold of the minds of men.

The Revised Version has the advantage of retaining the idiom of the Authorized which by now has become an integral part of our literary English speech, but it also gives a better clue to the original, it prints poetry as poetry, its marginal readings are very useful and its divisions into sections are more in accord with the sense. Other versions ought to be at hand but for ordinary study purposes this is the most useful as well as the cheapest basic rendering.

3 THE DEVELOPMENT OF THE CHILD'S MIND

So far we have considered principles of selection governing the subject-matter of Biblical study, namely its development as we find it. A further set of principles can be discovered related to the development of religion in the mind of the child.

There are in this, not one but *two* lines of development which therefore determine grading. First, there is the growth of the child's own apprehension of the literary subject-matter. Secondly, there is the growth of the child's own religious experience—a process which may have very little to do with the Scripture syllabus at all, but from which the teaching of Scripture will gain enormously if it can be co-ordinated with it. It is this intersection of so many lines of development that makes the teaching of Scripture at once more interesting and far more difficult than the teaching of almost any other subject. We have now noticed *four*— (1) the development of the religion of Israel and of the Church, (2) the development (quite separate) of the literature which records that development, (3) the growth of the pupil's own ability to understand both (1) and (2), and finally (4) the pupil's own religious development. These four are continually acting and reacting on one another, for they are all present at the same time, and no *one* can be taken as regulative of the other. This complicated situation arises from the peculiar nature of the documents themselves. Somehow we have to allow for this at every stage of our teaching.

CHAPTER IX

A CRITICAL ANALYSIS OF AN AGREED SYLLABUS

I REASONS FOR EXAMINING THE 'CAMBRIDGESHIRE SYLLABUS'

In choosing a particular syllabus for our consideration we shall be concerned not so much with the syllabus itself as with the principles on which it is based and which are more or less accepted by all the Agreed Syllabuses. I have taken the Cambridgeshire one for various reasons. It was the first of its kind, it has been the basis of considerable experiment, and it has suffered two drastic revisions in the light of experience. It is also the syllabus with which I myself have had some slight responsibility and I believe it to be a good one, but still open to considerable criticism in the light of further experience.

It should be noticed that no agreed syllabus is to be taken as a prescribed scheme. The Cambridgeshire book states in so many words:

The compilers wish to make plain that the object of the *Syllabus* is to serve as a guide and not as a hard and fast scheme of actual lessons. The passages and notes grouped under each course are primarily intended for the use of the teachers who, it is hoped, will study the *Syllabus* as a whole, and, in using any section of it, freely adapt the material or add to it in accordance with his own ideas and the needs of his pupils. A school should not feel bound to adhere strictly to the age groups suggested for the courses; but, if alteration is made, care would naturally be taken to secure continuity.

The *Syllabus* is concerned with more than the teaching of Scripture. Its full title is *The Cambridgeshire Syllabus of Religious Teaching for Schools*. Religious influences which are not those of instruction in Scripture naturally come in, and particularly is this the case at the earlier stages. 'Atmosphere' counts most. This depends on the temperament of the head teacher and the staff, the confidence (or lack of it) between teacher and taught, the general attitude of unselfishness and kindness which people show or are encouraged to show to one another, and the respect that they have for the subject. All this is necessary at every stage of development, but the older child is better able to appreciate ideals in the abstract and can even witness to a position which the school itself may not exemplify. The *Syllabus* therefore begins by asking questions such as these.

Is the school so organized as to encourage co-operation as well as proper forms of competition?

Are opportunities given whereby the stronger and cleverer may help the weaker?

Is the love of animals and birds encouraged?

What does the child do for his school?

What does the school do for the village or town, or for wider causes such as homeless children, hospitals, or missions overseas?

Is the grace of courtesy taught and encouraged?

In all these ways a right atmosphere is suggested which enables the child to appreciate the teaching of the Bible when it comes to it. There is, however, a warning to be observed here. Self-consciousness ruins moral growth. The right way to influence a young child is not by talking about these qualities or activities but by taking them for granted so that he grows up to feel that these are things which are 'done', and no decent person would think otherwise. A good deal of religious teaching in England and America is ruined by the over-insistence on awareness of what is going on. Teachers and children alike become more concerned with the idea of what they are doing than with the doing of it. This leads to a useless insistence on the teacher's way of doing things as being the 'best' way and some impatience if it is not followed.

A second more specific factor in the suggestion of atmosphere favourable to the appreciation of religion is the conduct of school assembly. The *Syllabus* gives a number of hints which are as relevant to a Sunday school as to a day school, and which are suggestive of others. Entry and exit of the children should be orderly and quiet. Matters of school order and discipline should not be brought into the religious service. Each act of worship should be planned a long way ahead and should constitute a unity, and should not be too long. In the planning of a series a wide range of religious interest and truth should be covered with attention given to special occasions such as the beginning and end of term, harvest time and national events. Scripture readings should be complete in themselves and if not immediately intelligible might be prefaced by a very brief explanation, but the reader must not let himself get in the way of the reading itself. The Authorized Version is best for reading with such alterations as are justified by the fact of a mistranslation. Prayers should be short and terse, and the Lord's Prayer should be said with care and proper pauses. Ancient prayers and collects should be used as much as possible, and if necessary the language should be briefly explained rather than altered. They were written by men with a real liturgical gift and they have helped to form the English language itself. Hymns need careful choice and tunes even more so. The kind of syncopated rhythm in many hymns of the Sunday type is most unsuitable, and so also are a great many hymns written by older people to express what they think children think. There are no better children's hymns than 'O God of Bethel' and 'O God our help in ages past', although these were not written specially for children.

It is of value occasionally to get older children to read the Scriptures. It ought not to be done casually and they will need preparation and practice. Seniors in a secondary school, particularly in a boarding school where they can meet often informally, might even be given the task of arranging a whole act of worship. There is a risk in this and it must be recognized and freely accepted. In a famous public school for girls in the west of England a few years ago the progressive Head wished the older girls to take full responsibility for the evening chapel services. I was the preacher on the first Sunday of this new regime. The girls had responded enthusiastically and had devised a form of service which contained almost as much as could be got in. It had full evensong as a basis, but there was also the Nicene Creed, part of the litany, special prayers for the school, the staff, the Church in various branches, commerce, industry, fishermen, and for everything and everybody that they could think of. It took a long time, and the Head was furious and said she would never let it happen again! Good government was obviously considered to be better than self-government. The children had acted all for the best but they got no credit for it and were made to feel like culprits. The Head had forgotten that risks have to be taken and it is no good getting annoyed.

2 STAGES OF CHILD GROWTH

The *Syllabus* itself is built on a graded plan according to the psychological growth of the children. The scheme follows, or perhaps it ought to be said, 'is followed by' the English day school structure with its primary and secondary stages each with subdivisions. We begin with the nursery school children under 5. Then follow infants (5–7), early Juniors (7–9), and later Juniors (9–11). All up to this point are classed in the schools as 'primary'. Then comes the secondary stage with children from 11 to 13, children 13–15, and children 15–16, followed by 'the Sixth Form' of children 17 and 18. This secondary period is to be found from 11 to 15 in the secondary modern schools, from 11 to 18 in the grammar schools, and from 13 to 18 in the English Public Schools. The American system is different and goes right through in a series of annual 'grades' from 5 to 17.

At the beginning of the scheme it is recognized that with young children 'atmosphere' is even more important than it is at a later stage, although of course it is important at *all* stages. With the younger ones, however, there is little intellectual instruction that can be given, and religious education is clearly something more than Scripture teaching.

Little children at the nursery school age are prepared to take God for granted and to talk about him and to him as naturally as they would to anyone else. The teacher's own attitude to God therefore is of more effect than merely what the teacher says. Little children like routine and expect stories to be told and actions to be done in the way with which they are familiar. In the 'morning ring' when they talk freely about home and the events of the day, and also at other times they will come to expect prayers and hymns as a normal expression of their interest in people and animals and events. God will be known to them as a loving heavenly Father caring for his creatures. They will know some stories about Jesus, especially the Christmas story.

As far as religious education goes there is not much difference between infants of 5-7 and children just below 5. Again it is 'atmosphere' that counts and the idea which they get of God from the teacher's attitude. The line between 'natural' and 'supernatural' is still very thin and awareness of God is something to which such children are very sensitive. The child's every-day experience can be made the basis of talks about God, a sparrow fallen to the ground, a playmate taken seriously ill, a holiday, even a fine day. Nature is the child's great outside interest at this stage and the wonder of living things leads to recognition of their Creator. 'Learning through doing' is characteristic of this stage and the preparation for the festivals of the Christian year gives many opportunities. It is an *activity* corresponding to a 'project' in other subjects and prevents staleness and the passive listening to stories. The syllabus works out as follows:

1. Celebration of the Christian year. (*a*) The harvest: stories from the New Testament about cornfields, flowers and grass. (*b*) The Christmas stories (see Chalmers and Entwistle's *Bible Books for Small People* (S.C.M.)). (*c*) Springtime and the renewal of life. (*d*) Easter—told very simply.

2. *Children aged 5.* Daily life as Jesus saw it (see Entwistle's *The Bible Guide Book* (S.C.M.)). Stories told by Jesus. Stories about people whom Jesus met.

3. *Children aged 6.* The boyhood of Jesus. Stories told to him by his mother. Jesus' friends. Some of his stories and kind deeds.

3 THE JUNIOR SCHOOL COURSE

The junior school age is from 7 to 11. It is marked by a transition from make-believe to increasing reality. The child more and more desires independence instead of security and he begins to look for outlets for his new-found energy. The Old Testament is excellent lesson material at this stage for there is plenty of action and picturesque detail. This, however, must be linked up with the New Testament otherwise the child may get quite a false view of God, and therefore, as already suggested, it is best to preface the Old Testament material with the rubric 'stories told to Jesus by his mother'. It is at this point that the teacher must be very clear in his own mind of the distinction between literal history, legend (which is embroidered history) and myth (which is not history at all). The Exodus, for instance, is history, Elisha making the axe to swim is legend, Noah's ark is myth. The overruling consideration, however, is that the Bible is a book about God, and myth and legend are both pressed into the task of explaining who God is, what is his character, and what he does. This should help the teacher when faced with the inevitable question 'Is it true?' There are truths of history, but there are also spiritual truths and these latter are often best taught by a made-up story, just as we our-selves use 'illustrations'. Moreover, even a historical account of an event does not give the full truth about it. Older children may enter into the significance, for instance, of the Crucifixion as St Paul did, over and above the actual physical fact, but with younger children a different technique will be needed. To tell the story of the Exodus from the point of view of an Egyptian mother who has lost her son in the Red Sea, or stories of the life and death of Christ from the point of view of an unknown disciple or a Roman soldier, will bring freshness into the story and expand the notion of the truth of it. Dramatization and hand-work (model-making for infants) are useful at this stage and continued hearing of certain passages will enable them to be learned by heart.

The *Syllabus* here divides into two parts.

1. *Children aged 7–9.* (a) The childhood of Jesus, 'bed-time

stories', stories from Genesis, the story of Moses, selected stories about Joshua, Gideon and Samson. (*b*) Jesus in his relations with his people: a selection of scenes from the Gospels. (*c*) Jesus as teacher: a selection from the parables. (*d*) Some stories of Peter.

This seems to be a considerable amount, but it is spread over two years and is so arranged that the Old Testament and the New Testament can be read concurrently.

2. *Children aged 9–11.* (*a*) The life of Jesus. It is here suggested that 'some attempt should be made to give a first impression of what may be described as the drama of the Life and Death of Jesus'. (*b*) The Old Testament in the form of 'the Bible' that Jesus knew. This would include some psalms as selections from the hymn-book, a few stories of Saul, David and Solomon, the early prophets (Elijah and Elisha), and selected incidents from the lives of Amos, Isaiah, Jeremiah, and the Exile. (*c*) Some stories of Paul.

The *Syllabus* at this point suggests that the Scripture scheme should be interrupted occasionally to insert stories of later 'followers of Jesus' such as Bede, Bunyan, Khama and Livingstone.

A further section deals with Prayer under various headings, as it is referred to in various Bible passages to the end that children may learn the nature of prayer themselves. This is one way of linking the Scripture lessons with the School Assembly.

4 THE SECONDARY SCHOOL COURSE

With the secondary school course (children aged 11–16) we arrive at the age of self-consciousness. The child can see himself from outside and is beginning to form ideals of himself. He becomes interested in character, and so the character of Jesus and not merely his sayings and doings can make a special appeal to him. It is here that we can begin connecting the Jesus of history with the Jesus who was 'the Way, the Truth, and the Life'. The method of dealing with this, however, needs careful thought. No two schools are alike and no two children are alike. This is not the stage for doctrine as such, nor indeed does it come in anywhere *as such* in a school syllabus, but in so far as it is in the mind of the Biblical writers themselves it can come in, although in a historical rather than a metaphysical connexion. At the same time the character of Jesus can be appreciated without raising *as a doctrinal question* the problem of 'the divinity of Christ'. It is at this secondary school stage that so many teachers give way to over-anxiety concerning their pupils' orthodoxy, and it is well therefore to keep in mind just how much the school can do and how much is really the function of the Church. The following of Christ is a more important matter to understand and accept at this stage than the acceptance of any theory of his person.

At the same time as regards the Old Testament teaching, children in the secondary school course are beginning to appreciate consecutive history. In the later stages the children will be able to grasp the history of Israel not only as the story of a nation but also as the development of religion. It is this latter that determines the choice of material for the former.

In accordance with this general scheme, the secondary syllabus is subdivided into three sections as follows:

1. *Children aged 11–13.* (*a*) The Life of Christ, based on St Mark's Gospel and Acts i–iv. In this, three main lines of study are to be kept in mind—Jesus' own conception of his mission and the suitable methods to be employed for bringing in the Kingdom; the progressive realization of his mission by others, coming to a climax in Acts; the opposition that he aroused, and its culmination in his death. (*b*) Outstanding events in Old Testament History. A connected history should here be given with the relevant Biblical references, beginning with the promise to the Fathers, and proceeding through the Exodus, the monarchy, the divided kingdom, the warnings of the prophets, the fall of the kingdoms, the Exile, the return, and ending with the Maccabean revolt.

2. *Children aged 13–15.* It is at this point that almost all the Agreed Syllabuses including the *Cambridgeshire* begin to go astray by overloading the syllabus not only with detail but also with interpretation. When we think of the history syllabus or the geography syllabus of a child of 14 and realize how many more years are to elapse before he can be expected to have a grasp of the

principles underlying these studies, and, in the case of history, of the character interpretation that is necessary fully to appreciate them, it is questionable whether the suggested Scripture syllabus is compassable by children of this age. A few syllabuses indeed, at this age begin a course not unlike that expected for an Intermediate B.D. It is here where we have to have regard to the principle of covering the same ground twice rather than continuing to pile up more and more detail. The *Cambridgeshire Syllabus* recognizes this in so far as it suggests alternative courses for the secondary school age. The wise teacher, however, will follow the general rubric at the beginning and use just as much of the syllabus as suits his purpose and his children.

(*a*) The Gospel of Christ, particularly in relation to the Messianic hope and in relation to the universal message. It might be suggested, however, that Luke's Gospel would make a better basis than selections from all the Gospels, as it is the universal character of this Gospel rather than the strongly contemporary character of Matthew that would make the chief appeal. The story in Acts (not neglecting some account of the Epistles) naturally continues the Lucan interest.

(*b*) 'The Development of ideas about Behaviour, Man and God in the Old Testament.' This of course is concerned chiefly with prophecy, and the link between the New Testament and the prophets of the Old should be remembered. It is important to stress the contemporary nature of prophecy—that the prophets were only 'foretelling' the future because they had a right understanding of the present. The eighth century is the period on which to concentrate, although the *Cambridgeshire Syllabus* gives a conspectus of the whole story right down to the Maccabean era. It would be a pity, however, for children who are going to leave school at fifteen not to have had a closer first hand acquaintance with Old Testament prophecy. And the eighth century lends itself so easily to treatment. There are two pairs, Amos and Hosea in the north, Isaiah and Micah in the south. Then again Amos is the prophet of justice, Hosea of mercy; Isaiah is the courtier, Micah the working man. The period and the problems are not quite but more or less the same for all of them, and to have four separate and very distinct points of view is an excellent way to treat the period. And above all it is important for the Bible itself to be read and not simply books about the Bible.

(c) The *Cambridgeshire Syllabus* here inserts 'Stories from the lives of Great Christians' classified under eight headings. This is very helpful as it brings home to children the fact that the Bible is a book by which great men have lived and died. Whatever may be the present-day view of the Bible out of school it cannot be said that William Penn, General Booth, Dr Barnado, Sir Ronald Ross, Luther, Cranmer, Henry Martyn and Edward Wilson were stupid or ignorant men, and these are in this list of 'Great Christians'. This kind of study, however, should be only occasional and not take the place of the study of the very Book which these men loved so much.

(d) *Concerning the Bible.* A very useful set of lessons could be made with this heading, showing how the Bible had come into existence, how and why and to whom and when the various writers wrote their message. Here the position should be that of responsible scholarship, neither taking the fundamentalist position nor dismissing it as of no account. Above all, a positive statement should be given and it should be emphasized that the Bible is concerned with religion and not with science. The formation of the canon and the sense of unity in the Bible is important. There is one theme throughout and if children can grasp this fact they will *not* be put out by shallow sceptical questions based often on the contradictions in the report of the same incident. An account of the manuscripts and of the English versions is also useful. What is not so useful is the introduction of the symbols J, P, E, D, Q, etc., and the syllabuses that suggest this as a subject for 14-year-old children are surely misjudging child psychology altogether. A great part of this section might be replaced by the study of some particular book, even an Epistle such as that to the Philippians. It will teach the children how to handle such a subject for themselves when they leave school.

(e) The fifth section in the *Cambridgeshire Syllabus* is called 'The

Universal Gospel'. As the suggestion is that this should be a condensed version of the main subject of religious teaching for the 15–16-year-olds we may consider it under that heading.

3. *Children aged 15–16.* The *Cambridgeshire Syllabus* here suggests a very considerable study of Church history and it works out a wide conspectus beginning with Paul and coming down to the Amsterdam Conference of 1948. It is admirably done and of course it is relevant for the whole scheme of religious education although not strictly coming under 'the teaching of Scripture'. It is difficult, however, to see how all this can be got into the time. A good deal of it should in any case come into the history lessons and might well be left there if the teacher of history and the teacher of Scripture are sympathetic to one another. It would, however, be a useful thing if before the child leaves school he is given just sufficient knowledge of present-day denominations and of how they grew up, to make him willing to study a little further later. At any rate he can be shown how and where to seek information if he wants it.

The *Syllabus* at this point groups together a good many New Testament passages under the two headings of personal religion and corporate religion. It is a very comprehensive scheme, but again if it is compared with a mathematics syllabus or history or English, it is clear that the children are expected to be much more advanced in their Scripture studies than in these others.

Accordingly, an alternative scheme of study has been suggested for the whole period 11–15 which is much simpler and more compassable. Both schemes are worth trying out with a class so long as it is understood that if either breaks down in the teacher's hands it should be heavily modified.

5 THE SIXTH FORM COURSE

With the Sixth Form we enter upon somewhat different ground. These are the children of our grammar schools who are staying at school till eighteen and are then going to colleges of various sorts or into business or the professions. They are more and more accustomed to responsibility, they ask questions and have views of their own and are critical of their pastors and masters. Accordingly it is perhaps not to the point to suggest a syllabus at all except for the fact that in so many schools it is assumed that by the time boys or girls get to the Sixth Form they have learned all they need to know about the Bible and they can now discuss 'problems'. It is extraordinary with how little material problems are taken up and discussed. The absence or the apparent absence of an accepted and authoritative corpus of knowledge in this subject such as there is in 'secular' subjects seems to exempt many people from making use of what knowledge there is. Accordingly it is essential at this stage that the Bible should not be left out but should indeed come into its own. Again it is important to remember that children can expect to have a considerable length of life before them and the aim of Scripture teaching should be to equip a young person with the intellectual knowledge, appreciation, and tools which will enable him to continue in this way when he no longer has the school to guide him.

The *Cambridgeshire Syllabus* has a very thought-provoking section on the needs of the Sixth Form. It points out that there is a variety of ways of tackling them. Some would make Sixth-Form work primarily Scripture teaching. Others would regard it as a setting forth of the Christian faith and life. Within each group there is the further division between the people who prefer the direct approach, beginning with the Bible or the Christian faith, and the people who prefer to start indirectly from the point where the children themselves are. Whatever approach is followed there are several things to be attempted. The first is free questioning and discussion on the part of the pupils. They are encouraged to do this in other subjects; it is more than ever important here. Secondly, the pupils must be made familiar with the historical authentication of the Bible. The excesses of earlier historical critics have been left behind and there is a far more solid ground of history underneath the Bible than was once assumed to be the case. Thirdly, it should be made clear to the pupils how very shaky is the ground occupied by materialists and determinists. The writings of Dr Fred Hoyle will doubtless be known to many pupils and it is worth exhibiting just what are the limitations of a mechanistic hypothesis, and what indeed are the limitations of science in general. 'The general approach to Sixth Form religious teaching should be intellectual rather than devotional.' Christianity should be presented as something as much able to stand up to critical scrutiny as any other serious subject of the curriculum. All this will be a *praeparatio evangelica*, a preparation for the day when the pupil will make his own decision and will we hope accept the faith as his own. But this last is the task of the Church rather than the school.

The *Cambridgeshire Syllabus* sets out as the concern of the Sixth Form three main courses.

1. *The Christian Faith* under the eight headings of belief in God (the sense of mystery, mind and design, and the moral sense), the Fatherhood of God, Jesus Christ, Redemption, the Holy Spirit, the Church, the Forgiveness of Sins, Eternal Life.

2. *The Bible and Christian Teaching*, again under two headings. (*a*) History (Revelation in the Bible); (*b*) the Teaching of Jesus, and the history, faith and worship of the Christian Church. This includes a study of the Fourth Gospel.

3. *Specific Books as separate courses* (e.g. Dorothy Sayers, *The Man Born to be King*; C. Skinner, *The Gospel of the Lord Jesus*; C. S. Lewis, *Christian Behaviour*; A. D. Lindsay, *The Two Moralities*; to which others can be added).

Under this heading comes the comment 'The type of book chosen for such a course will always involve the Bible, directly or indirectly; but the Bible at large is a most discouraging wilderness in which to search for the corroboration of some fact or quotation vaguely remembered from an earlier lesson' and there is a criticism of Bible commentaries—'the majority deal overmuch in notes on abstruse points and tend to obscure the contours of the wood in their attention to individual trees'.

These comments have much substance, but there are certain omissions. In the first place it is not necessary to make, say, C. S. Lewis or A. D. Lindsay the main subject of a discussion in which the Bible is consulted to see if it has anything to say. It is just as helpful, and from the Scripture teacher's point of view, more helpful, to pose a problem which the Biblical writers themselves posed and which is equally a problem today, and then see how it is handled both by our contemporaries and by the Biblical writers. For instance, there is the problem of social justice (Amos); the dilemma of a little country like Belgium hemmed in between two big countries like France and Germany (Isa. i-xxxix); the working man's point of view of foreign policy (Micah); Are there as good Christians outside the Church as inside? (Jonah); Ought Christians to drink intoxicants? (a similar problem to that in I Cor. viii); Was Jeremiah a Quisling?; What are we to say about *apartheid*? (the book of Ruth). Anything which removes the Bible far off into a situation so apparently different from ours is unfortunate, for the pupils will be given an impression of its irrelevance except for looking up quotations. The other attitude, however, will put a greater strain on the teacher, for it demands a certain *wholeness* of attitude on his part and a very extensive and intelligent understanding of the Bible. It is he himself rather than a book that should be the commentary.

In the second place the Sixth Forms are not entirely or even largely composed of intellectual giants. At any rate the level of knowledge shown by first year students at the University or in the teachers' training colleges suggests that the Sixth Forms are a good section of the intelligent young people of the country with only a few that are very outstanding. The proportion of this number who have really understood the philosophy of their own specialisms and its bearing upon life in general is not very large and there is no reason to believe that it will be any larger in the case of Scripture which in any case is not a specialism. Not all of the questions asked at Sixth Form Conferences under the auspices of the Student Christian Movement show very deep thought although they often show considerable anxiety, but not more so than a body of young apprentices would show in a large factory. It is well not to underestimate the interests of Sixth Forms but it is almost as easy to overestimate them.

Thirdly, it is a genuine difficulty that while there are good educational reasons which justify the study of the Bible in schools open to all-comers of different denominations and of none, the introduction of doctrinal questions inevitably has the character of propaganda. A conscience clause protects the rights of the parent although it is hardly ever invoked in a grammar school, but there are many cases not so serious as matters of conscience in which nevertheless the suspicion of propaganda or proselytism creates resentment.

6 SPECIAL OCCASIONS

The *Cambridgeshire Syllabus* concludes with some notes on the use of the *Syllabus* for special purposes, e.g. classes in the small school, usually a rural school, and the single teacher school, and with supplementary chapters on (1) the language of the English Bible (taken chiefly from Quiller-Couch); (2) making the Bible familiar to children (by hymns, dramatic passages, dramatic work and choral-speaking); (3) history, legend and myth; (4) miracles in the New Testament; (5) the artist and the Christian faith. It finally gives an annotated and classified bibliography of twenty-four pages.

7 AGREED SYLLABUSES IN USE

In 1953 there were forty-nine Agreed Syllabuses in use in the schools of England and Wales. Many authorities produced their own and the enterprise provided great occasion for fellowship among the Churches, the teacher and the officials. Of those which were simply adopted by other authorities the *Cambridgeshire Syllabus* was in use in twenty-three areas, the *Sunderland* in twenty-one, the *West Riding* in thirteen, the *Surrey* in ten, the *Durham* in eight, the *Lancashire* in four, and the *Middlesex*, the *York*, and *Lindsey* in three each. This distribution is far from being local. Thus the *Sunderland Syllabus* is in use as far afield as Brighton, the Isle of Wight, and East Sussex. The *Cambridgeshire Syllabus* is used in West Sussex, Wiltshire, Shropshire, St Helens and Burnley. Oxford made use of the *West Riding Syllabus*, and the *Durham Syllabus* was used in East Suffolk and Bedfordshire. A great deal of thought has gone even into the adoption of a syllabus, for with forty-nine from which to choose the task has been formidable.

The Agreed Syllabuses have now been in operation since 1944 and enough information has been collected about their working to justify the preparation and publication of a report.[1] It has been carefully compiled with the collaboration of groups of teachers in widely different areas in the industrial Midlands, for example, and rural Norfolk. Its sections cover the organization of teaching, the content of the syllabuses, staffing problems, Sixth-Form work, school worship, technical equipment, and indeed every aspect of the subject. It is a very valuable document, factual and practical. One conclusion which it makes clear is that there is no foundation for the criticism (only heard outside the school) that the Agreed Syllabuses offer a very attenuated variety of religious instruction. Such criticism tends to ignore not only the actual content of the Syllabuses but also the stages of the religious development of children.

[1] *Religious Education in Schools:* The Report of an Inquiry made by the Research Committee of the Institute of Christian Education into the Working of the 1944 Education Act. Published by the S.P.C.K., 1954.

SECTION D
METHOD

CHAPTER X
GENERAL OBSERVATIONS

I THREE POSSIBLE AIMS

It has already been pointed out that there are at least three aims in the modern teaching of Scripture. It may be taught for comprehension, for appreciation and for interpretation. The first two of these are common to other subjects also and are a matter of technique. The third is, as we have seen, a matter of attitude and is, so to speak, a resultant from the other two.

In a historical subject comprehension is essential, and in the case of Hebrew history something like a philosophy of history is needed almost from the outset. The historical books, for instance, are 'the early prophets' and some realization of the implication of that fact must be in the teacher's own mind. The notes in Chapter XIII (p. 200) of a lesson on Naaman the Syrian illustrate what that means.

In the earlier classes no real difficulty arises. The central figure is Our Lord and the Old Testament stories are told either for their own sake as good narrative or as stories which he would have heard as a child. The Cambridge *Little Children's Bible* makes this approach, and, as we have already seen, one advantage of it is that it provides an easy answer to the question 'Is it true?' If they are stories at two steps removed from ourselves, the question 'Is it true?' may even not be asked at all.

It is in the later stages, when stories are replaced by connected history, that difficulties appear. Shall we follow the history of the

Hebrew people from the Age of the Patriarchs down to the Maccabees taking the history just as we find it in the English Version or shall we follow the history as it came into existence *as history*? In the first case we begin with Genesis and go straight ahead. In the second we begin either with Amos, the first of the writing prophets, or with Moses, the first point at which myth and legend most surely give way to history, or with David and the so-called 'Court History' which is the earliest historical narrative of any length (II Sam. ix–xx). With senior forms or with adults the procedure is again as simple as it is with infants: we undoubtedly begin with Amos. It is the stages in between that present us with the problem and the fact that there are so many alternatives indicates how difficult the problem is. On the whole the best place to begin is with Moses and to continue in one sweep down to the reign of Jeroboam II. This of course means that we have to accept the prophetic 'editing' of the earlier historical documents before we come to the prophets themselves, but it is most important to get clear the various steps in the progress from a wandering tribal people to the two settled kingdoms. The steps are marked by a succession of great names—Moses, Joshua, Gideon, Samson, Samuel, Saul, David, Solomon, and then the leading kings in each of the separated kingdoms. The history can be gone over again at a later stage when the eighth-century prophets have been studied, and the significance, for instance, of I Sam. xv. 22[1] can then be seen as a Deuteronomic comment belonging to the eighth rather than to the eleventh century B.C.

At this point we may introduce a principle which affects all Biblical teaching, particularly of the Old Testament. It has often been said that it is better to know an elementary subject in an advanced way than an advanced subject in an elementary way. Nowhere is this more true than in Scripture teaching. It is a mistake to assume that the older the pupils are the more detail they must be given, and the further into Church history they must be taken. Genesis is full of admirable stories for the very young, but it is also excellent material for the older children. The historical

---

[1] 'To obey is better than sacrifice and to hearken than the fat of rams.'

books are full of colour and excitement, but as edited by the prophets they exhibit a philosophy of history, and it is in this form and with this emphasis that they have come down to us. Consequently to go over later the ground that has already been covered by the infants and junior school is to do more or less the same thing that the ancient writers themselves did. In so doing we shall notice not only their comment and emphasis but also their method of selection. When we come to the prophets we shall see this principle at work. Why, for instance, does Isa. xxxvi–xxxviii. 8 'repeat' the story of Sennacherib as given in II Kings xviii. 13–xx. 1–6, 9–11? Is it a repetition or is Isaiah the 'source' of the apparently earlier narrative? It is a superb story and has upon it the genuine prophetic touch. Clearly, therefore, at some point in teaching the narrative in Kings this duplication in Isaiah must be brought in. It cannot be done with young children, but it strengthens the case for a second reading at a later stage.

The prophets must obviously be put into their historical setting. And this will not only help to make a connected narrative of the period after Jeroboam II, but it will also bring out the sequence of the prophetic development. Micah and Isaiah are contemporaries and the duplication of Isa. ii. 2–4 with Mic. iv. 1–3 gives some indication of it. Yet we ask why is Isaiah so completely obsessed with the Assyrian menace and Micah mentions it hardly at all? Must it not be because their circumstances and background are different? We notice therefore that Isaiah is the court attendant and Micah is the working-man of the countryside. A study of the similarities and the differences in their messages will be very enlightening on this point. To Micah the capital city is not his concern; he is more concerned with his own village and his neighbours. Consequently he is not found in the Books of Kings in which Isaiah has found a place.

This principle of revision holds good in the New Testament also. Just as the prophecies have to be worked into the histories so have the Epistles to be worked into the Acts of the Apostles. Take the Corinthian problem, for instance. We get a certain amount of information in Acts but we get much more in the two Epistles.

From these we realize that there were originally four Epistles and that two are lost. To try to reconstruct the life at Corinth and its difficulties from all the various facts before us in Acts and the two surviving Epistles is a far more worthwhile way of teaching Scripture than to draw a map of Greece 'putting in Corinth, Athens, etc.' Thus Acts provides vivid and exciting narrative for younger children, but it needs later on to be supplemented by a revision in the light of the Epistles.

A good deal, of course, necessarily depends on one's view of the Epistles. Are they expositions of a coherent body of doctrine or are they letters written off quickly to deal with some specific problem that has arisen? Surely the second is right. The very structure of Romans with its four separate endings, supports this view, and so also do Paul's many digressions and repetitions and, to us, irrelevances and even contradictions. On this second view the natural framework of the Epistles is Acts, and it is a very profitable study to find out from internal evidence, from the history itself and from contemporary sources, if any, just what the situation was to which a letter of Paul's was a reply. In this way we may go over the story not twice only but three times—once as interesting narrative, again with the Epistles put into their approximate setting, and yet again from the point of view of the generalizations that Paul draws from the specific problem.

It is, however, not only the historical parts of the New Testament narrative that lend themselves to revision. Nowhere is this more needed than in the teaching of Jesus, particularly in the parables. In a subsequent chapter we shall see how the Parable of the Prodigal Son, for instance, can be used as excellent material both for young children and also for the Sixth Form. A parable exhibits the Eastern habit of expressing truth not as an abstract argument but as a concrete story. We must get out of the Western habit of looking upon the story as nothing more than an illustration of something else. The story form of teaching exhibits truth in a specific situation in which the personal and emotional factors are all present, in a way in which they are not present in a casuistical treatment of a moral question.

The continual interpretation and re-interpretation of the life and character of Our Lord in theological literature is an indication of the value of the same process on a smaller scale in the teaching of the classroom. The historical narrative taken as it stands is excellent material for young children. At a later stage it raises the whole question of the nature of history. That 'contingent truths of history can never prove eternal truths of reason' was the way in which Lessing stated the problem, but the problem constantly recurs in the experience of men. And the Synoptic Gospels, written as they were after the Epistles, give rise to this very question. To use the content of the Gospels for only younger children as if they were 'simple' or even to treat the Gospels with older children as if the 'synoptic problem' is the only thing that matters, is to miss the biggest question of all, the facing of which will certainly be the most profitable of all.

'Comprehension' therefore, in Scripture teaching, is a very wide subject. With the pupils it has many levels, but the deepest one of all must be something firmly understood by the teacher himself *even though he may never have to use it as such* with the particular class with which he is dealing. By comprehension, however, we refer throughout to the text of Scripture itself. It is not meant to be a subjective opinion. For example, the famous text in Matt. xvi. 18, 19 concerning Peter and the power of the keys, raises very many difficulties as it stands, but they must be faced in their *contemporary* context. What is not legitimate is to teach that this text refers to the Pope and the present Roman Catholic Church. This is a purely subjective opinion and is held by no reputable scholar in the theological faculty of any university in Britain. It is imposed upon the text and does not arise from it. Similarly Jesus' counsel to the young ruler that he should sell all that he has and give to the poor cannot be generalized without doing violence to the true nature of teaching as shown by the Gospels. It was a specific answer to a specific situation and in a sense (only in a sense) does not teach 'us' anything.

Nor is allegorizing a legitimate form of teaching. Of all subjective methods of teaching Scripture this is probably the worst.

It makes nonsense both of history and of literature, and it puts the text at the mercy of every kind of personal fad and fancy. Augustine's treatment of the Parable of the Good Samaritan is a classic example of the wildness of this method. The inn is the Church, the innkeeper is St Paul, the priest and the Levite are the Old Testament, and so on. Yet it has been a favourite method of teaching the parables and unfortunately it appears to gain justification from the fact that one parable in the Gospels is so treated. This is the Parable of the Sower, which is followed by a detached exposition of every item in the story. On this point Professor C. H. Dodd's book *The Parables of the Kingdom* should be consulted, especially in regard to the vocabulary of the parable. The general treatment is quite alien to parabolic teaching, for elsewhere each parable has one point and one only, and the individual details do not really matter. The assumption in this case is that here we have a bit of early Christian sermon-making which has been written after this particular story as an appendix. It was clearly a favourite parable with the early Church.

A form of allegorizing which was common in earlier days and has not entirely passed away was 'typology'. The sort of question that would be asked of a pupil would be: 'Show in how many ways Joseph is a type of our Lord.' The answer consisted in taking the Joseph story and seeing how many incidents could be paralleled in the life of Jesus. He went down into Egypt, he was rejected by his brethren, he forgave his brethren. A great deal of ingenuity was shown in collecting types and amplifying the similarity. Yet even though the similarities are present they are purely superficial and what does anyone gain by observing them? It shed no illumination whatever on the text and it debases the Old Testament. It ceases to have value in its own right and becomes a rag-bag of odd bits of information, the only value of which is that they can be made to mean something or anything that the reader cares to make them mean.

That every parable has one point only is very important to observe in teaching, although that point may not always be one that can be grasped by younger pupils. But it avoids a great deal

of difficulty in certain cases. The stock example is the Parable of
the Unjust Steward. Whether 'the Lord' in that parable is the
Lord in the story itself or refers to Jesus who tells the parable it
still leaves us with the difficulty of a commendation of shady conduct. But the point is surely that if Christians were as circumspect
about their spiritual interests as this rogue was about his material
ones, they would be much better Christians. No moral gymnastics
are needed in this interpretation.

2 APPRECIATION

Appreciation is here taken as referring to the *form* of Scripture and
not merely its content. We have already seen what Quiller-Couch
and George Sampson thought about it in general. It is now time
to come down to particulars.

There is often held to be a distinction between the study of the
Bible and the devotional use of the Bible, and we have already
indicated that there is a difference between study and appreciation.
It is very far, however, from being an exclusive difference.
Difficulties in understanding or downright disagreement with
what is written may be so acute as to make appreciation impossible.
You cannot 'appreciate' something which worries you by its
improbability. For instance, the story of the Garden of Eden is
wonderful narrative and an excellent subject for 'appreciation'.
But if we are concerned all the time with its bizarre account of the
origin of human sin and are wondering how we can accept it as
true, appreciation of the story itself becomes possible only by
shutting our eyes to all this and simply appreciating the story for
the sound of the words alone. This is what many people do when
they read the Bible 'devotionally'. They give their critical faculty
a rest and are content to use the narrative simply as a peg on which
to hang their own thoughts.

But this procedure puts asunder those things which in a work of
art are most truly joined together—namely, form and content.
The form of a literary work is what it is because it is the best
possible way of expressing the intention and the ideas of the writer.

Why is it that Lamb's *Tales from Shakespeare* are such a parody of the real thing—excellent though they are in themselves? Surely because Shakespeare was not concerned just to give information. He was concerned to produce an effect, and the only right and proper way to produce that effect was by dramatic action. The form of *Macbeth* is integral with the story of Macbeth and is not to be divorced from it. Similarly the story of the Garden of Eden is superb narrative not because the writer was trying to write a literary masterpiece but because he had something to say and this was the way to say it. Yet we disagree with what he says, and the child asks 'Is it true?' We may say, therefore, that it is 'just a story'. Or we may start off by saying 'This is the kind of thing which people of those days believed. They saw that there was a lot of wrongdoing in the world, and they asked one another how it had arisen and this was what they thought was the reason.' For this sort of thing there are many other examples from folk-lore. The essential thing therefore is to keep intact this connexion of form and content, and so when the content is not in question the mind is open to appreciate the form.

But is it *really* the form? Is not the Bible a translation? What is here said may be true of the Greek or Hebrew originals but can it be true of a translation into another language? If the writers chose their own form of expression by inward necessity, that can hardly apply to a translation.

This is a serious question and it applies not only to appreciation of the form of the material but also to the material itself. It is for this reason that, for example, in some churches every candidate for the ministry is still required to have a working knowledge of the Hebrew language. Not one in a hundred will ever know enough to be able to pit his knowledge against that of George Adam Smith or Wheeler Robinson, but it is somehow thought that more of the meaning of the Bible can be acquired from the painful use of a lexicon in the hands of an amateur than from a knowledge of the judgements of the best Hebrew scholars of the day. Nearly all people who themselves are good at languages postulate a direct knowledge of the language itself as the only key to the meaning of its literature. There are Greek scholars who write about Plato in the same way, and in the old days at Oxford it was not possible to get into touch with Plato or Aeschylus without first qualifying as a linguist.

But this is a poor way to treat the classics of the world's thought and the labours of the world's scholars. What is required is a knowledge of the way of life and the way of thought of the writers with whom we are dealing and then a good translation can convey the *exact* message of the original. It may mean occasionally a long explanation of what in the original is a single word or a metaphor, but once the meaning has been grasped the 'form' itself can be enjoyed. It is sufficient for instance to know that ἀνήριθμον γέλασμα is Aeschylus' way of describing sunlight on the sea—'the countless smiles' of the waves of the sea—a poor translation in itself, but with the explanation quite enough to catch the flavour of the original. It is enough to know that *tribulatio* is the Latin for threshing wheat, and therefore its use by the early Christians— 'trials and tribulations' in our version—indicates that kind of painful experience which in the end makes for good and not for evil. To be able to recognize the letters in Hebrew or Greek so as to be able to look up a word in a lexicon or recognize it in a commentary, and then to have access to the work of the scholars— George Adam Smith's *Isaiah* for instance, or C. H. Dodd on *Romans*—is enough for appreciation. Teachers who come to the teaching of Scripture from other disciplines, say geography or mathematics, often find themselves at the outset non-suited by the pedants because of their linguistic deficiencies. There is no need whatever for them to accept this position, for it is simply nonsense.

But in the case of the Bible this is not all. Here the translation *itself* is a classic. In the English literature lesson it has its own place alongside the other treasures of English literature. But in the Scripture lesson a working knowledge of the English Bible itself is of far more value than merely a detailed knowledge of its 'background'. It must be remembered that many of the men of earlier ages who lived and died by the Bible had no commentaries at all, nor had they any Greek or Hebrew learning. Consequently they made mistakes in interpreting individual words and texts and they also made mistakes through ignoring the background of many passages. But the strange thing is that they managed to get at the heart of the message and to them through English it came to mean just what it meant to the people who first heard it. Take for instance (as Quiller-Couch has reminded us) the connotations that have gathered round the word 'Jerusalem'. To the Christian it meant heaven, the home of their spirits, but is there anything which expresses more adequately the feeling of the exiled Hebrews for their home country than the poignant verses of the unknown sixteenth-century writer 'F. B. P.'—

> Jerusalem my happy home,
> Name ever dear to me,
> When shall my labours have an end
> In joy and peace and thee?

This, however, is but an expansion of Pss. cxxii and cxxxvii. And is there anything in the Hebrew that is lost in the English version of these psalms? All we need to know about these two psalms is that the first was part of the song of the pilgrim Jesus going up to Jerusalem for the feasts, and the other was written in bitter exile in Babylon. Rowland Prothero's book *The Psalms in Human Life* bears witness to the way in which, in a translation, the psalms speak to our condition.

Or take Isa. liii, that great 'Servant' passage. It is not known to whom the writer refers and a knowledge of the Hebrew will not help us to discover him. There are misunderstandings in the passage in the Authorized Version, but George Adam Smith will help us here. With all this in mind and a knowledge of the conditions of the Exile and of the life of Jeremiah, we turn again to that Authorized Version which has thrilled generations of Englishmen and we can understand it both for the Hebrews and for ourselves.

'Appreciation' is thus possible in every way to the English reader and we need not have a bad conscience about it. Quiller-Couch knew no Hebrew (although he was a 'classic'), nor did George Sampson, and yet these two men did more to open up the Bible to the schools of England than any theologians of our time. Comparisons no doubt are odious, but when they are already made between those who know the original language and those who do not, it is worth making this further comparison and remembering that it is with English children that we are to deal.

What then are the characteristics of appreciation of the English text of the Scriptures?

First of all there is the excellence of the plain narrative itself. It is astonishingly economical of words and yet it obtains its desired effect. The parables are outstanding examples of this. Here for instance are two verses from the story of the Great Supper (Luke xiv):

> And the servant came, and told his lord these things. Then the master of the house being angry said to his servant, Go out quickly into the streets and lanes of the city, and bring in hither the poor and maimed and blind and lame.
>
> And the servant said, Lord, what thou didst command is done, and yet there is room.

There is no pause between these verses although there might well have been a pause in the telling of them. Yet we know that between the first verse and the second the servant must have been away for quite a while. It is not necessary to say so and so it does not say so. Note, too, that in the parable every verse begins with And. This is in the Greek of course, but this co-ordinate conjunction makes of the story one whole and also emphasizes the annoyance of the host. And in these two verses there are only ten words of more than one syllable, and each of those ten has but two.

How many times has the Parable of the Prodigal Son been paraphrased but has it ever been told in as few words as the original translation or in words as simple?

This brevity is present even in long sustained passages. The Joseph cycle in Genesis or the Elijah and Elisha cycles in Kings, the stories of Gideon or Samson in Judges, the long narratives in Daniel, the story of the Crucifixion in all the Gospels, the account of the riot at Ephesus in Acts xix, and the shipwreck, ch. xxvii, have the same quality of succinctness. For that reason when they are read aloud they need to be read slowly in order to allow time for the succession of events to suggest itself to the listener.

The reference to Daniel may raise a doubt of another kind. In Dan. iii, the continued repetition of the words 'cornet, flute, harp, sackbut, psaltery and all kinds of music'—so embarrassing to a reader in a hurry!—looks as if brevity was certainly far from being a characteristic of Hebrew narrative. So also is the telling in dialogue of a message all over again when it is being delivered. But these are not really contradictions nor are they exceptions. They rather indicate that brevity is a genuine form of a story, and is not a way of cutting out 'non-essentials'. When the form of the story requires graphic detail, that detail is duly put in. There is no virtue in brevity as brevity and the Hebrew story-teller knew how to tell a story and how many words were needed for the right effect. The English reader of Dan. iii needs to keep a very tight hold upon himself if he is not to ruin the effect by too great speed. And the writers of the Gospels showed the same Hebrew characteristics of the good story-teller. The Crucifixion story, for instance, is told with extraordinary brevity, with no comment save 'that the Scripture might be fulfilled' and with not a single expression of sympathy intruded into the narrative. Consequently, if it is read slowly, but not too slowly, each word given its due place, the story has its own tremendous effect, and any comment of the writer would be distracting—as indeed the phrase 'that the Scripture might be fulfilled' is to the modern listener (but not to the ancient listener) a distraction.

A further characteristic of Biblical writers is their understanding of the value of climax and their equal understanding of the need not to overdo it. II Kings v begins thus: 'Now Naaman, captain of the host of the king of Syria, was a great man with his master and honourable, because by him the Lord had given victory unto Syria: he was also a mighty man of valour, (but he was) a leper.' Notice that in the Hebrew all that appears after 'man of valour' is the word 'a leper'. Nothing else is said about it but coming at the end of a list of Naaman's excellences it neutralizes all of them in a single word. Belshazzar's death is given us without comment in one short sentence in Dan. v at the end of a narrative of twenty-nine verses. And who can miss the effect of the astonishing conclusion of the long story of Elijah on Carmel? 'And the hand of the Lord was on Elijah: and he girded up his loins and ran before Ahab to the entrance of Jezreel.'

A few other good examples in the Old Testament are Judges v. 31; Ruth iv. 18–22 (which gives the reason for telling the story at all!); II Sam. ix. 13; II Sam. xviii. 33; II Kings xix. 33 (and its repetition in Isa. xxxvii); Ezek. xxxvii. 10. But if the teacher will read his Bible carefully, he will continually come upon examples. And the climax—although the word means a 'ladder'—is more than the last rung of the story. It is a summary of the story, and needs to be noticed in order to get the full flavour of the narrative. It is of course a familiar device in poetry, and narrative in the Old Testament has many of the characteristics of poetry. It has compactness and finish and its aim is to touch the emotions and not just to inform the mind.

The New Testament also has the same quality. The most notable examples, of course, are in St John's story of the Last Supper (xiii. 30): 'He then having received the sop went out straightway: and it was night', and the devastating climax in the last three words of the long catalogue of the merchandise of Babylon the Great in Rev. xviii. 13, 'and souls of men'. There are, however, other examples such as Phil. ii. 11 and the great climax in I Cor. xv. 57 at the end of the chapter on immortality followed by a deliberate anticlimax in v. 58 which heightens its effect. There is a similar anticlimax in Mark's story of Jairus' daughter (v. 43). Matthew's grouping of the sayings of Jesus into the 'Sermon on the Mount' finishes with the comparison of the two builders, on the sand and on the rock, which rounds off this whole body of teaching. In the light of after events, Acts viii. 1 is a significant climax to the story of Stephen: 'And Saul was consenting unto his death.' The last two verses in Rom. viii are a fine climax to the argument of that chapter, and so too, the verses at the end of II Cor. iv and the last verse of ch. iii.

The appreciation of Hebrew poetry has already been discussed but we may look at one other prose form, namely prophecy. To describe this as oratory is to bring in too much of an element of self-consciousness, for the professional orator cannot but be aware of his own technique. To call prophecies 'sermons' is even more inept for it at once sets up a resistance in the mind of the reader. Prophecy has a form of its own. The nearest we have to it in this country is the Welsh *hwyl* or the type of utterance that used to be heard in Quaker meetings a century ago where the speaker almost chanted his words. As we have it in the Bible it is a spoken form put into writing and this accounts for some of its peculiarities, its cadences and its refrains. The first two chapters of Amos, for instance, have a refrain—'for three transgressions, yea, for four'— which comes eight times and in each case the section ends with an emphasis on the word 'palaces'. To get the full flavour of prophecy therefore, it should be read aloud. Isa. liii, already referred to, Ezek. xxxiv and Jer. viii are examples of passages which particularly require this treatment.

The question is often asked whether children should learn by heart that which they do not understand. The answer is yes, although much depends on how it is done. Children have no difficulty in learning anything so long as it has a good rhythm. Many 'count out' games have words that are quite meaningless, but they go with a swing and are easy to remember. And prophecy is particularly suited for this kind of oral repetition—indeed that is how in the first place it was transmitted. Isa. xxxv, xl. 1–11 (already familiar to some from the music of Handel), xlii. 1–9, 53, lv. 6–13, Ezek. xxxvii. 1–10, xlvii. 1–5, are examples of prophetic passages that are easily remembered in this way. We need to be clear, however, of the purpose in view. It is not to 'exercise the memory' nor to provide the sort of home-work that can easily be tested. Its aim is enjoyment and to make of it a task is to defeat its purpose. The enjoyment of the sound of the words is an aesthetic appreciation and the meaning of them will come later. Learning by heart, however, is very much easier for younger children than for the adolescent, but it is best done by hearing passages well read again and again. The astonishing repertoire that some children have of music-hall songs has been gained not by sitting down to them and making the effort of learning but by continual repetition.

Good reading of Scripture, therefore, is a very essential part of Scripture teaching, for it can create that source of pleasure which for the hearer makes learning easy. And to have at command a knowledge of Scripture passages is to have readily available the raw material on which later study is but a commentary. Passages such as those indicated will, however, not come much in a child's way at a time when his capacity to learn them is at its best, and so they may have to be taken by themselves but provided with suitable background in exactly the same way as a child learns pieces of music. But most Scripture lessons will provide phrases and even words which should be noted in passing for their aptness and beauty.

> The sound of a going in the tops of the mulberry trees...
> sowing the wind and reaping the whirlwind...
> redeeming the time...
> the burden and heat of the day...
> possess our souls in patience...
> these are they which came out of great tribulation...
> Is there no balm in Gilead? Is there no physician there?

It is in the production of phrases such as these that a literature is created. There is in the Bible an absence of banality and bathos. The word is always apt and characteristic and full of colour. In the graphic story, for instance, of the healing of Jairus' daughter we have at the end what appears to be a bald statement—'and he commanded that something should be given her to eat' (Mark v. 43). But this is far from bathos. It is a graphic sign of the historicity of the story as well as characteristic of Jesus. No one making up a story of that kind would have thought of such a homely conclusion.

The reading of Scripture aloud needs to be well done, and giving a passage piecemeal to different members of the class is not a suitable method. For people have to be cast for the part of reader just as they have to be cast for parts in a play, in order to get the full effect. Normally, therefore, it will be the teacher who does it, and it would be well if in every lesson in which the Biblical text itself is being studied the teacher should begin by reading the appropriate passages from beginning to end without note or comment. Reading should be slow but not too slow, and no attempt should be made to hurry over passages which in the ancient idiom involve either repetition or itemizing. If this is done it is surprising how effectively the cadences of the original come through in a translation.

On the other hand the over-dramatizing of passages not in themselves dramatic should be avoided. This is where recordings of Biblical passages by actors and others so often miscarry. They draw attention from what is said to the way in which it is being said. This is particularly the case in dialogue whether as between two persons such as the father and the son in the parable of the prodigal, or in Isa. xl where the prophet is discussing with an imaginary interlocutor, or Amos vii, with a real one. It is important that these differences should be marked, particularly in passages of the second type, but the range of modulation of the voice need be very small—just enough to indicate that two people are concerned. For all such passages were in the first place written not as works of literary art—it is of the genius of the Bible that they are such—but to convey a very specific message. It is the message therefore that should be 'got across' and a too dramatic reading will undoubtedly prevent it. If the reader 'fancies himself' as a reader it will simply attract attention to himself.

CHAPTER XI

CORRELATION WITH OTHER SUBJECTS

I SCIENCE

We have already noticed the importance of the correlation of school subjects with one another. We may now discuss in more detail the correlation of Scripture with geography, history and English.

The question is often asked, 'Why not correlation with Science?' There are books on the market such as *Modern Discovery and the Bible* by A. Rendle Short which purport to smooth away all the apparent difficulties in reconciling scientific facts and Biblical statements. Genesis can be 'squared' with the doctrine of evolution, whales have been discovered which can swallow men, the sun standing still for Joshua's benefit is a picturesque way of describing a fact of nature which is capable of scientific explanation, and so on.

It is not too much to say that such books are quite worthless both as science and as Biblical exposition, and they should have no place in the school library. For the most part they fall between two stools—the desire to exhibit the fundamental reasonableness of the Biblical way of putting things and the desire to claim them as miracles. The Jonah story, for instance, is sometimes taken as a miracle, to be accepted as such, and sometimes as an account of scientific 'fact'. The uncertainty of which it is indicates only the passionate anxiety of the writers to cling to the literalness of the story. It is the Philistine's attitude to everything poetic and symbolic. Genesis, of course, provides a paradise for such unscholarly reconciliations.

The teacher, however, would do well to consider what he himself thinks about this question of correlation with science. The Bible quite obviously deals with literature and history, and in so far as it is concerned with the land of Palestine there are also geographical factors which influence the religious development of the people. But it is not and does not claim to be a book of science in our sense of the word, and so there is no real conflict between them.[1]

The following distinctions, however, might be noted:

1. The Bible, in so far as it is concerned with one God who is personal and who is righteous, assumes a uniformity of God's character over against the capricious deities of Greece, Rome and other nations. This might well be considered a correlation with science because science too must assume a reliable uniformity of nature, but unfortunately it is not the uniformity but the absence of it which attracts the attention of fundamentalists. They are more impressed with odd happenings which make impossible any scientific view of the universe rather than with that uniformity which is the basis alike of science and of the Christian view of God and the world.

2. The word 'science' has two meanings. It refers to *content*, i.e. the subject-matter of 'natural science', and when we say 'science' we mean physics, chemistry, biology, etc. It also refers to *method*, i.e. the strict regard for evidence, the elimination of preconceived ideas, and the classification of material in a consistent schematic form. In the latter sense there can be and often is an unscientific attitude to science, and there is also a scientific attitude to history or literature or any other 'arts' subject. By both standards, books such as *Modern Discovery and the Bible* fall down. They are unscientific in their method because they have already decided on other grounds what it is they are determined to prove, and they are not really dealing with scientific facts so much as with opinions. Literature has its own appropriate method of approach and to apply to one subject such as literature the method appropriate to another subject such as physics, is of all unscientific attitudes the most unscientific.

[1] Father Waggett, a popular preacher of fifty years ago, used to say that you could not get up a controversy between sweeping a room with a broom and sweeping it with a purpose. The room is swept in either case, but the two categories of action are quite different.

2 GEOGRAPHY: THE DESERT AND THE SOWN

The correlation of Scripture with Geography does not mean the substitution of one for the other. The travels of St Paul have often been treated as a geography lesson, and the drawing of maps and the insertion of all the places mentioned in Acts were somehow supposed also to be 'Scripture'. Correlation means a study of the way in which geographical factors have had their effect on occupations, religion and history.

Let us begin with the most obvious factor of all—that feature of the Middle East which Breasted called 'the Fertile Crescent'. Here you have on the East the valleys of the Tigris and the Euphrates and the fertile land between them—Mesopotamia—and at the south-west the fertile valley of the Nile. Here were two ancient centres of civilization both dependent on great rivers. They are separated by the northern part of the great Arabian desert. The road from one to the other follows the fertile land up the Euphrates valley and then westward to the coast of Syria and so down the coast and across the Serbonian Bog to Egypt. This is the fertile crescent and all the migrations from East to West have followed this track. A visual illustration of this is to be found along the mountain road that follows the Dog River in Syria. Here cut into the rocks are inscriptions of ancient Assyrian and Egyptian kings as well as the later monuments of Napoleon III and Allenby. Every army passing from Egypt to Mesopotamia or from Mesopotamia to Egypt has had to pass that way.

This of course has its importance in the history of Israel. From the north the southern kingdom was the safer. Between it and the Assyrian lay the northern kingdom and Syria, both of which would have to be conquered before Judah could be reached. On the other hand Judah lay right in the track of an army advancing from Egypt. These two little kingdoms of Israel and Judah were thus buffer states between Egypt and the North. In this their position was not unlike that of Belgium between France and Germany, or still better, that of Burgundy in the time of Charles the Bold. What ought to be the foreign policy of a country in such a position? There was an

Egyptian party in the nation for which the Assyrians had a very proper contempt. Egypt, said the Assyrian envoy, was 'this broken reed whereon if a man lean it shall go into his hand' (Isa. xxxvi. 6). Isaiah himself had a contempt for it. 'The Egyptians are men and not God, their horses flesh and not spirit' (Isa. xxxi. 3). The counsel of the prophets therefore was a policy of neutrality. If the people sided with either of the two empires they would be overwhelmed in its defeat and they would be ignored in its victory. 'In quietness and confidence' therefore lay their strength, and they should do as little as possible to provoke the enemy. Thus the great problem of Isa. i-xxxix arises directly out of the geographical situation of Palestine, and it is interesting to trace the references to it not only in Isaiah but also in the Second Book of Kings.

This, however, is not the only problem that arises out of this situation. It is the desert that is responsible for the configuration of the fertile crescent, but it has an even greater importance in its contrast with the fertile land. This contrast between what Professor Fleure calls the Steppe and the Sown,[1] is felt not only in this situation but also throughout the world. The desert means a hard life dependent upon flocks and herds, with no fixed habitation, with no neighbours, and it is the breeding-ground of stern independent spirits impatient of control and yet strongly susceptible to the presence of the one God ruling over all. The desert silences and the wide vault of the sky both foster a monotheistic religion and an ascetic way of life. The fertile land, however, dependent upon crops and the succession of the seasons, compels more settled habitation, and where men gather together in companies for any length of time the natural differences between strong and weak, wise and foolish, provident and carefree, not only show themselves but become the basis of civilization. Oppression and deception raise their heads and the community splits into classes. Luxury and indulgence become desirable and the gods of fertility become the gods of the people, so that a sex-centred religion becomes almost inevitable. Consequently for many reasons the contrast between the desert and the sown land deepens into a conflict.

[1] Fleure and Peake, *Corridors of Time.*

Here is the real inwardness of the Cain (who 'builded a city') and Abel story, and here too is the message of Amos. His scornful reference to the palaces of the rich are the refrain of chs. i and ii. Amos was a desert-dweller, who lived by what he could gather of sycamore fruit, and he had nothing but doom for the townsmen of Samaria. Isaiah was a townsman and saw the desert as something which has to be redeemed. In the day of the Lord the desert will blossom as the rose (Isa. xxv) and even the unknown prophet of the Exile looks for the day when the desert thorn bush shall give way to the myrtle tree (Isa. lv. 13). The prophetic 'Song of Moses' in Deut. xxxii exalts the fertile land over against the desert

> The Lord's portion is his people
> Jacob is the lot of his inheritance
> He found him in a desert land
> And in the waste howling wilderness.

But to the desert-dweller it was not the desert that needed to be redeemed but the towns.

It is an interesting exercise to make a note, from a concordance or in other ways, of all the references to this distinction between the wilderness or desert and the fertile land. Early prophecy arose out of the desert. To Elijah God was to be found in Horeb. To the psalmist in Habakkuk God came from Teman and both he and the writer of Deut. xxxiii refer to Sinai as Mount Paran whence God appeared to show himself to Israel. Sinai—wherever that was—was in the desert land and there God had his home. But in the fertile land there was not one God but many. The Baals were the gods of fertility and on every bit of rising ground there appeared the crude altar, the tree and the pole which were the apparatus of their worship.

3 GEOGRAPHY: PHYSICAL FEATURES

The standard text-book on Palestine is of course Sir George Adam Smith's *Historical Geography of the Holy Land* together with its accompanying Historical Atlas. This great work was published in 1894 and has continually been reprinted. It not only brings together the results of extensive researches in Palestine by American, British, French and German geographers, particularly in the period from about 1870 to 1890, but it is also based on long personal visits mainly in 1880 and 1891. The author at one time or another went over the whole of the ground himself, and he was fortunate in being able to see the land at a time when very little interest was being taken in it by the native inhabitants. Consequently he saw, for instance, Jacob's well outside Nablus as it had been for centuries—a lonely spring in a field—before the Greek Church had capitalized it as a source of revenue, and had covered it over with a huge and ugly building. His book contains well over 1200 Scripture references and a careful study of it re-creates the physical and historical background of the Bible as no other book has ever done. It is too large for classroom use but it is indispensable for a school library. It has one slight weakness. There is not sufficient relationship between the text and the maps and so it is very difficult to localize many of the places mentioned in the text. A smaller, more recent work is the American *Westminster Historical Atlas to the Bible*, published in England by the S.C.M.

As an illustration of the difference that has been made both by the emergence of geography as a science and by the historical method of studying the Bible we might compare Smith's book with an older and deservedly popular book on the same subject, Thomson's *The Land and the Book*. This is in the form of a travel diary made on the spot in 1857 by a man of keen observation and considerable Biblical knowledge. It is well written and very entertaining but is content simply to wander over the countryside among the 'sacred sites' and to fit apt quotations from time to time. H. V. Morton's *In the Steps of the Master* is a modern travel diary of the same kind and even more interesting although without Thomson's Biblical knowledge.

This, however, is not what we mean by 'correlation' although it has its uses, and both of these latter books should be in the library. George Adam Smith's book, however, is of a different kind and any correlation with geography will need to have constant reference to it.

It is often forgotten that Palestine lies in one of the most extraordinary areas that there are on the earth's surface. The valley of the Jordan is the beginning of the great Rift valley which continues across the Red Sea and down to the great African lakes. An air photograph of the Jordan valley shows a most grotesque landscape through which the river winds its tortuous way.[1] The river itself is only 100 miles long and it falls from 7 ft. above sea-level to 1292 ft. below at its entrance into the Dead Sea. The constant evaporation, of course, accounts for the increasing saltiness of that region. The Jordan runs between long strips of arable country which at the southern end gives way to a barren country region called the wilderness of Judaea. This even now is an area frequented by robbers and the road from Jericho to Jerusalem is as dangerous as ever. How could the ancients account for this withered and blasted region except that it was some mighty devastation wrought by the hand of an angry God? The tradition of buried cities and pillars of salt was strong in the minds of the people and the appearance of the country gives colour to the tradition. Men's ideas of the character of God are often determined by what they see of his works in nature.

An interesting example of the same thing is the effect that 'Sinai' had upon the Israelites. It was clearly a volcano and the pillar of cloud by day and the pillar of fire by night showed that in early times it was in active eruption. But where exactly was 'Sinai'? From the third century onwards the traditional site has been in the present peninsula of Sinai. On the other hand the 'land of Midian' is closely connected in the Bible with Sinai and this is generally held to have been towards the north end of the gulf of Akaba, the eastern arm of the Red Sea. This moreover, is, or was, a volcanic region and the sub-tribe of Kenites to which Moses' father-in-law belonged, was a clan of hereditary blacksmiths whose patron deity was a god of fire. The siting of Sinai, although a matter of conjecture, is of less importance than the influence the region had upon the religion of the people of the

[1] See J. H. Stembridge, *The World: a general Regional Geography*, pl. 27, or A. C. Bouquet, *Everyday Life in New Testament Times*, p. 3.

neighbourhood. Jehovah was the God that answered Elijah by fire, and the writer to the Hebrews as well as the authors of Deuteronomy speak of God as 'a consuming fire'.

Fig. 2

Terrain. The configuration of Palestine has greatly affected its history. It is a small country. From Dan to Beersheba is only 150 miles and the width from east to west at the latitude of Jerusalem is 55 miles. Yet within this small area there is quite an astonishing variety of climate, terrain and vegetation.

From north to south the land falls naturally into two sections divided from one another by the plain of Esdraelon. Galilee to the north was markedly different from the rest of the country.

Its people spoke with a different accent and they were temperamentally different. The plain of Esdraelon is crossed by a road going from Tyre and Sidon down to Samaria and Jerusalem, and by another which comes from the coast and skirts Carmel in a north-easterly direction making for Damascus. Accordingly Esdraelon was a natural battlefield for contending armies and 'the plain of Megiddo' as it was called in ancient times, 'in the Hebrew tongue Har Megeddon' (Rev. xvi. 16), came to be the symbol for the final battle of Armageddon at the end of the ages.

The land both north and south of Esdraelon takes the shape of a long slope from sea-level on the west to a mountainous ridge in the centre varying in height from 4000 to 1500 ft., with a steep slope on the eastern side down into the valley of the Jordan. At the latitude of Jerusalem these contours are very distinctive and form well-marked strips of country. There is the Maritime Plain in the west, then the low hills called the Shephelah, then the central ridge falling away steeply to the Jordan valley. Beyond this there are the still higher mountains of Moab and Ammon.

The characteristics of these various regions are outlined very clearly in Sir George Adam Smith's book but there are two features which are of particular importance for the teacher of Scripture. The first is that there was a great deal of difference (in both senses of the word) between the hill people and the people of the plains—a distinction which is noticeable in other regions of the world also. The highlander and the lowlander even in a small country tend to develop antagonisms. Benhadad's servants remind him that Israel's God 'is a god of the hills: therefore they were stronger than we, but let us fight against them in the plain and surely we shall be stronger than they' (I Kings xx).

The second point is that the contour of the land, divided as it is into many separate valleys, lent itself to settlement on tribal lines. These tribes had very little to do with one another and were full of mutual suspicion. They came together only when there was a threat to their common existence but once the crisis was over they again fell apart. The Book of Judges is the history of a series of crises which from time to time united Israel, but even in a crisis the tribal feeling was strong and could easily wreck the common effort. The attitude of the men of Ephraim, for instance, in the days of the Midianite peril (Judges viii) was not unlike that of Macdonald clansmen at Culloden. It was not until the greatest and most continuous peril of all arose—that of the Philistines—that the tribes were sufficiently of one mind to have unity of command under a king of the whole nation, King Saul. Yet even then the difference between the northern tribes and the southern was such that the united kingship lasted less than a century.

Frontiers. Palestine as a whole has four 'natural' frontiers—the Mediterranean, the mountains of Lebanon, the Jordan valley, and the southern desert. But within these there was a political division, the frontiers of which were very far from being 'natural'. This was the division between the northern kingdom of Israel and the southern kingdom of Judah. A cursory reading of the narrative in I Kings xii might make it appear that the cause of the split was political—revolt against a king who overburdened his people with taxation, but the sixteenth verse makes it clear that it was tribal: 'What portion have we in David? Neither have we inheritance in the son of Jesse. To your tents, O Israel.' This was an echo of a similar revolt even in the days of David, when Sheba raised a rebellion against the king (II Sam. xx).

The frontier between these two kingdoms was never very certain and it changed at least three times in the later history. These changes are shown in Fig. 3. If the plan is consulted along with even a large-scale physical map it will be noticed how difficult it is to identify all these small rivers and even when they are identified it is difficult to believe that they ever constituted a territorial frontier. This is not surprising because the division between north and south was tribal rather than territorial. Political divisions never meant much in Palestine even in Roman times. The frontier was constantly being pushed backwards or forwards. In I Kings xv. 17, for instance, we read that Baasha, king of Israel, went up against Judah and fortified Ramah which was well inside the borders of Judah. Then Asa, king of Judah, came along and destroyed these forts and himself fortified Geba (*v.* 22). 'Geba to

Beersheba' became the usual description of the length of Judah (II Kings xxiii. 8). But when the northern kingdom fell Judah extended its boundaries and took in Bethel, which Josiah destroyed (II Kings xxiii. 15), and in the Maccabean period the frontier, such as it was, had advanced well beyond the earlier line. Modin, where the Maccabean revolt began, is well north of the first frontier.

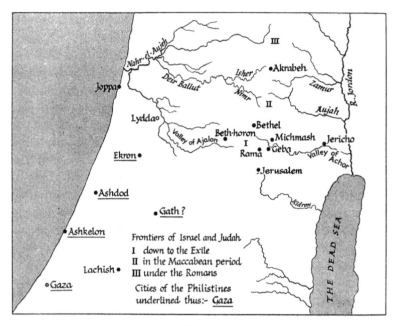

Fig. 3

Rivers. A physical map of Palestine shows an almost countless number of little streams pouring down the sides of the central range and falling into the Jordan or the Mediterranean. Yet there is no large river except the Jordan, and most of those that are recognizable are waterless in the dry season. The river Kishon which swept away Sisera's army, for most of the year finds a wide shallow outlet over the sands of the Bay of Acre. The immense amount of detritus brought down by the Jordan in its rapid flow makes the stream brown with mud, and it was not surprising that

Naaman compared it to its disadvantage with the rivers of Damascus (II Kings v). The hot steaming valley of the Jordan has a strip of dense vegetation on the western side which now, as in ancient times, is the haunt of dangerous wild animals. Its ancient name was 'the pride of Jordan' (Jer. xii. 5, R.V.).

The sea. The sea had no attraction for the Jews. They were poor sailors and they were content to leave seamanship to the foreigners. It was to be one of the attractions of heaven that there would be 'no more sea' (Rev. xxi. 1). Consequently the Maritime Plain in the south was occupied by the Philistines and that of the north by the Phoenicians. These were both seafaring people who had come, the Philistines from Crete ('Caphtor' according to Amos) and the Phoenicians from North Africa. In New Testament times, however, the Mediterranean was a Roman lake. North Africa was as much within its influence as southern Europe, and the propagation of the olive tree was a characteristic of all its shores. Yet the constant sea traffic in the summer months was carried on by every other nation except the Jews.

Towns. The siting of towns in Palestine reveals the same variety of reasons as elsewhere. The five cities of the Philistines show at any rate four different types of origin. Ashkelon is on the sea coast and had once a harbour so convenient that it was a port of landing for the Crusaders. Ashdod was inland, a fortified place bestriding the junction of the road to Joppa and the road to Ekron. Gaza was the nearest point to Egypt and was on a well-watered eminence. It was also the starting-point for the caravan road going south-east to Beersheba and Petra. Ekron possessed the oracle of the Philistines' god and was also an outpost towards Israel. The site of Gath is unknown except that it was certainly inland.

Jericho is of special interest owing to the legendary account of its capture by Joshua. It lies near the valley of Achor of unhappy memory (Joshua vii, Hosea ii), at the mouth of a mountain pass. It can easily be dominated from the hills around and have its water-supply cut off. It was luxuriously fertile but the great heat had an enervating effect on its inhabitants and it never withstood a siege. It was captured in turn by the Syrians, by Aristobulus, by Pompey, by Herod, and by Vespasian and its gates were freely opened to the invader every time.[1]

Other Palestine towns of geographical importance are Samaria, fortified by Omri as his capital in place of Tirzah (I Kings xvi. 23, 24); Tyre, holding a strong natural position improved by Phoenician engineers; Nazareth, almost on the brow of a steep escarpment which looks across the plain of Esdraelon; Tiberias and Caesarea, two artificial cities created by the Romans, and, of course, Jerusalem. The siting of Jerusalem calls for comment. It is on the crest of the central range but in a far from defensible position as it is only on one side that it is protected by the deep valley of the Kidron. Yet it has consistently maintained its position ever since the days of the Tel-el-Amarna letters. If Palestine is the part of that central region where Europe, Asia and Africa meet, Jerusalem is the point at which all the life of Palestine has converged. It is not surprising that a full description of the site and importance of the city takes up the two large volumes of George Adam Smith's *Jerusalem*.

Nomenclature. Geographical nomenclature is the point at which so much history and geography meet. Most names go back to Canaanitish times and refer to physical features. Geba means a hill; Ramah, a height; Carmel, a garden; Ekron, barren; Horeb, dry; Beer (in compounds such as Beersheba), a well; En, a spring; Lebanon, whiteness; Kidron, dirty coloured. It was also the habit of ancient writers to try to account for names by assuming a historical origin. The names Oreb and Zeeb, for instance, were given respectively to a rock and to a winepress because of Midianite leaders who were slain there (Judges vii. 25). The word Ebenezer means 'Stone of help' and recalls a great victory of Israel (I Sam. vii. 12). As we have seen, one of the concerns of the compilers of Genesis is to give an explanation of both place-names and personal names.

---

[1] There is a mass of information about Jericho in J. Garstang's *Joshua and Judges* which, however, tends to accept the Biblical narrative as it stands except that it assumes the coincidence of an earthquake with the blowing of Joshua's trumpets.

4 HISTORY

As has already been indicated the best kind of correlation of other subjects with Scripture is that which can take place in the staff common room. When the teachers of history, literature and geography are willing to use Bible material as part of the illustration of their own subject, the artificial barriers that divide off Scripture from other subjects can be broken down. This requires on the part of the Scripture teacher an awareness of the parts of his subject that have this relevance, so that it is not necessary for him to repeat in one context something already presented in another.

Nevertheless, there are correlations with history which are very particularly the concern of the Scripture teacher. We may consider four. These are in method, style, standards and content.

1. The historical method is sufficiently familiar to the modern teacher of Scripture. In brief, it involves the effort to put oneself at the date and point of view of the writer with whom we are dealing. It is the very opposite of the fundamentalist approach which ignores historical sequence altogether. A historical narrative necessarily requires historical treatment. It is this which clarifies, for example, the Book of Isaiah. The quite plain gap between the time of Hezekiah, king of Judah, and the time of Cyrus, king of Persia, indicates a difference of date between Isa. i-xxxix and Isa. xl-lv. When the literary conventions of the ancients are also taken into account it is quite clear that the author of the first part could not be the author of the second part. The historical approach means the attempt to date these two sections and to consider what the two situations were with which the writers were dealing. That is not only the scholarly, but also the common-sense way of studying Isaiah. The fundamentalist approach is concerned not with the question of how we in our time can put ourselves back into the past, but with the question of how the people in the past could project themselves into the future. In the case of Isaiah it is postulated that the historical Isaiah 'must have foreseen' that in two hundred years' time there would be a king of Persia called Cyrus who would lead his people back from that captivity which

the historical Isaiah had never even contemplated. Similarly it is held that there is no difficulty in accepting Deuteronomy as having been written by Moses even though it contains the account of his own death, because—so it is postulated—God 'must have revealed' to Moses the details of his own death. All this is purely gratuitous reasoning, aimed not at finding the truth, but at justifying a position arrived at in spite of the evidence. It requires a subjective interference with the documents which the historical method does not require at all.

The historical method therefore is that which is employed whenever we are dealing with records of the past. It is the method employed when studying Livy's history of Rome, Clarendon's history of the Rebellion, or the tortuous diplomacy of the Russian government.

There is a very good illustration of the need for it in the New Testament, namely the Synoptic problem.

One of the most notable books of the second Christian century was the *Diatesseron* of Tatian. The name indicates what it is. It is the first attempt to rewrite as one narrative the Gospel which has come down to us 'through four' documents. It was by no means the last attempt, for such 'harmonies' of the Gospels are familiar to us in our own day. They are quite arbitrary, for they necessarily ignore the basic fact that our Gospels are selections made and arranged by the respective evangelists according to some aim which each had in view. Matthew, Mark and Luke, for example, put the cleansing of the Temple at the end of Jesus' ministry. John puts it at the beginning. A Gospel 'harmony' does not discuss the reason for this nor does it try to collate it, but necessarily has to content itself with stating that it happened twice.

The Synoptic problem, however, represents something which is inherent in *all* historical study. Here are three documents, indeed four, all of which deal with the same subject. There are slight differences noticeable among the first three, and between the specifically Synoptic Gospels and the Fourth Gospel there is a very wide difference. What is the cause of these differences and what sort of impression of their subject do we reach because of them?

It should be clear that we get a far better impression of the life of Christ through four varying witnesses than we should get were the *words* of the four arbitrarily combined into one narrative.

But this is true elsewhere. A reference to Sabatier's life of St Francis of Assisi shows that there was a Synoptic problem there also. The life and character of St Francis have to be reconstructed from the impressions that they made on different writers. It is the same with Oliver Cromwell and with any great man who has been the centre of a movement or a cause of controversy. And this applies not only to men but also to institutions and movements. The method of research is always the same—the study of circumstances, motives and relationships and thus 'evaluating' the sources of our information. Langlois and Seignobos' *Introduction to the Study of History* and G. M. Trevelyan's *Clio: A Muse* discuss the method in great detail. It holds good over the whole field of history whether of so-called 'sacred' history or so-called 'profane'.

2. The style or form of history has an importance of its own although in this regard the Bible will not give us much in the way of illustration. It can recount an incident extremely well, such as the Assyrian envoy's visit to Hezekiah, or the story of Belshazzar's feast, but in what we should call the specifically 'historical' books there is no history in our sense of the word. We have here, as the Hebrew Bible reminds us, *prophecy* rather than history, and the main concern of the writers gets in the way of their work as chroniclers. For purely historical records we have to go to the Apocrypha, and we shall find I Maccabees to be a quite admirable example of historical writing. It gives a balanced account of the warfare against Antiochus Epiphanes and provides the background for the book of Daniel. The author writes history after the manner of Livy or Polybius.

3. The standard by which the Biblical historians dealt with their material has already been indicated. In all history unpopular kings and notables have been given a bad press and most historians have naturally considered anything that hurts their own vested interests to be reprehensible. It is very difficult, for instance, to get a true account of the Peasants' Revolt of 1381 because every

one of the authorities has his own reason for being biased against the peasants. How far have King John or Richard III suffered at the hands of contemporary chroniclers?

The Biblical historians had one standard of measurement, and that was the conception of God that was current among their own particular group. It is necessary to state the fact in this way for two reasons. First, the prophets had this in common with modern verbal inspirationists, that they tested the past by standards of their own time and not of the past period with which they were dealing. The classic case of this is Omri, one of the greatest kings that Israel ever knew. But he is given a bad press: 'And Omri did that which was evil in the sight of the Lord, and dealt wickedly above all that were before him. For he walked in all the way of Jeroboam the son of Nebat, and in his sins wherewith he made Israel to sin' (I Kings xvi. 25, 26). If we inquire what was this particular sin we find that it was that he worshipped God elsewhere than at Jerusalem. And if we ask why Jeroboam did it, the answer is that after the division of the kingdom Jerusalem was the capital of a foreign country and the northern kingdom necessarily had to have its own sanctuary (I Kings xii. 26–7). Nevertheless, the prophetic writers of the Deuteronomic school made no allowances for this. It was a sin whichever way you looked at it, and so, but for the Assyrian inscriptions, Omri would have been almost disregarded by historians. Of course Jeroboam had done other things as well. He had made two golden bulls and sacrificed to them, and had priests who were not of the sons of Levi. But the cardinal sin was his worship at Bethel.

Now this is not mere prejudice. Every historian, even Hallam, has to have a point of view. He must have some measuring rod by which to judge his material and some principle of selection. The prophetic historian's standard was a religious one and that which made for religious edification was put in and emphasized and everything else was either condemned or left out.

It is well to notice that they were not merely following oral tradition. They had before them many earlier writings and they themselves indicate, usually at the end of their account of each ruler, that they had made judicious use of their material.[1] 'Now the rest of the acts of Omri which he did and the might that he shewed, are they not written in the book of the Chronicles of the Kings of Israel.'

The second reason for stating that the standard of judgement was one that prevailed among the prophet's own community is that the prophetic standards were by no means accepted by the whole of the people. What we call 'the religion of the Old Testament' is often the religion of no more than about a dozen men. Over against that was the popular religion of animism, magic, fertility cults and other remains of the Canaanitish religion, and even of the religion which the Hebrews brought with them into Canaan. Allowance has always to be made for this fact. The rapidity, for instance, with which the message of the prophet of Isa. xl-lv, was forgotten is a token that it had never really been accepted.

4. It is in the content of Biblical history that we have most scope for correlation. Israel lay between Egypt and Mesopotamia and the history of those two regions is bound to include references to the history of Israel. Indeed the history of Palestine is very largely the history of relationships with the successive empires of the ancient world of the Near East. Syria, Assyria, Egypt, Babylon, Persia, the Seleucids, and Rome come one after the other into the picture while in the patriarchal ages there were still earlier contacts with Egypt and Babylon. Consequently Israel is set amid the nations. An excellent short book which the teacher ought to have at hand is Professor Norman Baynes' *Israel among the Nations*

[1] Many of these sources are now lost and it might be useful to make a list of them.
 The Book of Jashar (Jos. x. 12; II Sam. i. 18).
 The Book of the Wars of the Lord (Num. xxi. 14).
 The Book of the Acts of Solomon (I Kings xi. 41).
 The Book of the Chronicles of the Kings of Israel (I Kings xvi. 14, etc.).
 The Book of the Chronicles of the Kings of Judah (I Kings xiv. 29, etc.).
 The history of Nathan the prophet (II Chron. ix. 29; I Chron. xxix. 29).
 The prophecy of Ahijah the Shilonite (II Chron. ix. 29).
 The history of Shemaiah the prophet (II Chron. xii. 15).
 The history of Iddo the seer (II Chron. ix. 29; xii. 15; xiii. 22).
 The history of Jehu the son of Hanani (II Chron. xx. 34).
 The history of Samuel the seer (I Chron. xxix. 29).
 The history of Gad the seer (I Chron. xxix. 29).

(S.C.M.). It deals with each of these nations in turn quite fully enough to provide a background for school lessons, but also including over a hundred pages of notes and references.

We begin with the coming of the Semites first into ancient Babylonia and then into Egypt. The important period of Egyptian history for us is the Eighteenth Dynasty, 1580–1321 B.C., during which Thutmose III widely extended Egypt's dominions and Amenhotep IV, commonly called Ikhnaton, 1375–1358 B.C., led a religious revolution in the direction of monotheism. It was some time during this reign that the Habiru or Hebrews invaded Canaan which was then an Egyptian province. The Tel-el-Amarna letters from Jerusalem to the Egyptian foreign office graphically illustrate the anxieties of the times.[1]

The connexion of the Hebrews with Canaan brings to light the fact that there are two religions of Israel—the popular animism and the more spiritual religion of the prophets. This indeed is a fact of wider application. It has often been true of culture as well as of religion. The culture of Greece was the concern of a minority. Horace and Virgil and the other Latin poets give us a picture of the thoughts and habits of the intellectual smart set in Rome. Juvenal, however, shows us the conflict between popular religion and popular irreligion at the end of the first century and so is of more value for understanding the background of the early Church than almost any other contemporary author.

The discoveries of Sir Arthur Evans at Knossos has helped us to 'place' the Philistines of the Bible, and their kinsmen the Phoenicians of Tyre and Sidon who were in constant contact with Solomon. It is when we get to the break-up of the United Kingdom of Israel, however, that Israel becomes more and more linked with world history. The continual pull towards Assyria or Egypt is what we should expect of a buffer state. It was an anticipation of the later history of Burgundy under Charles the Bold, and Belgium in the twentieth century where a similar situation arose. Even a brief study of Assyria, illustrated as it can be from the archaeological discoveries, will show us with what courage

[1] A selection is published in the S.P.C.K. Texts for Students.

Isaiah and Hezekiah stood up to the Sennacherib's ambassador (Isa. xxxvi and xxxvii; II Kings xviii and xix).

The history of Babylonia is important for its influence on the Hebrews during the Exile both for good and for ill. It is well to note the character of Nebuchadnezzar as it affords justification for the belief that many of the Hebrews were well-treated in Babylon. Indeed Babylon became one of the three later centres of Judaism. The deliverance at the hand of Cyrus is recorded in Isaiah as a special providence of God towards the Hebrews, but the Cylinder of Cyrus records that Cyrus was also an emissary of Marduk, the god of Babylon, and one of his first acts was to restore the temple of the god. Persian religious ideas infiltrated into Hebrew religion as a result of the connexion with Persia, but the Persians were mild rulers, and the Jews of Palestine lived their lives in comparative peace. The exact dating of Zerubbabel, Ezra and Nehemiah is a matter of some difficulty but the sequence is clear. The possession of the Law, the Temple worship and the institution of the Sabbath sufficiently marked them off from their neighbours without any strong desire for political independence. They naturally idealized their own past and the last of the historians—the Chronicler—rewrote the history of David as that of a period of golden splendour.

With the death of Alexander the Great and the coming of the Seleucids, Israel came once more to play a leading part in world history of the Near East. The fierce nationalistic passions that were aroused by Antiochus Epiphanes gave a new character to Judaism which it never lost until the nation was wiped out by the Romans. Modern Zionism has shown some of this same quality.

Two very necessary parallels need to be drawn here. First, the inscriptions of Assyria, Babylon and Persia are of great importance in helping us to look at Israel as these ancient contemporaries looked at her. Secondly, a time chart is useful in order to bring together facts which are usually kept far asunder in history teaching. Thus Homer is of the period about the time of Solomon, Buddha is contemporary with Zechariah, Socrates with Nehemiah, Plato with Ezra, the battle of Marathon with the Book of Malachi.

Most illuminating of all is the fact that the date of Amos is the traditional date of the founding of Rome, 753 B.C.

With the New Testament we are very much within world history, and it is important that pupils should realize that the Apostolic Church was not operating in a vacuum. The admirable article on 'The Roman Empire in the First Century' by Professor Haverfield in Peake's *Commentary* is a good introduction together with the article by Professor Gilbert Murray on 'Pagan Religion at the coming of Christianity'. These put the New Testament in its historical setting, but the pupils should be encouraged to look out for indications of this in the Bible itself. What terrible event, for instance, unrecorded elsewhere, is behind the casual reference in Luke xiii. 1, 'There were present some that told him of the Galileans whose blood Pilate had mingled with their sacrifices'? Here is a contemporary event which everybody must have been discussing at the time. It is followed by another reference to the collapse of a tower at Siloam killing eighteen people. The Book of Acts, of course, is full of contemporary references (who, for instance, was Gallio?), and it is important to notice the character and organizations of the Roman government at the time. This should be compared with the entirely different situation in which the Apocalypse was written. Tacitus' judgement on Nero should be taken into account, as it will help to justify the savage anger of the Book of Revelation against the regime. At the same time selections from Josephus provide a relevant source with which our forefathers seventy or a hundred years ago were more familiar than we are today.

The study of pagan religion as it is given both in Gilbert Murray's article and also in his *Five Stages of Greek Religion* brings home to the reader that St Paul was not the only missionary using the Roman roads at the time. There are missionaries of other religions also, particularly of the Oriental cults. In Deissmann's *Light from the Ancient East* opposite page 105 there is an illustration of a receipt given to someone for his subscription to the Isis Missionary Society. At p. 451 of the same book there is an interesting illustration of a stone notice-board from the theatre at

Miletus indicating the seats reserved for Jews (see p. 173 below). Did St Paul go to the theatre? It would appear from this and from references in the New Testament[1] that he probably did.

5 ENGLISH

The correlation of Scripture with English has already been dealt with elsewhere in passing. The Authorized Version has taken its rightful place both among English anthologies and also—more important—in the histories of English literature. It is a great deal more than a translation. It stands in its own right as an original, for it is from this point that there begins an influence both on the English language and on English literature which has continued for over three centuries.

In judging this influence of the Bible it would be a serious underestimate if we confined our attention simply to literary men. Milton, Isaac Walton, Sir Thomas Browne, Bunyan, Dr Johnson, the Brontës, Scott, Carlyle, Thackeray, and many more require in us a knowledge of the Bible if we are to appreciate both their style and their point of view. It is for lack of this that some of our moderns fall short in their estimate, for instance, of Milton. They have grown up within a generation that does not know the Bible as our forefathers knew it. When John Richard Green declared that in the Elizabethan age the English became the 'people of a book' he was speaking the sober truth. The Bible was the one book available for all to hear if not to read. The sonorous prose of the English versions, chiefly of Tyndale's, was heard in every parish church in the land and became familiar to noble and peasant alike. It gave them a vehicle in which to express their thoughts and by which to extend their thoughts. It had already given shape and vocabulary to the Book of Common Prayer and Cranmer had created a beautiful Litany out of the very words of Scripture. The Psalms in the Prayer Book version became even better known to

[1] I Cor. iv. 9 where 'spectacle' is the same Greek word as in Acts xix. 29, 31 'theatre'. Heb. x. 33, 'gazingstock', comes from the same word and means a spectacle or stage play.

the commonalty of the seventeenth century than the Old Testament stories to their medieval forbears. Nor should we forget the immense services in this regard to the country and to the language rendered by what nowadays are sometimes called 'our unhappy divisions'. If sects divided off or were cast out from the Established Church it was usually on some Biblical reason that they staked their separatism. The seventeenth-century sects and the later Methodist and Evangelical movements were both caused by and resulted in a searching of the Scriptures which mightily affected the common speech of the whole country. Meanwhile in Scotland Presbyterianism was even more the religion of a book than Anglicanism and Burns' *Cotter's Saturday Night* shows how the tradition persisted right down to his time. Accordingly the chief influence of the Bible was upon the language of the common people, and the works of the great writers could be appreciated because they had this measure of common ground with their readers.

Accordingly, one of the necessary reference books to keep handy is the *Oxford Dictionary of Quotations*. It is an illuminating exercise to work through the pages of familiar quotations from the Bible and to discover how unexpected many of them are. How many people, for instance, have used some such phrase as 'science, falsely so-called' without realizing that it was from the Bible.[1] It is this which shows so clearly how much the Bible has entered into the very texture of our language. It is here where Puritanism had its revenge on the Restoration, for although it was laughed out of court by Butler's *Hudibras* it contributed a vocabulary on which even its enemies were compelled to draw. No one was more temperamentally different from the Puritans than Dr Johnson but the characteristics of Johnson's style are equally characteristic of the Bible and were modelled upon it. And as Johnson was the arbiter of letters during his time Biblical diction became very marked in the great writers of the period.

[1] In an earlier book, *How to know your Bible*, I have collected a large number of these into a connected narrative. It was possible from twenty-six quotations to make up an intelligible paragraph of no more than 219 words.

Perhaps in none is this more noticeable than in Burke in whom the grand style was matched with the equally grand manner in treating his themes.

Many Biblical themes occur in other literature also and it is interesting to compare their respective ways of treatment. Greek tragedy, for example, has already been mentioned in connexion with a story in Daniel and the story of Jeroboam II. The Book of Job exercised a fascination over Milton and Shelley, both of whom meditated a poem on the subject, for they were both attracted by Job's robust attitude towards the Almighty. The note of defiance comes into both Milton's Satan and Shelley's Prometheus. Milton's greatest success was with the story of Samson, an expansion of Judges xvi. 23–30, with Manoah introduced as the interpreter of the whole story.

Sir Thomas Browne wrote of death and immortality after the grand manner of the fifteenth chapter of I Corinthians. Isaac Walton's *Compleat Angler* is as much a deliberate justification of the ways of God to man as is *Paradise Lost*, and it is steeped in knowledge of the Bible. Bunyan of course has the true Biblical touch and he also has the Biblical psychological insight. Addison's *Spectator* catches the familiar accents for lighter and more humanist themes. And so we might continue through the 'classics' right down to the present day. Wherever the prophetic note has to be sounded the Bible makes itself evident either in style or in ideas or in both. Milton's *Areopagitica*, Burke's speeches on America, Carlyle's *Sartor Resartus*, William Lovett's address to the working-men of England like Mazzini's address to the working-men of Italy, all show the same pervasive influence. In another and deeper way so also does Newman's *Apologia*.

If we cross the Atlantic we shall find the influence of the Bible on American literature quite as great as on that of the mother country. Tom Paine's *Common Sense* appeals to the Old Testament and has the prophetic touch, the Declaration of Independence has the grand manner in both style and subject-matter. Lincoln's Second Inaugural is of the same quality as the first chapter of Isaiah—'Come, let us reason together, saith the Lord.' Melville's

Moby Dick has a hero of the Old Testament patriarchal type. The Romantics think they have little in common with a Biblical religion but they cannot escape now and then a Biblical style. Channing, Emerson, Thoreau and Oliver Wendell Holmes feel the influence just as Thomas Henry Huxley and Matthew Arnold exhibit it on this side in the same period.

We must not of course allow coincidences such as these to be exalted to the status of cause and effect. Because a writer chooses an acute spiritual problem or a religious theme, it does not follow that he has been reading the Bible any more than the use of the Johnsonian antithesis proves that the user is acquainted with Hebrew parallelism. But there is such a thing as a literary atmosphere and the heritage of a literary style, and men breathe it and inherit it often completely unawares. It is in any case an interesting exercise to consider when any author is being read, whether there are reminiscences of Biblical themes or Biblical style to be discovered in his writings. Such an exercise will not be possible without a steadily growing acquaintance with the words of Scripture and a love for them. It is in its correlation with English more even than with history that the Bible becomes most alive, for literature involves appreciation both of form and of content. Too much can be made in school studies of what is called the 'background' of the Bible. It sometimes completely precludes the reading of the Bible itself. The various correlations with English should help to restore the balance.

CHAPTER XII

TEACHING AIDS

There is one general rubric which must be observed in any discussion of the use of teaching aids. They are intended to be *aids* and not to take the place of teaching. It is very easy in a colourful subject like the Old Testament to put the illustrations in place of the text. What is called the 'background' of the Bible becomes so interesting that there is almost no foreground.

It is as well therefore continually to ask oneself what is this particular illustration intended to do? Is it really necessary? Not every lesson will need visual illustrations and even when they are needed their use will be mainly incidental. It is a good plan to use visual material as a focus of what has already been taught in the lesson rather than to allow the lesson to be a comment on the picture.

I PICTURES

Pictures are the main visual aids to teaching, and in the case of Scripture they fall into two main classes, those objects that are contemporary with the Bible, and those that are modern illustrations of Biblical stories. On the whole the first class are for older children and the second for the younger. The first class again can be divided up into pictures of (*a*) contemporary inscriptions such as the Moabite stone, (*b*) contemporary art such as the Assyrian reliefs in the British Museum, (*c*) reconstructions of ancient buildings and sites, (*d*) views of natural scenery which has not changed since Biblical times, such, for example, as the view of Esdraelon from the escarpment south of Nazareth. All these pictures of whatever class should have a bearing on the Bible narrative and be a definite illustration of it with a certain observable importance. For instance a picture of Galilee as it is today or of some nondescript bit of a river valley, does not illustrate anything in particular, for it might be anywhere, but a picture of Esdraelon gives a view that Jesus himself must have seen scores of times with Carmel to the east, Tabor on the west, Gilboa across the plain, the mountains of Moab in the distance, and the road crossing the plain from north to south. And by 'contemporary' is meant contemporary with the particular period with which we are dealing. A picture of David as a shepherd boy is not a contemporary picture and the function of such an illustration is quite different from that of a contemporary 'document'.

An adequate collection of pictures is not difficult to acquire. For the first class of illustrations the following list of books will be referred to although it is recognized that the pictures may be found in many other publications as well.

Reference	Name
A.E.	*The Art of Ancient Egypt.* (Phaidon.)
A.T.	BREASTED. *Ancient Times,* 2nd ed. (Ginn.)
A.N.T.	CAIGER. *Archaeology and the New Testament.* (Cassell.)
B.I.P.	KIRBY, R. *The Bible in Pictures.* (Odhams.)
B.M.	British Museum publications.
B.S.	CAIGER. *Bible and Spade.* (Oxford.)
D.	DEISSMANN. *Light from the Ancient East.* (Hodder.)
D.P.	DEISSMANN. *Paul: A Study in Social and Religious History.* (Hodder.)
F.	FINEGAN, J. *Light from the Ancient Past.* (Princeton and Oxford.)
G.	GADD, H. J. *History and Monuments of Ur.* (Chatto and Windus.)
H.	HALL, H. R. *Ancient History of the Near East.* (Methuen.)
O.H.	*Oxford Helps to the Study of the Bible,* new ed., 1931.
S.B.	*The Story of the Bible.* (Fleetway House publications.)
W.	WOOLLEY. *Ur of the Chaldees.* (Penguin.)
W.O.P.	*Wonders of the Past,* 3 vols. (Amalgamated Press.)

(a) *Contemporary inscriptions*

A warning has already been given concerning the use of archaeological material (p. 59), especially if it is looked upon as 'proving' something for which there is otherwise no corroboration. There is, however, a good deal of material that is parallel with the Old

Testament narrative which often enables us to see the Israelites as others saw them. It is suggested therefore, that as a minimum the teacher should possess himself of pictures of the following:

B.S.   The stele of Hammurabi. This is a good example of a 'table of stone', and it also has a bearing upon the laws of Moses. The story of its discovery would interest older children and so too would the controversy as to whether Moses had 'borrowed' from it. The differences as well as the similarities when compared with the 'laws of Moses' should be noted.

B.S. and   The Moabite Stone. This gives the Moabite view of the
O.H.   relations between Mesha king of Moab and Israel in the time of Omri, Ahab and Jehoram (II Kings iii).

B.S. and   The black obelisk of Shalmanezer III which mentions the
O.H.   homage paid to Assyria by Jehu in 841 B.C., a fact not recorded in the Biblical narrative (II Kings x). This is a beautiful bas-relief of more interest to children than most because it has pictures as well as words.

F.   The prism of Sennacherib. A most important historical document. It describes the siege of Jerusalem in the reign of Hezekiah (II Kings xviii).

B.S.   Defeated Israelites bringing their tribute to Sennacherib engaged in the siege of Lachish. (*Oxford Helps*, new ed., Pl. 67.) Thus Hezekiah brought his gifts (II Kings xviii. 14–16).

O.H and F. The stele of Esar-haddon (Ezra iv. 2; II Chron. xxxiii. 11 (margin): 'the captains of the host of the king of Assyria which took Manasseh with hooks'). This shows the king leading two captives by strings hooked through their noses.

F.   The Cyrus cylinder. This narrates the fall of Babylon and credits Cyrus with appointment by Marduk, the god of Babylon, just as the Unknown Prophet of the Exile credits him with appointment by Jehovah (Isa. xlv. 1).

The contemporary material for the New Testament is of course much greater than that for the Old Testament. Pictures of the following will be found useful:

O.H.   Augustus as *imperator*. The well-known statue in the Vatican.

O.H.   Heads of contemporary emperors—Tiberius, Caligula, Claudius, Nero, Vespasian, Titus and Domitian.

O.H.   Reliefs from the Arch of Titus—showing the trophies taken at the capture of Jerusalem.

D.P. and   The Gallio inscription—fragment of a letter from the
O.H.   Emperor Claudius to the city of Delphi, mentioning Gallio as Governor of Achaia A.D. 52 (Acts xviii). This is an important document for New Testament chronology. The fragmentary nature of it will convey a sense of the difficulty with which archaeologists have to contend.

D.P. and   An altar to unknown gods, discovered at Pergamum, or
A.N.T.   alternatively an altar to 'a god or goddess' on the Palatine Hill, Rome (there is an excellent picture or photogravure in *The Story of the Bible*, p. 1355). (These illustrate Acts xvii. 23.)

(b) Other contemporary material

Among contemporary objects of art other than the inscriptions, the following will be found useful. (For purposes of ancient history *as such* a much larger list will be needed especially of the art of ancient Egypt. But we are here confining ourselves to illustrations for use in Scripture teaching.)

B.M.   The Rosetta Stone. This gives the clue to Egyptian hieroglyphics.

Postcard   Cleopatra's needle. This is the absurd title given to the obelisks of Thothmes III now in London and in New York.

B.S., A.E.,   Heads of Thothmes III (*B.S.*), Amenhotep IV (Ikhnaton)
O.H. and F.   and his beautiful queen Nefertiti (*A.T.*). Thothmes was the great king of the Egyptian XVIIIth dynasty who subdued Syria and Palestine. Ikhnaton was a religious reformer, a pacifist king, who allowed Palestine to be overrun by the Habiru (? Hebrews). The letters that passed between the governor of Jerusalem and the Egyptian foreign office at this time were discovered in 1887 and are now known as the Tel-el-Amarna tablets. The head of his queen is one of the most beautiful art treasures in the world. The dates of Ikhnaton's reign are 1376–1362 B.C.

B.S.   Statue of Ramases II who reconquered Palestine and may possibly be the Pharaoh of the oppression.

O.H.   Strangers coming into Egypt. This is a wallpainting from a tomb of the XIIth dynasty and may be typical of the visit of Jacob's sons as recorded in Gen. xlii. 5.

O.H.   Egyptian forced labour. Brickmaking and the hauling of stone.

B.S.   Portrait reliefs of Hittites (showing the origin of the Jewish nose?), Canaanites and Philistines.

F.   The Ziggurat at Ur, a Babylonian temple tower, the sight of which is recalled by the story of the tower of Babel (Gen. xi. 4–9). It was also the pattern of the later 'hanging gardens' of Babylon.

B.M.   Assyrian bas-reliefs from the collection in the British Museum, notably (a) the war scenes of Tiglath Pileser III, (b) a siege by Sennacherib, (c) war scenes of Assur-bani-pal, (d) Assur-bani-pal's lion hunt, (e) Assur-bani-pal dining with his queen (almost the only Assyrian sculpture with a female figure and the only one dealing with a domestic scene). These reliefs show both the quality of Assyrian art and the savagery of the Assyrian character. The glee of the prophet Nahum at the fall of Assyria is all the more understandable.

F., *O.H.*, G., F. and W.   The mosaic 'Standard' from Ur (British Museum). This consists of a wooden frame and two scenes in mosaic— on one side a war scene and on the other a domestic scene. 'The date of this priceless illustration of early Babylonian life which is for the Sumerians what the Luttrell Psalter is for the medieval English, is before 3000 B.C.' This and other ancient works of art help to reconstruct the life of those days which was clearly far more 'civilized' than it was thought to be a hundred years ago.

O.H.   Phoenician ships of the kind probably used by Hiram, king of Tyre in bringing materials for Solomon's temple.

O.H.   Phoenician women. There is an almost startling picture on an ivory plaque found at Nimrud, showing a Phoenician woman dressed in fashionable Egyptian headdress and looking through a window.

F.   Steles from Ras Shamra (1) With the God El, (2) with the god Baal. These were discovered in 1929 with a large number of clay tablets from the site of Ugarit, a city on the Syrian coast opposite Cyprus. The names of both gods appear in the Old Testament, but El has a wife Asherat and their son is Baal. Asherat is probably the Asherah of I Kings xviii. 19 and II Kings xxiii. 14.

W.O.P., vol. II Rock of Behistun with its sculpture showing the triumph of Darius over ten rebels. The inscription is in the cuneiform characters of three languages, Persian, Elamite and Babylonian, and the deciphering of this, chiefly by Rawlinson, opened up the study of cuneiform texts everywhere.

A.T., p. 496 Alexander the Great at the battle of Issus. A floor pavement from Pompeii.

B.S. The Sphinx of Gizeh. Any photograph of this should have been taken after 1926 when the front was cleared of sand and revealed the dream stele of Thothmes IV between the paws. There is an excellent coloured picture on p. 94 of *Story of the Bible* (Fleetway House).

D. A Roman milestone erected by Quirinius (Luke ii. 2) and bearing the date of the year 6 B.C., on the road from Iconium to Pisidian Antioch, passed by Paul and Barnabus (Acts xiii. 51). It is still standing.

D. An ostracon receipt for the Isis collection A.D. 63, illustrating the fact that there were other missionaries than Christians.

O.H. A Roman road. There is a photograph of a Roman road in Syria in the *Oxford Helps*, pl. 98, or a photograph can be obtained of the remains of the stone Roman causeway over the moors at Levisham near Whitby.

A.N.T. The Wiegand Cup. This is one of half a dozen glass goblets dating from the first century and which were in common use among the humbler classes. This one has an inscription in Greek which is also found in Matt. xxvi. 50, and it has the best chance of being of the type used at the Last Supper. At any rate it is quite certain that the so-called 'holy grail' was not of gold or silver or anything valuable. The cup is now at the Selly Oak Colleges, Birmingham, and Caiger gives a photograph of it opposite p. 17.

W.O.P., p. 158 The Pont du Gard, built across the Gardon near Nîmes about 19 B.C., the finest Roman aqueduct in existence, which gives a vivid idea of the might of the Roman Empire even far away from the capital.

W.O.P.,   The statue of Diana of the Ephesians—the image that was
p. 600   said to have fallen from heaven (Acts xix. 35).
W.O.P.,   A Roman amphitheatre, e.g. the Colosseum at Rome or
pp. 1057–62   the theatre at Orange, Arles or Nîmes. This again helps
   to bring back the world of the first century, and if to
   this we add—
D.   The inscription in the theatre of Miletus—'the place of the
   Jews, the God-fearers'—(the word occurs in John ix. 31)
   —we begin to understand something of the circumstances in which St Paul was brought up.

(c) Reconstructions

Archaeology is a science that requires considerable skill and
experience in order to appreciate it. Especially is this the case with
sites of towns or buildings. Imagine St Paul's Cathedral completely
vanished except the ground plan and here and there a portion of
wall and a column or two. How would the ordinary non-expert
get any idea of what it was in its complete state? In the same way
it is of little use to put before children or indeed any ordinary
adult a picture of an excavated site. It all needs so much interpretation before it can mean anything at all.

It is much more helpful to have an expert reconstruction, as then
we can understand what the place or the building was in the times
which we are studying rather than as it appears now. Look, for
example, at the *Oxford Helps*, pl. 71, at a picture of the Ishtar Gate
of Babylon built by Nebuchadnezzar about 600 B.C. as it appears
today, and then turn to Breasted's *Ancient Times*, plate II, and see
what it looked like in its original coloured setting, and there is no
doubt which is the better 'illustration'.

The following 'reconstructions' are all to be found in *Wonders
of the Past* at the pages indicated:

A nobleman's hall in Tel-el-Amarna, p. 1156.
The Palace of Sargon, p. 309.
An Assyrian palace (in colour), p. 296.
Nineveh (in colour), p. 294.
The entrance to Sennacherib's palace, p. 290.

The Hanging Gardens of Babylon (in colour), p. 348.
The Palace of Xerxes (Ahasuerus) at Persepolis, pp. 761–3.
General view of ancient Athens, p. 694.
The agora of Athens (in colour), p. 696.
The Acropolis, p. 704.
The Acropolis (in colour), p. 693.
The Parthenon (in colour), p. 814.
Temple of Diana at Ephesus (in colour), p. 590.
The Roman Forum, pp. 476, 478.
Jerusalem, p. 1006.
Jerusalem, the golden gate (in colour), p. 1008.
The Catacombs in Rome (in colour), p. 1109.

The book *The Story of the Bible* (see below) gives a reconstruction of Herod's temple at p. 1044.

(d) Views

The American Colony in Jerusalem publishes a very large and usually admirable series of views of Palestine. Many of the pictures in books are reproductions of these. The book from which the following are taken is *The Story of the Bible* published by The Fleetway House, Farringdon Street, E.C. 4 in two volumes. The text is written by well-known scholars and there are 1200 illustrations some in colour and some in photogravure. These illustrations need to be used with great discrimination. In pictures of sites it is not always made clear whether the view is as it is today or as it used to be. Nor is it always clear which are the few genuine identifications, which are simply traditional, and which are frankly bogus. For example, we have a picture of El Bireh 'where Mary is said to have missed Jesus', another of the obviously untrue 'inn of the Good Samaritan', and on p. 70 we are shown a picture of the excavations at Kish entitled 'Story of the Deluge confirmed' and referred to as 'visible proof'. This, as every scholar knows, is purely gratuitous and is very far from being 'proof'. The views of the various tombs called after Rachel, Isaac, Sarah and other Old Testament characters may easily mislead the reader into thinking that they are genuine. In the case of the tomb of Absalom we are very properly told that this identification is no earlier than the sixteenth century A.D. The greater number of the New Testament sites are notoriously untrustworthy, and even a genuine one such as Jacob's well has been despoiled by the ignorant treatment of ecclesiastical Philistines. But many of them appear in pictures either with or without the tendentious caption 'tradition says', which for many people is almost the same as proof.

Having allowed for these limitations, however, it is still true that *The Story of the Bible* has a large number of most useful pictures for classroom use. Of these we select the following (pages indicated):

> The Dead Sea and Wilderness, pp. 30, 743, 922, 977.
> The table-land of Moab, p. 242.
> The plain of Esdraelon, pp. 252, 869, 1129.
> Jerusalem to Jericho, p. 1038.
> The Ladder of Tyre, p. 905.
> A caravan in the desert, p. 58.
> The Sea of Galilee, p. 256.
> Cedars of Lebanon, p. 671.
> Capernaum—the synagogue as it is today, p. 1050.
> Capernaum—the synagogue reconstructed, p. 1046.
> Paphos, p. 1302.
> The Appian Way, p. 1337.
> Reconstruction of Herod's temple, p. 1044.
> The Fabrician Bridge at Rome, p. 1373.
> The pyramid of Cestius, p. 1374.
> The Arch of Titus, p. 1351.

(e) Modern pictures

Modern pictures of Bible stories also need to be chosen with great discrimination. It should be remembered that an illustration tends to fix itself permanently to the thing it illustrates and so may not only be in any case a limitation but may also give quite a wrong impression of a historical character or incident. How many people who have grown up with *Alice in Wonderland* with Tenniel's illustrations, feel that any other illustrations are somehow 'wrong'? Similarly it is difficult if not impossible to imagine

Mr Pickwick apart from Cruikshank's illustration, or *The Water Babies* illustrated by anyone else than Linley Sambourne. These, however, are fiction and it is due to the genius of the artist that the pictures and the story are so truly blended as to become inseparable.

With historical characters, however, and a known contemporary setting, it is not so. Doré, Tissot and other modern painters as well as Titian, Rembrandt and other old masters, interpreted the Bible stories in their own way without caring too much about possible accuracy. It was not every painter who took such labour to get genuine local colour as did Holman Hunt in 'The Scapegoat'. In all these cases we are necessarily dealing with interpretations and this has to be allowed for in our choice of material to give to children. Some of the resistance that has been put up to the modern historical study of the Bible doubtless arises from the recollection of pictures in childhood.

In recommending, therefore, certain publications as being useful for illustration particularly with young children, these general principles have been kept in mind. Not historical accuracy but historical probability is to be observed.

Among publications which will give all that we need for reference, mention might here again be made of *The Story of the Bible*. There are a number of excellent camera studies of Palestine today and these on the whole are to be preferred to the studies by painters (there are exceptions). So many customs have not changed. There are pictures of occupations such as sowing, reaping, buttermaking, water-carrying, ploughing, weaving and harvesting; of customs, of eating, marrying, buying and selling, funerals; festive seasons, holidays and processions; and scores of other interesting studies from life.

A more recent publication is *The Bible in Pictures* edited by R. Kirby, with Professor S. H. Hooke, Professor E. D. Jones and Father C. C. Martindale as consultants (Odhams Press). Nine artists have co-operated to make the drawings which are simple and clear and have no particular value in themselves but only as illustrations. They have the merit of being *possible* and they are simple enough to be guides to children who wish to act the parts.

The book falls into three sections—the story of Jesus, the story of his people (the Old Testament), and the story of his Church.

In addition to these there are various series of modern drawings and pictures, chiefly for young children, among which the following are samples.

Macmillan's Bible Pictures.
Nelson's Bible Wall Pictures.
Shaw's Bible Wall Pictures (National Sunday School Union).
S.P.C.K. Bible teaching pictures, by Elsie Anna Wood.
S.P.C.K. The Parables, by Nina K. Brisley.
S.P.C.K. Palestine cards.

A full list of these and other publishers' series is put out by the Institute of Christian Education. It is well, however, to see the pictures themselves before acquiring them, in order to be sure that they are really necessary. History and Geography teachers will be able to supplement the Scripture teacher's choice from more general illustrations of their own.

2 COINS

It is not always realized how relatively cheap (at any rate for a school if not for an individual) are certain ancient coins which illustrate the Bible. Some may be obtained from local antique dealers or application could be made to Messrs B. A. Seaby, Ltd, 65 Great Portland Street, London, W. 1, whose catalogues are a useful guide to current prices. The connoisseurs tell you that you must not clean old coins, but for our purpose as illustrations of lessons they are much better cleaned. A gentle application of some non-abrasive substance will make the coins more easily decipherable.

The following are a good collection with which to begin:

(1) Any silver coin of Alexander the Great showing the head with the lion skin of Heracles. Reverse: Zeus seated, with the word ALEXANDROS.

The importance of this type of coin is that it shows the beginning of the deification of the emperor. The story of Alexander fired Julius Caesar with ambition for his own deification and when his turn came he became 'divus Julius'.

(2) Any copper coin of Augustus showing on the obverse the title Divus, or, still better, the sestertius of Julius Caesar and Augustus. On one side is the head of Caesar and the legend DIVOS JULIUS and on the other the head of Augustus and the legend DIVI·F. This carries the evidence for emperor worship one step further. This cult became the great opponent of Christianity and the Emperor became the Anti-Christ of the Apocalypse.

(3) A silver denarius of Tiberius, with head on obverse, and on reverse a figure seated and the letters PONTIF. MAXIM. This is the tribute money (Matt. xviii. 28, etc.).

(4) An orichalcum coin of Vespasian bearing on the reverse a seated figure and JUDAEA CAPTA, or a silver denarius with the word JUDAEA. The first was struck in honour of Titus' capture of Jerusalem in A.D. 70.

(5) A silver coin of the Roman republic, P. Porcius Laeca, with the word 'PROVOCO' (I appeal) struck in honour of the Lex Julia which established this right. It was to this law that St Paul appealed (Acts xxv. 11).

(6) A copper coin of Herod Archelaus (Matt. ii. 22) with a helmet on one side and a bunch of grapes on the other.

(7) A copper coin of Herod Agrippa I (Acts xii) with a royal umbrella and the words BASILEUS-AGRIPA on one side and on the other three ears of corn.

These last two coins illustrate the Jewish hatred of idolatry. To have a man's head on a coin was idolatry, and so no Roman coins were acceptable for the Temple offerings. They had to be changed and consequently the money-changers became part of the Temple organization.

Two other coins may be added but they are very difficult to obtain.

(8) The half shekel of Simon Maccabaeus which was the normal Temple tax (Matt. xvii. 24).

(9) The silver stater of Augustus commonly known as the tetradrachm of Antioch. (The stater in the fish's mouth, Matt. xvii. 27, and probably also a 'piece of silver', Matt. xxvi. 15).

These can be added to from time to time from the list given in the new edition of the *Oxford Helps*, pp. 260–3.

3   TIME CHARTS

For all history teaching a time chart is a most useful device. It is a means of translating time intervals, which are very difficult to grasp, into space intervals, which are very easy. It can give a visual conspectus of an entire period so that the relationships of events are clearly seen. It also can be used to show parallel lines of development of different countries and cultures.

It is best to make one's own time chart, as the making of the framework and the selection of dates and events to fit into it is a help to remembering their sequence and relative importance. Moreover, the making of a time chart is often the most effective way of making notes. For this purpose a large sheet is needed and if notes can be added by the side of an event, a whole chapter in a text-book may be presented in an easily recognizable form. For the making of a time chart a really good text-book is needed in order to supply the main theme and the leading events. This can be augmented from other books but the scheme as a whole is always kept well in view.

For Scripture teaching various time charts are needed. The period we are to cover begins about 3000 B.C., and continues to about A.D. 100. In the earlier period there will not be many entries, and such dates as there are will be largely conjectural. Nevertheless, the fixing of dates is an exact science and not very relevant here. What really is important is the sequence of events and the parallel events going on at the same time. As we get to the later period, events begin to crowd in thick and fast and dates become more certain. We need, therefore, to alter the scale of the time charts, and as this can scarcely be done on one sheet we shall need a number of them.

Time charts, however, can be a snare. There is a strong temptation to put in as much as possible and so to lose sight of the wood for the trees. It should be kept in mind that our purpose here is to present the Biblical history in its setting, it is not the teaching of ancient history. Consequently, there must be a rigid principle of selection and everything excluded except that which bears upon the development both of Biblical history and Biblical religion.

A word should also be said about the spelling of ancient names. There are, for instance, about half a dozen current ways of spelling Akhenaton. These are not so much spellings as transliterations, and it does not really matter how the names are spelt as long as they are recognizable. Ikhnaton, for instance, is obviously the same person as Akhenaton. The teacher must not let himself be intimidated by the scholars on these matters!

It is suggested that we should have five time charts, namely:

(1) From 3000 B.C. to 1550 B.C.
(2) From 1550 B.C. to 1000 B.C.
(3) From 1000 B.C. to 300 B.C.
(4) From 300 B.C. to A.D. 70
(5) From A.D. 14 to A.D. 135.

(1) *3000–1550 B.C.*

This period takes us from the IIIrd dynasty of Egypt down to the expulsion of the Hyksos and the accession of the XVIIIth dynasty. It includes the Pyramid Age and the Feudal Age, and shows leadership passing from the North to the South. The IVth dynasty builder of the great pyramid, Khufu, and the builder of the Sphinx, Khafre, appear in the list and also the last king of the XIIth dynasty, Amonemhet III, but no other names are necessary.

The history of the city-states that eventually made up Babylonia comes into this period. At the beginning the region was called Shinar but it became Babylonia when the Amorites established Babylon. Here again is the contrast between north and south—the south or Sumer mainly dominated by Ur, and the north by Akkad. In the IIIrd (united) dynasty of Ur, about 2300 B.C., we have the building of the great Ziggurat, extension of trade and the stories of Etana, Adapa and Gilgamesh, and these might be entered on the chart. The land of Sumer was greatly harassed by the Elamites for about two centuries and was finally invaded by them, only to be attacked in their turn by the Amorites. The Amorites invaded Akkad about 2050 B.C., and the sixth Amorite king was the famous Hammurabi. The dynasty was extinguished and the

Babylonian civilization with it, by the invasion of the barbarous Kassites in 1750 B.C.

Assyria began as a Sumerian colony about 2900 B.C., and seven centuries later had to maintain itself against the Mitanni and the Phoenicians, but there is nothing of importance to go on to the chart. About 1900 B.C., the Hittites entered Anatolia—another collection of small states which ultimately became dominated by one of them, Hatti. The Hittite old kingdom began about 1740 and lasted till 1460 B.C.

The traditional history of Israel begins round about 2300 to 2100 B.C. with the Elamite raids on Sumer, during which Abraham migrated into Canaan. The migration of Joseph and others into Egypt appears to have taken place during the Hyksos (shepherds) occupation of Egypt, and their later oppression by the Pharaohs of the XVIIIth and XIXth dynasties may have been due to their association with these shepherd kings from the desert. (See Gen. xlvi. 34. Note should also be made of the fact that Palestine in the early period was a colony of Egypt.)

For this period the handiest authorities are Breasted's *Ancient Times*, 2nd ed. (Ginn), an admirable text-book with excellent illustrations and a wealth of maps; G. L. Woolley, *Ur of the Chaldees* (Pelican edition); O. R. Gurney, *The Hittites* (Pelican); N. Baynes, *Israel among the Nations* (S.C.M.); Oesterley and Robinson, *History of Israel* (Oxford), vol. I.

(2) 1550–1000 B.C.

This period begins with the XVIIIth dynasty of Egypt and ends with the election of Saul as king of Israel. It is the period of the first Egyptian Empire with its capital Thebes and the great names are Queen Hatshepsut; her brother Thutmose III, 1501–1447 B.C., whose conquests are recorded in the vast temple at Karnak; Amenhotep IV or Ikhnaton, 1380–1362 B.C., the religious reformer who shifted the capital to Amarna; and Tutankhamen, the boy king whose tomb was uncovered in 1922 by Howard Carter and the Earl of Carnarvon. These were all of the XVIIIth dynasty.

The chief names in the XIXth dynasty are Ramases II, 1301–1234, and Merenptah, 1234–1225 B.C.

This is the period of the Hittite empire, 1460–1190 B.C., and the great kings, Suppiluliumas who became king in 1380 and Hattusilis III who became king in 1275 B.C. This empire passed away through the effect of war and the new Hittite kingdom which arose on its ashes in 1190 B.C. was the one which was brought into contact so much with Israel (Num. xiii. 29, Joshua i. 2–4, I Sam. xxvi. 6), and Hittites were to be found among Solomon's multitude of 'strange women', I Kings ii. 1.

The traditional date of the fall of Troy also comes into this period, 1184 B.C.

The early history of Israel now begins to take shape. The Tel-el-Amarna letters which cover the reigns of Amenhotep III and Amenhotep IV, report the continuing raids of the Habiru or Hebrews upon Palestine which had become part of the dominions of Thutmose III. It would look therefore as if the Exodus took place about the time of Thutmose's successor Amenhotep II. This of course is again purely conjectural. At the same time as the Hebrews were entering Palestine the Arameans were establishing themselves in Syria with a capital at Damascus, and there arose also the kingdoms of Edom, Moab and Ammon. In the reign of Rameses III (1204–1172 B.C.) of the XXth dynasty of Egypt, a Philistine invasion was driven back from Egypt and the Philistines settled in southern Palestine. From their five cities they raided the Hebrew settlements to the north and were finally beaten off only when the Hebrew tribes united under King Saul in 1025 B.C.

(3) 1000–300 B.C.

Israel is now the chief actor on our stage but there are also great events happening abroad. There is a succession of empires rising and falling, Syria, Assyria, Babylon, Persia and Macedon. Persia having overcome Babylon, overcomes Egypt and is in turn overcome by Alexander the Great. The city-states of Greece have their golden age towards the end of this period. Rome has not yet become a world power. In the East, Buddha, Confucius and

B.C.	EGYPT	THE UNITED KINGDOM OF JUDAH (South) and ISRAEL (North)	OTHER KINGDOMS	GREECE, ETC.	B.C.
					1025
1000		Saul, 1025–1000 David, 1000–974 Solomon, 974–937			1000
		JUDAH ISRAEL or EPHRAIM			
		Rehoboam Jeroboam I		Zoroaster?	
900					900
		J Omri, 887–876 Ahab, 876–853 ELIJAH Jehu, 841–814	Assur-nasir-pal, 884–859 Karkar, 853 (Shalmaneser III retreats)	Homer	
		ELISHA	SYRIA and ASSYRIA		
800					800
		Uzziah (Azariah), 784–739 Jeroboam II, 782–743 ISAIAH AMOS MICAH *E* HOSEA Ahaz 735–715 Fall of Samaria, 721	Fall of Damascus, 732 Sargon II, 722–703	Rome founded, 753	
700		Hezekiah 715–692	Sennacherib, 705–681 Esarhaddon, 681–668 Assur-bani-pal, 668–626		700
		D Josiah, 637–608 ZEPHANIAH JEREMIAH NAHUM	ASSYRIA Fall of Nineveh, 612		
600		Fall of Jerusalem, 586	Nebuchadnezzar, 605–561		600
		EZEKIEL B A B Y L O N THE EXILE 'ISAIAH II' Fall of Babylon, 539		Buddha, 568–488 Confucius, 550–476	
500	Darius I, 521–495	Zerubbabel's return, 538 HAGGAI *P*		Aeschylus, 525–456	500
	Xerxes, 486–466	ZECHARIAH		Sophocles, 496–406 Marathon, 490 Euripides, 485–406 Salamis, 480 Socrates, 469–399 Thucydides, 455–400	
	Artaxerxes, 466–424	MALACHI P E R S I A		Age of Pericles Plato, 427–348	
400	Darius II, 424–404	Nehemiah's return, 445 JOB Ezra's return, 397		Aristotle, 381–322	400
	Darius III, 336–322	JONAH Fall of Persia, 330			
300		Death of Alexander the Great, 323 *C*			300

Fig. 4

[To face p. 183

Zoroaster become the founders of new religions. The year 300 B.C. is chosen for the close because this brings us not only to the death of Alexander, but also to the end of all the Old Testament writings with the exception of the Book of Daniel.

Here selection is most necessary and Fig. 4 indicates the sort of thing that is needed. Old Testament writings and the names of the prophets are given in capitals. *J*, *E* and *P* are the three well-known documents of the Pentateuch; *D* is for Deuteronomy and *C* for the Books of Chronicles.

(4) *300 B.C. to A.D. 70*

It is very important to realize that the obvious break between the Old Testament and the New was not at all obvious to contemporaries. Accordingly it is suggested that this time chart should emphasize that fact and show how the Roman Empire went on its way completely ignorant of the great events taking place in Palestine.

We begin with the successors of Alexander the Great and the Seleucid rulers of Palestine. There is the brief Maccabean period, how brief will appear from the time chart. Then Rome enters the picture, and there is the reorganization of Syria and Palestine under the various members of the Herod family and the building of the third Temple. Christ is born in the reign of Augustus and the background of his life is the surging sea of discontent, bitterness and revolt. This finally overflows into the great war which ended with the fall of Jerusalem in A.D. 70.

In this time chart we shall notice the rise of Rome and the struggle with Carthage, Caesar's conquest of Gaul, and the triumvirate ending with Caesar's dictatorship and the foundation of the Empire. On the literary side we shall notice the dates of Euclid, Lucretius, Virgil, Horace, Livy and Cicero, names that are familiar in other contexts. It will be useful also to insert the conjectural date of the books of Ecclesiasticus, Tobit, Susanna (for the reference in *The Merchant of Venice*), I Maccabees, the Similitudes of Enoch, and Jubilees.

(5) *From A.D. 14 to 135*

This takes us from the accession of Tiberius to the Jewish revolt under Bar Cocheba after which Jerusalem was destroyed. The dates of the Roman emperors are important, of Pilate as Procurator of Palestine, and of Gallio as proconsul of Achaia. The chronology of St Paul should be attempted, thus equating the events in Acts with the dates of the Epistles.[1] Certain open questions may need to be provisionally taken as settled, such as whether Philippians was written during an unrecorded imprisonment about A.D. 55, or whether it was written from Rome during Paul's last imprisonment. The Latin writers Tacitus, the two Plinys, Seneca and Juvenal all come into this period and among the Greek writers are Josephus, Philo, Plutarch and Epictetus.

4 MAPS

Maps are essential in the teaching of Scripture, but as in the case of time charts they should be used as aids to teaching rather than as something needing careful elaboration.

When we deal with the movements of ancient peoples physical rather than political maps are more likely to give us what we want. A physical map or still better a relief model map of Palestine is most useful for illustrating the tribal divisions of the country, the extraordinary phenomenon of the Jordan valley, the difference between the hill country and the plain, the significance of Esdraelon, and very many more geographical facts. Such a model is very expensive to buy but it is not difficult to make although it requires a good deal of patience. The making of it could be a useful 'project' for a junior class. To be manageable it would have to be on a fairly large scale, say four miles to an inch, and the inset maps in George Adam Smith's *Historical Geography of the Holy Land* could be used as a basis. The floor should be of plywood and would mark the level of the Dead Sea, and from this the various levels

[1] An attempted outline will be found on p. 147 of my book *How To Know Your Bible* (Allen and Unwin).

can be built up by thin sheets of cardboard of a uniform thickness, each one representing say 200 ft. of contour. Six of these layers would be needed to build up to the Mediterranean level, and thirteen more to reach the contour of Jerusalem.

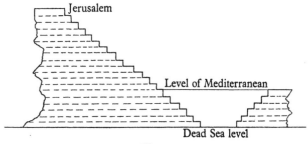

Fig. 5

After the layers are glued into position a thin covering of plasticene can be laid over the whole in the conventional colours—green for the lowest level followed by shades of brown increasing in darkness. The making of such a map would of course be a long business, but its usefulness never ends. The process can be short-circuited by buying a model ready-made but plaster models need careful handling and should be kept under glass.

Other obviously necessary maps are:

(1) One of the ancient world from the Hellespont to the Persian Gulf indicating clearly the region of the 'fertile crescent'. This would illustrate the difference between the desert and the sown, and also the centrality of Palestine in these tribal migrations. Its position also in relation to Europe, Asia and Africa, is clearly seen.

(2) The Mediterranean world. An enlargement of the map given in the first edition of Deissmann's *Paul* is most useful. I have made one 11 ft. long by 4 ft. wide on unbleached calico and traced in waterproof ink. It folds up into very small space and is washable. There is value in Deissmann's emphasis on the Mediterranean as a Roman lake with a similar civilization all round its shores, particularly of course at the eastern end. This helps to explain how Alexandria and Carthage became early centres of Christianity

equally with Rome and Ephesus. Such a map should show the roads and indicate the sea-routes. In the making of it reference should be made to Haverfield's article on 'The Roman Empire at the time of Christ' in Peake's *Commentary*.

(3) A map of Asia Minor in the first century A.D. is a useful adjunct to the study of early centres of Christianity as well as an indication of the places visited by Paul. The 'seven Churches of Asia' would be marked as well as the various provinces of the Roman Empire. The map itself would indicate the confusion that could arise between the Roman province of Galatia and the whole region generally called 'Galatia'.

(4) Two other maps of Palestine will be found useful—as it was in the time of Solomon (and the relation of the tribal divisions to the physical features should be noted), and as it was in the time of Christ, showing the various tetrarchies.

Not much more is needed on the large scale than these six maps. They can of course be bought but it is much more satisfactory to make them, as then the important places can be put in as they are seen to be important and the map does not get crowded up with details.

The teacher, however, should be ready to illustrate quickly on the blackboard the geographical factors necessary to the understanding of a lesson. A sketch-map of Esdraelon (see p. 149), for instance, can readily be made as the lesson goes along. The vulnerability of the fertile crescent from both the desert lands and the populated highlands can be brought out by a simple map. An outline plan of Jerusalem indicating the position of the temple and of the various gates, is not a matter for elaboration but for rapid illustration.

Sectional maps are also useful although they need more careful drawings as they must be drawn to scale. They could form an exercise for the pupils. They are made by laying a rule across a stretch of territory on a physical map, measuring off the distances between the contour lines, and noting the contour heights, and transferring the whole on to squared paper. Some remarkable discoveries are often made in this way, such, for instance, as the height of Jerusalem. The Israelites went 'up' to Jerusalem in a much more literal sense than that in which an Englishman goes 'up' to London.

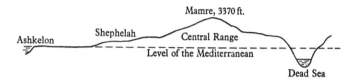

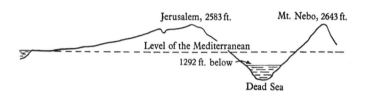

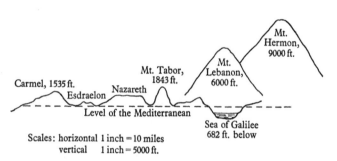

Scales: horizontal 1 inch = 10 miles
vertical 1 inch = 5000 ft.

Fig. 6

5 VERSIONS

As the Bible is a translation its interpretation depends in the first instance on the state of the knowledge of the original languages at the time when the translation was made. There has been continual progress in Hebrew studies ever since the first translation into English, and in Greek studies ever since Erasmus, and the establishment of a 'text' is the first duty of every translator.

The text having been established there arises the question of translation, and this requires an expert knowledge of two languages. A good Hebraist or a good Greek scholar is not necessarily a good translator into English for something more is needed than a knowledge of words and phrases. Contexts are important, and still more a sympathy with the mind of the original writer. In the case of the Bible it is remarkable how sympathy with its purpose has often helped the translator to convey its meaning even though his knowledge of the original tongues has not been so perfect as is possible today. It is this fact which gives the Authorized Version of the Bible the impression of being *itself* an original, which, in a manner of speaking, it is.

Translation therefore depends on the progress of knowledge of the original and also on the development of the language into which it is being translated. Tyndale caught the accents not only of Hebrew prophet and Christian evangelist but also of sixteenth-century England and consequently he produced a work of art so excellent that it was very little altered by the forty-seven translators of the Authorized Version of 1611. If we take a leap across the centuries we may say that Mr J. B. Phillips has caught the idiom of the twentieth century as well as the idiom of St Paul in his recent translation of the Epistles. The simplicity of the Gospels is not so easily caught by the modern translator, although E. V. Rieu in the Penguin series, R. A. Knox, and J. B. Phillips, have produced excellent versions. The preface to Dr Rieu's volume is of particular interest. The Scottish convenanting background of the late James Moffatt made him an admirable translator of the Old Testament.

In default therefore of knowledge of the Greek and Hebrew originals, the English teacher should be familiar with various versions and use them with his class to arrive at a more exact understanding than one version alone would give. Nevertheless, he should try to get as near to the original as he can, and for this purpose a most useful book for the Greek Testament is an old one called *The Englishman's Greek Concordance of the New Testament*. It was compiled by George V. Wigram, first published by

Bagster in 1844, and is still frequently reprinted. The only know-ledge of Greek needed is that of the alphabet. Young's *Analytical Concordance* to the whole Bible is also of particular use to the student anxious to be in touch with the original, as all the words are arranged under their Hebrew or Greek original. As translators often render the same original word by different English ones, or make the same English word do duty for a number of Hebrew or Greek ones, both these concordances are most useful for getting back to the original. They are, however, very expensive, although they ought both to be in a school library.

A Hebrew Old Testament and a Greek New Testament are very useful 'exhibits' to have available even if they are no more than that. To compare a page of the Greek of say the Codex Sinaiticus with the printed text is a useful introduction to the realities of textual criticism, and the British Museum publishes a useful series of cheap monographs. A copy of the Vulgate is also useful, especially if Latin is taught in the school. One of its minor uses is that it gives the Latin titles by which the psalms were so long known.

When we come to the English versions we can divide our material into two parts:

(*a*) *English versions up to 1611.* The chief version of the New Testament will be found in a large book often obtainable at second-hand, called *The English Hexapla.* It was published by Bagster in 1841 and is a very noble volume. It prints the Greek text at the top and underneath are the following six versions: Wycliffe (1380), Tyndale (1534), Cranmer (1539), the Genevan (1557), the Rheims version from the Vulgate (1582), and the Authorized Version (1611). Not the least useful part of this book is the long introduction or 'Historical account of the English Versions of the Scriptures' (160 quarto pages). At the end of this account appear the names of all the forty-seven translators of the Authorized Version with some account of each of them. This introduction should nowadays be supplemented and in some ways replaced by reference to H. Wheeler Robinson, *The Bible in its Ancient and English Versions*, which gives a full account of the versions of the whole Bible—Hebrew, Syriac, Greek, Latin and English. The chapters on the English versions give extracts which show the dependence of the versions on one another as well as the progress made in the knowledge of the original languages. The particular qualities of the Revised Version and the issues that arose on its publication are the subject of a whole chapter. It was a revision of the Authorized and not an independent translation.

(*b*) *English versions after 1611 and the revision of 1885.* In the chapter on the Revised Version in Dr Wheeler Robinson's book there are listed the various English translations made between 1885 and 1940, a list which has to be extended by the addition of translations made up to 1953. Of these *The Twentieth Century New Testament* (1898) and Weymouth's *The New Testament in Modern Speech* (1902) are often available, but they have been eclipsed by Dr James Moffatt's *New Testament* (1913) and *Old Testament* (1924). This was an extraordinary accomplishment for one man, based as it is on an expert knowledge of Hebrew and Greek. There are various editions and its sales have been phenomenal. For the first time it presented the Bible in the colloquial English of our own century. On the Roman Catholic side Monseigneur R. A. Knox was inspired also to attempt a one-man translation of the whole Bible. Being a competent Greek scholar his New Testament (1946) is an excellent rendering of the original. The notes, however, are not always in accord with the best modern scholarship and some of them (e.g. the bland statement about Paul's alleged authorship of Hebrews—'it is now accepted by the Church as his') are merely a reiteration of Roman dogma rather than a conclusion based on evidence. These considerations, however, do not affect the translation itself. The translation of the Old Testament (1951) was made from the Latin of the Vulgate, and as it is a translation of a translation it is not on the same line as his *New Testament*.

For class use, however, the translations of the New Testament by J. B. Phillips are by now almost indispensable. The Epistles came first in 1947 (*Letters to Young Churches*), and the book had an instant success. In some ways more of a paraphrase than a literal translation it makes crystal clear the arguments of the writers and with the short introductory notes is almost as good as a commentary. The translation of the Gospels followed in 1951 and even there, where the utmost simplicity seemed to have been achieved by earlier versions, the rendering shed new light on familiar passages.

The latest translation and the most scholarly is the American *Revised Standard Version* of which the New Testament was published in 1946 and the Old Testament in 1952. This has made use of the vast amount of manuscript and other material that has come to light since 1880. It is not always known that our knowledge of Hellenistic Greek has undergone almost a revolution by reason of discoveries made only within the last half century. Thousands of 'ostraca' have been found bearing inscriptions in the language of the New Testament, and they have enabled us to fix more accurately the meaning of many words not found in classical Greek. The Revised Standard Version translators have used all this material and have published two valuable booklets explaining the principles upon which they have worked, and giving some account of the present state of knowledge of the Biblical languages. One is an *Introduction to the Revised Standard Version of the New Testament* (1946) and the other is a similar volume on the Old Testament (1952). Both of these ought to be in a school library. One of the translators of the New Testament is Professor Edgar Goodspeed who himself in 1923 had published a translation of the New Testament based on the text of Westcott and Hort.

Without overloading the subject it is quite useful to have available some versions of the Bible in the languages studied in school—a French Bible, for instance, and Luther's German Bible. All this will help not only to elucidate meanings but also to take away the feeling of undue strangeness which besets all Biblical studies.

6 MODELS

There is no need to give any detailed advice to the teachers of young children concerning the making of models to illustrate the Scripture lesson. It is a customary technique in all subjects. Yet it needs discrimination in its application. Again it should be emphasized that model-making is a teaching *aid* and is not to be treated as a thing in itself. Often far too much time is taken in needless illustration in the flat or in the round and then since so much time has been spent it is felt that the models must not be thrown away. They are preserved in dust and decay in school cupboards.

With older children the chief value of model-making is that it is a second road to knowledge, reading and listening being the first. Building up a relief map, as already indicated, is a form of model-making and it is an excellent way of understanding the geographical background of the Old Testament. This knowledge is very necessary and this kind of model is a genuine teaching 'aid'. Models of buildings are of less value, although a reconstruction in cardboard of Solomon's temple or the agora of Athens in Paul's time, or a synagogue in the days of Christ, are undoubtedly a help to appreciation. If, however, the value consists in the making of them they should not be preserved for future generations of pupils nor should they be very elaborate.

7 BROADCASTING

The suitability of broadcasting as a teaching aid depends on the nature of the subject. In geography, for instance, talks by travellers and other people who have first-hand knowledge of a country are very valuable. The teaching and appreciation of music are enormously helped by wireless programmes. But in the teaching of Scripture as distinct from religious talks to Sixth Forms and stories for younger children, it is difficult to see what more can be done by broadcasting than can be done by a good teacher on the spot. As a novelty, and as a means of attracting attention it no doubt is a help, but in a subject which depends for its attractiveness more than in most subjects on the personality of the teacher, this vital medium is missing.

On the other hand, there are ways in which broadcasting could be of great assistance to the teacher who is not as yet very expert in his craft. First of all, the technique of Scripture teaching is very far from being familiar, and to have actual Scripture lessons given over the air would teach the teacher himself how to handle his material. They should exemplify the difference between propaganda and education, and between the technique of history and of English and that of Scripture. A series of such lessons for children of a given age-range (which would of course change from time to time) and based on one of the more popular agreed syllabuses would be very useful.

Then, of course, the link between the Bible and school worship is important. The school broadcast services offer an opportunity in this direction, not that they should continue to take the place of school services but that they should be models of how it could be done.

For senior scholars the many talks on religious subjects have stimulated attention. They have often, however, shown the same defect that is present in the senior sections of some of the Agreed Syllabuses, for they have given no hint as to how the Bible can be of any use in modern problems except as anecdotal illustration. It is just here where the seniors need more guidance, for otherwise they are left with one of two conclusions—either that the Bible is a kind of coloured story-book for younger children which the seniors leave behind, or that the Bible is a collection of texts to adorn, or, alternatively, to clinch any argument that might arise.

Nevertheless, when we note the great success of Dorothy Sayers' *The Man Born to be King*, both as a drama and as a series of broadcasts, it is clear that a good deal can be done by wireless to bring home to pupils the fact that the Bible deals with real people. And broadcast drama of Scripture scenes has the advantage of keeping the attention fixed on what is being said rather than being diverted to costumes or, often irrelevant, action.

Broadcast talks for adults by Biblical scholars have an important place in religious education by stimulating teachers to keep up their own studies. From the point of view of actual classroom work they often fail of their purpose just as lectures by such experts at summer schools often bewilder the teacher who has not yet learned how to mediate technical knowledge to less mature minds.

8   FILMS AND FILM STRIPS

As teaching aids films and film strips come under the heading of 'pictures'. They are, however, more convenient, as everybody can see the picture at once and they need the minimum of explanation. What has already been said about pictures applies here as well, namely that the material should be chosen because it is good and because it is a *necessary* illustration. Many of the pictures mentioned in the previous section could be shown on the screen by an epidiascope or film strips on frames could be made from them, having due regard to the law of copyright. But Bible scenes or views of the Holy Land should be used only if the teacher can be certain that nothing else will do for his purpose.

There are very few religious films that are suitable for classroom use, and the commercial cinema type of pseudo-religious film such as *Samson and Delilah* is about as far removed from the significance of the Bible story as it well could be. Old Testament scenes lend themselves only too easily to spectacles and as such have no place in genuine teaching of Scripture.

The teacher will want to know where he can get help in these matters. The Religious Education Press, 85 Manor Road, Wallington, Surrey, and the S.P.C.K., 69 Great Peter Street, London, S.W. 1, publish useful lists of film strips and are ready to give advice on the use both of film strips and of films.

9   A SCHOOL LIBRARY OF RELIGIOUS EDUCATION

Bibliographies on this subject are numerous and the teacher will no doubt be guided by the classified list of books in his own Agreed Syllabus. There is, however, a bewildering number and quite often the amateur scarcely knows where to begin in forming a good school library.

A few hints therefore may not come amiss as long as it is understood that these are simply suggestions.

It is important to bear in mind the divisions of the subject and to see that every one is represented in any collection however small. Such a scheme might include the following: (*a*) General reference, (*b*) Background, (*c*) History of the Bible, (*d*) Versions, (*e*) 'Introduction', (*f*) Commentaries, (*g*) Maps and Atlases, (*h*) Archaeology, (*i*) the Life of Christ, (*j*) Church History, (*k*) Worship, (*l*) Method.

An indication has already been given in previous chapters of books suitable for some of these sections. The principle on which to go is to obtain first of all books that are standard works rather than to get the latest book because it is the latest or the cheapest because it is the cheapest.

(*a*) A good *general reference* section might contain as a beginning Hastings' *One-volume Dictionary of the Bible* together with the fifth (additional) volume of the larger dictionary.

A Companion to the Bible, edited by T. W. Manson. A concordance, preferably Young's but at any rate Cruden's, and also, as already mentioned, Bagster's *Englishman's Greek Concordance*.

(*b*) For *background* such books as:

J. N. Schofield's two books, *The Historical Background of the Old Testament* and *The Religious Background of the Old Testament*.
J. M. Breasted, *Ancient Times*.
Oesterley and Robinson, *History of Israel*.
The People and the Book, edited by A. S. Peake.
T. R. Glover, *The World of the New Testament* and *Paul of Tarsus*.
A. C. Bouquet, *Everyday Life in New Testament Times* (see also under Archaeology, p. 197).

(*c*) For History, etc., of the Bible the following:

Sir F. Kenyon, *The Story of the Bible*.
C. H. Dodd, *The Authority of the Bible*.
Introduction to the Revised Standard Version of the New Testament and of the Old Testament (two separate pamphlets).

H. Wheeler Robinson, *Ancient and English Versions of the Bible*.
Rowland Prothero, *The Psalms in Human Life*.

(d) *Versions*

If a second-hand copy of the *English Hexapla* can be obtained
it is very useful. It contains the Greek of the New Testament with
six English versions parallel.

The modern versions of Weymouth, Moffatt, Phillips, Knox
and Rieu, and the Revised Standard Version should be available,
particularly the last.

(e) '*Introduction*'

This is a technical term and has a meaning much wider than the
ordinary one. It means the study of the text, dates, authorship,
background and structure of the various books of the Bible. There
are two very useful volumes in the London Theological Library,
namely H. Wheeler Robinson's *Making and Meaning of the Old
Testament*, and F. B. Clogg, *An Introduction to the New Testament*.
To these might be added:

F. C. Burkitt, *The Gospel History and its Transmission*.

'Introductions' will also be found at the beginning of most
commentaries on individual books as well as in the general articles
in the one-volume commentaries.

(f) *Commentaries*

A one-volume commentary is valuable as covering the whole
ground. There are three that are outstanding, Peake's (which is
rather overloaded with detail but is valuable for its general articles),
Gore's S.P.C.K. one-volume commentary (entirely written by
Anglican scholars and including the Apocrypha), and the Abingdon,
published in America but written by British as well as American
scholars and the most 'expository' of the three.

The Student Christian Movement *Teachers' Commentary* is a
very useful work as it is concerned with methods of teaching as
well as with the text.

J. B. Thomson Davies' *The Heart of the Bible* (three vols.) sets out the text of the Bible in the order in which the writings come into existence. It has good introductions and is a most useful work.

Among individual commentaries it is important to have a good one on Genesis as this is the book that most often comes up for discussion. Driver's commentary is the one most accepted and along with this should go Chapman's *Introduction to the Pentateuch* in the Cambridge Bible. George Adam Smith's commentaries on Isaiah and on the Twelve Prophets and Skinner's commentary on Jeremiah called *Prophecy and Religion* have about them a quality of inspiration as well as of scholarship.

J. M. Thompson's *Synoptic Gospels* is essential for the English reader.

A useful commentary on the Gospels is Major, Manson and Wright's *The Mission and Message of Jesus*.

C. H. Dodd's commentary on Romans and E. F. Scott's on Hebrews will be useful as specimen commentaries on the Epistles.

(g) Maps and Atlases

These have already been mentioned in a previous section.

(h) Archaeology

For the Old Testament Finegan's *Light from the Ancient Past* and S. Caiger's *Bible and Spade*.

For the New Testament, Deissmann's *Light from the Ancient East* and *Paul*, Caiger's *Archaeology and the New Testament*.

Archaeology is a dangerous subject for it can so easily be misapplied. It will therefore be useful to have in the library G. H. Richardson's *Biblical Archaeology* and Millar-Burrows' *What Mean These Stones*, a very excellent book published by Yale University.

(i) The Life of Christ

Major, Manson and Wright's book has already been mentioned. To it should be added two smaller books, Glover's *The Jesus of History* which by this time has become a classic, and Gore's *Jesus of Nazareth*.

(j) Church History

This has not been dealt with in this volume, but the school religious knowledge library will need to have a few standard books as a nucleus from which to expand.

Suggested are:

C. H. Dodd, *The Apostolic Preaching.*
A. D. Nock, *St Paul.*
H. Bettenson, *Documents of the Christian Church.*
T. R. Glover, *The Conflict of Religions in the Early Roman Empire.*
H. M. Gwatkin, *Early Church History to 313 A.D.* (2 vols.).
K. S. Latourette, *The Unquenchable Light.*

These all are concerned in the main with the earlier period. For books dealing with the later and modern periods the Agreed Syllabus bibliographies should be consulted.

(k) Worship

This again lies outside the scope of this volume but it should be represented in the school library. The Oxford University Press and the S.P.C.K. are two publishers among others who publish books of school worship. It might, however, be useful to have two books on the nature of worship itself. A very handy general book is W. D. Maxwell's *An Outline of Christian Worship.* There is also a useful book of essays by members of Mansfield College edited by N. Micklem, *Christian Worship: Studies in its History and Meaning.*

(l) Method

It is difficult to suggest specific books on this subject, but there are one or two general books which might be helpful, such as:

G. L. Heawood, *Religion in School.*
Mary Entwistle, *The Bible Guide Book.*

The Appendix to the Oxford Little Bible ('for parents and teachers') will be found useful.

The *Teachers' Commentary* already mentioned, is useful for classroom purposes. It is not overcrowded and it deals with the material not in verses but in sections.

A note might be added concerning 'Text-books' for use in class. It may be a counsel of perfection to affirm that the Bible alone should be the text-book and that any explanation of it should come from the teacher and from reference books, but this indeed is the ideal arrangement. Whereas in an earlier generation the Bible in the text of the Authorized Version was considered to be all that was necessary we are apt in our time to substitute books about the Bible for the Bible itself. Some text-books even in such excellent series as the *Cambridge Bible for Schools* or the *Clarendon Bible* tend to take the place not only of the Bible but also of the teacher and often give the impression that the Bible is a far more difficult book than it is. Some text-books are so overloaded with 'notes' that the pupil is apt to feel that 'Bible Study' means learning the notes. There is, however, a certain modicum of assistance needed for the pupil apart from the teacher and the sort of scheme laid out in a series of colloquial English translations published by the National Adult School Union seems to me to meet the need. The pupil has his own Bible (and let it be one with decently large print!) but he also has one of these books. The series up to date includes *Genesis* (T. H. Robinson), *Micah* and *Habakkuk* (Naish and Scott), *Jeremiah* (A. C. Welch), *Amos* (T. H. Robinson), *Hosea* (J. W. Povah), *Ruth* and *Jonah* (C. M. Coltman), *Samuel* (J. Skinner), *Isaiah i–xxxix* (Allan), *Deuteronomy* (Cadoux), and the most expensive of these is only 1s. 3d.

For the New Testament the additional book for use in class might be Rieu's *Four Gospels* as it is only 2s. 6d. Other translations unfortunately are published at a price prohibitive to school children.

Where the Bible itself is made the main subject of study the teacher will need to do a good deal of preparation. It will have the great advantage, however, of familiarizing the pupil with the text of the English Bible. Opportunity should be given both in class and in assembly for the children to hear the Bible well read and so gradually to learn some of it by heart.

CHAPTER XIII

SOME SPECIMEN LESSONS

I NAAMAN (II KINGS V)

[This is a plain piece of narrative, but no 'moral' is drawn from it except such as is evident in the story itself. These are not so much 'notes' as a report in full of a lesson actually given to a class of twenty-four children aged 12, in forty minutes.

This story is concerned with Gehazi as well as Elisha, but the Bible used by the children was 'The Little Children's Bible' (Oxford University Press. The Leicestershire Authority's *Syllabus*) and in it the story stops at *v.* 19. It *ought*, however, to continue to the end of the chapter in order to bring out the contrast between Gehazi and Elisha, just as the earlier part contrasts Naaman and Elisha. This interplay of personalities is very characteristic of the Old Testament writers, and the aim of this lesson is to exhibit it. The Gehazi story could form a second lesson, beginning with revision of the first.]

The children have already read about Elijah.

I. *Revision:*

Elisha followed on after Elijah.
>What do we know of Elijah?
>He met the priests of Baal on Mount Carmel.
>Where is Mount Carmel?
>It is the nobble on the coast of Palestine. (Quickly do a map on the board of the coast line. Jordan and Carmel.)

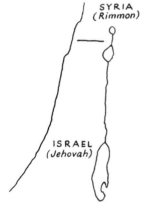

SYRIA
(*Rimmon*)

ISRAEL
(*Jehovah*)

II. *Introductory:*

>1. Draw a line across the map north of Carmel.
>What is the country south of the line?
>Israel or Samaria. (Write Israel on map.)
>What is the country north?
>Syria. (Write Syria.)

2. What would you call the part of the country that is on the line?
The Border Country.

Would it be a quiet place?
Probably continued raids and fights. (Any other Border country?
Scots and English.)

We are going to read about something that happened after one of
these raids.

3. What was the name of the God of Israel?
Jehovah.

Name of the god or *a* god of Syria? (Tell them 'Rimmon'.)

So that we have Jehovah on one side of the border and Rimmon
on the other. (Write them in on the map. This is important
because of Naaman's request.)

III. *Reading:*

The teacher reads II Kings v. 1–19 without note or comment. Children
listen.

IV. *Exposition:*

Children open their Bibles and follow the scheme.
Recall the border raids just mentioned.

1. Verses 1–4. This little maid had been captured and became a
servant. She finds out that her master Naaman is a leper.

What is a leper? (Importance of this is seen in *v.* 27 later.)
A man with a horrid skin disease that turns his flesh white and
makes it waste away.

The maid tells them of Elisha in her own country.

2. Verse 5. Naaman departs. With a letter from the king of Syria
to the king of Israel. He takes with him: 10 talents (hundred-
weights) of silver; 6000 pieces of gold; 10 changes of raiment.

Why?
Because he thinks that Elisha is like one of our 'specialist' doctors,
and he will want a large fee.

This is Naaman's *first mistake.*

3. Verses 6–7. He seeks out the king, because surely such a specialist
must be near the king.

This is Naaman's *second mistake.*

(Did anyone else ever make a mistake like that? Recall the wise men coming to see Jesus, who thought he must be known to the king, and so they went to see Herod.)

The king is angry and he rends his clothes. Why? (Eastern custom.) Declares 'Am *I* God?'

Do you see any difference here between the king and Naaman? Naaman clearly thinks that healing is the work of a professional doctor.

The king clearly thinks it is the work of God.

Which do *you* think it is?

Let us see what Elisha thinks.

4. Verses 8–12. Elisha asks the king to send Naaman to him 'and he shall know that there is a prophet in Israel'.

He doesn't say 'doctor' he says 'prophet'.

Then does he agree with Naaman or with the king of Israel concerning the work of healing?

Has Naaman changed his views yet?

No.

How do we know?

He comes to Elisha's door with his chariots and horsemen and is *still* thinking of the importance of the occasion.

What did he expect Elisha to do? (Read *v.* 11.)

He expected Elisha to have what we call a 'bedside manner'.

So it was Naaman's *third mistake.*

What did Elisha actually do?

Sent him to wash in the Jordan.

What did Naaman say to that?

He was very angry. 'Are not Abanah and Pharpar...'

Was that true?

Yes. The Jordan is a muddy, swift-flowing river, and the rivers of Syria are blue, clear, cold and slow. So the rivers of Damascus (the capital of Syria) would *look* more useful for healing than the dirty Jordan.

So Naaman was *still* thinking of medicine and Elisha's patent 'cure'.

Naaman's *fourth mistake.*

He refuses to go. (It is not so much the refusal that matters as the reason for it. He has no more faith when he goes than when he refuses to go.)

5. Verses 13–16. Naaman's servants advise him to go.
Notice how full of common sense their remarks are.
He goes, and is cured.

What does he say after that?
'No God except in Israel.'

Has he then at last changed his mind about how healing is done?
It looks as if he has, doesn't it? *But* see what he does next.
He offers Elisha gifts.

Does that show that he has changed his mind?
No. He still thinks it is the Jordan water that has done it.
What do *you* think?

Naaman's fifth mistake.

Why then does Elisha refuse gifts? (Ask the class.)
(It is to make it quite clear that it is God and not Elisha who had
done this. Rubbing his hand on the place would not cure him.
Washing in the Jordan or Abanah or Pharpar would not cure
him either.)

Then what exactly *has* Elisha done?
Shown him (as he said he would, *v.* 8) that 'there is a prophet in
Israel'.

What does that mean?
What does a 'prophet' do?
Showed that God was at work.
So it is God and not Elisha that matters.

6. How do we know that Naaman *at last* believed this? Read *v.* 17.
Because he asked for two loads of earth.

Why?
The class discussed this for some time and finally came to the con-
clusion that it must be because of the God of Israel being some-
how connected with the *soil* of Israel.
Point out that this is a very ancient idea.
Look at the map again on the board.
Jehovah lives south of the border, so if you go north you leave
him.
But it you take some soil with you and stand on it you are once
again in the land of the God of Israel and he can hear you.

7. But what about the God who lived *north* of the border? Read *v.* 18,
and explain by an analogy.

Our royal coronation is a Christian service. But some people, like Indian princes, who are Hindus or Moslems, have to attend whether they are Christians or not. It is also a *Protestant* service, and yet the Duke of Norfolk has to attend, although he is a Roman Catholic.

They attend because of their *official position* and if they give up their 'official position' they need not attend.

Naaman, too, had an 'official position' with the king and so he had to go to the Temple of Rimmon whenever the king went. So he asks Elisha for forgiveness when he has to carry out his official duties. Elisha agrees.

There this part of the lesson ends, although the story might be read through again without note or comment.

V. *Appendix:*

Read the story of Gehazi, *vv.* 20–7.

Ask class if Gehazi's mistake was like any of the mistakes of Naaman.

He thought it was Elisha who had done the healing, and that Elisha ought to have been paid for it and so he pretended that Elisha had changed his mind.

Notice Naaman's gratitude and lack of suspicion. 'Be content: *take two.*'

What was Gehazi's sin? Was it telling a lie?

Much more than that.

Notice Elisha's remark: 'Is this a time to receive money, etc.' (*v.* 26).

He wanted Elisha to take credit for something that only God had done—Naaman was cured of thinking like that and also of his leprosy.

So Gehazi who still thought like that was punished with the leprosy also.

Suppose Gehazi had then gone out and washed in the Jordan seven times, what do you think would have happened?

2 LUKE XV

[The following notes are of two lessons on the same subject, but completely different, as they are for children aged 10–11 and of children aged 16 respectively. This repetition of subject-matter for older children is to be preferred to the overloading of later lessons with detail and with new matter before the full significance of the earlier material has been grasped. Even though the first reading is with children aged 10–11 the *whole* parable is to be studied. Attention to the context (*vv.* 1 and 2) shows that it is a parable about *two* sons and not about one only. Thus if the story is ended (as it often is) at *v.* 24 the whole point of the parable as it concerns the Pharisees and scribes of *v.* 2 is lost.]

1. *Parable of the Prodigal Son (Luke xv) for children aged 10–11*

Aim: to know the story

1. *The nature of parables.* The teacher asks the class if they know what a parable is. A story. What kind of story? (Avoid the popular grotesque definition of a parable as 'an earthly story with a heavenly meaning'!) An illustration. *Æsop's Fables* parables? Why not? Is Bunyan's *Pilgrim's Progress* a parable? Why not? Hence a parable is a story drawn from ordinary life to illustrate a lesson.

Hence a parable, not a fable in which animals talk; not an 'allegory' in which every sentence has a separate hidden meaning. And so we try to find the meaning in the story as a whole.

2. *Reading the parable.* The parable is read through aloud with expression, by the teacher, the children's Bibles being *closed*.

3. *Paraphrase in writing.* They are then asked to write down the story briefly in their own words. This is to enable them to judge the value of the exposition that the teacher himself gives later, during which they will be asked if they have observed this or that point.

4. *Blackboard scheme.* Bibles are opened and the story is gone through and the scheme is built up on the blackboard (see diagram on p. 206), getting the points from the children.

5. *Character study.* Each person in the story is taken in turn and characterized by questioning, so that the good and bad points (if any) are brought out.

6. *Interpretation.* What is it that Jesus wishes to teach by this parable? Who is the father? God. What is God like? Is he an angry, cruel being of whom we should be afraid? Why not? Then are we

justified in behaving as we like? Why not? Because of the misery of being separated from God—*the far country*. Much nicer to be at home. Note the happy nature of the home. What does the parable teach *us about our relation* to other people?

THE HOME

THE FAR COUNTRY
Waste
Want
Repentance

HOME AGAIN
Forgiveness
Resentment

2. Parable of the Prodigal Son (Luke xv) for children aged 16

Aim: to study Jesus' view of the nature of sin and repentance

[This is by no means the only possible aim for a lesson on this subject with children of this age. It could be taken, e.g. with the contemporary reference to the Pharisees, scribes and sinners and Jesus' attitude to them, or it could lead to a discussion on forgiveness or on the nature of loyalty. The present notes, however, of a lesson actually given, indicate—(1) how doctrine may be taught without dogmatism; (2) the use of Biblical cross references; (3) correlation with English literature.]

1. *The parable is read through aloud.* The class is then questioned as to its possible *point*, and if it is thought useful the answers are noted down on the blackboard for reference later. As each answer is given the other members of the class are asked if they think it reasonable and only if so are the points written down. Thus possible suggestions are that the parable deals with 'forgiveness', or 'the nature of God', or 'hypocrisy', or 'contrast between duty and pleasure'.

2. *The context is studied* and is found to consist of four items:

(1) The publicans and sinners draw near to hear Jesus.
(2) The Pharisees and scribes object to this.
(3) The parable of the lost sheep.
(4) The parable of the lost coin.

These items are obviously all connected. The publicans and sinners are closely represented by the lost sheep and the lost coin. Who then are the Pharisees and scribes? Attention is drawn to the elder brother in the parable of the prodigal son. He clearly stands for the Pharisees and scribes.

3. *Parable of the Prodigal Son* is thus a dramatic story in which are three characters:

The younger son standing for the sinners; the elder son standing for the Pharisees; the father standing for God.

What is the plot of the play if any? It is not just a 'moral' story, teaching a truth. Is the common title of the parable a good one? The plot centres round a story of wrongdoing and repentance, and the attitude to it of three persons.

4. *Three attitudes.* We look at the story therefore from each point of view in turn, like Browning's *Ring and the Book* or Thornton Wilder's *Bridge of San Luis Rey.*

(*a*) Begin with the *elder* son's attitude to his brother. Note his resentment. Consider whether he had any just cause for it? Have the Pharisees any cause for *their* resentment? What is the *father's* attitude to the son's resentment?

(*b*) *The father's attitude.* In what sense had the father been wronged? Notice the quality of his forgiveness. Unquestioning. Is there any conflict here between justice and forgiveness? Why did the father forgive him? Is it right to forgive people?

(*c*) *The younger son's attitude.* Can it fairly be described as repentance? What is repentance? Notice that he does not ask for *forgiveness*, but for punishment. Is this related at all to the father's attitude? Apart from this would the forgiveness have been right?

5. What can we infer from this as to the nature of sin and repentance? Is it better that the acts should be wrong and the spirit
right (younger son—sinners) or that the acts should be right and
the spirit wrong (elder son—Pharisees)? Compare Jesus' other
parable concerning two sons. (Matt. xxi. 28–32). Were there any
precedents for this in the Old Testament? (Jacob and Esau?) Can
you think of any modern stories or poems on the same theme?
(See 'How Dossy saw God' in Winifred Holtby's *Truth is not
sober*, and Kipling's *His Private Honour*.)

3 SEVEN LESSONS ON ST PAUL'S CONNEXIONS WITH CORINTH

These notes cover the relevant sections in Acts and the two
Epistles to the Corinthians. They are concerned to place the
Epistles in their context of history, to show the nature of Paul's
correspondence and what might appear to be the precarious
chances of its survival.

The lessons are for older children (16+) although the *Cambridgeshire Syllabus* optimistically puts this subject in the scheme
for children aged 11–15. The *London Syllabus* specifies no particular age between 11 and 18, and it separates the study of the
Epistles from the context in Acts. It does, however, warn teachers
against treating them simply as expositions of a doctrine called
'Paulinism'.

A modern translation should be in constant use along with the
R.V. The best for class use is J. B. Phillips' *Letters to Young Churches*,
but Moffatt will be needed for I Cor. xiii. The *Clarendon Bible*
volume on Corinthians is useful, but is so heavily overlaid with
doctrine that it is not very suitable for class use in a non-deno-
minational school or indeed for children. The handiest school book
on the Pauline Epistles is H. N. Bate, *A Guide to the Epistles of
Saint Paul*, and the Home University book on *St Paul* by A. D.
Nock should also be readily available. The teacher himself should
have ready for reference Deissmann's two books *Light from the
Ancient East* and *Paul: A Study in Social and Religious History*, and
W. M. Ramsay's *St Paul the Traveller and Roman Citizen*.

The subjects of the lessons are:

1. The situation of Corinth and the circumstances of Paul's first visit.
2. Paul's residence at Ephesus from which the Epistles were written.
3. The letters to Corinth: (*a*) the first (lost) letter, and I Cor. i–vi.
4 and 5. (*b*) The second letter: I Cor. vii–xvi.
6. (*c*) The second visit (unrecorded) and the third (lost) letter: II Cor. x–xiii. 10.
7. (*d*) The fourth letter: II Cor. i–ix; xiii, 11–14. Summary.

It is assumed that with children of this age the lessons will be mainly discussions, *guided, however, by constant reference to the text*. It is most important to cultivate the habit of discussing not in the air but with some definite situation in mind. 'Should women wear hats in Church?', for instance, could give rise to discussions that might be both vigorous and useful. The point here is to see *why* St Paul spoke of the veiling by women, what were the circumstances in Corinth in his time. All this should be taken into account *before* launching into a discussion on the rightness or wrongness of the Archbishops' ruling that *in our churches and in our time* hats are not necessary. The aim of the lesson is to train pupils in this use of the historical method and so to appreciate St Paul's attitude. It is better throughout to avoid the word 'church' which has associations for a twentieth-century child quite different from that of the Corinthian communities which met at home. The word 'community' is a useful and accurate substitute.

Lesson I

1. The situation of Corinth. Refer to the maps (as large a scale as possible). This is the 'city by two seas' of Horace, *Odes* I, 7, the place that attracts tourists. 'It's not everybody that can get to Corinth' (Horace, *Epistles* I, 17). It was cosmopolitan, rich and licentious.

2. Read Acts xviii. 1–17. Possible date of Paul's visit A.D. 50. (How can we tell?) He arrives from Thessalonica via Athens where he had failed with the intellectuals (xvii. 32–4). He determined not to fail at Corinth (I Cor. ii. 1–2). No more argument, but demonstration. (How?)

He stays eighteen months and while there he writes to the Thessalonians on the information brought to him by Silas and Timothy. (Note I Thess. iv. 16 and 17. He expects the end of the world soon. We shall come across this idea in these Epistles also.)

3. Only three events of this period are recorded:

(a) Priscilla and Aquila. Were they Christians already? If so, Christianity must have reached Rome before this date. Note the date of Claudius' decree. Note that Aquila was a fellow-craftsman with Paul who lodged with them.

The synagogue is Paul's base. He persuades both Jews and Greeks—so there would be different races in the Christian community at Corinth. What sort of 'Church' was it? See I Cor. i. 11 and xvi. 15, and note that they were groups who met in people's houses.

(b) Note Paul's friends. We shall come across them in other contexts. Note his opposition from the Jews, so strong that he changes his lodgings, and compare the attitude of the Jews with that of the Romans. If Paul was eighteen months in Corinth much must have happened in that time. Why then are only these three incidents recorded?

(c) Importance of Gallio. Who was he? How do we know the date of his appointment? (Refer to Deissmann.) Why did the Jews beat Sosthenes? Was he, like Crispus, a Christian convert? (See I Cor. i. 1.) If so, was it possible for a Christian to be a ruler of a Jewish synagogue?

4. Discuss the relations of Jews and Christians then and now. *Note.* Translation of Acts xviii. 17: 'Gallio took no notice.'

Lesson II

1. Read Acts xviii. 18 to the end of ch. xx.
2. Note the order of events:

> Paul, Priscilla and Aquila come to Ephesus (xviii. 19).
> They stay at Ephesus and he travels further afield (*vv.* 19–23).
> Apollos comes to Ephesus (*vv.* 24–8).
> Paul returns to Ephesus and Apollos goes to Corinth (xix. 1–20).

Do *vv.* 21 and 22 mean that Paul only *wished* to go into Europe again, but that he sent Timothy and Erastus instead while he himself stayed on at Ephesus?

3. The situation of Ephesus. Its importance. Worship of Diana. Read the vivid story in Acts xix. 23–41 noting that the earliest name for Christianity was 'the Way' (*v.* 23). Note also the favour with which the Town Clerk viewed the Christians (*v.* 37).

4. The importance of Apollos.

In what ways were Alexandrian Jews different from others? (xviii. 24). What is meant by 'the baptism of John'? (xviii. 25, and xix. 1–6). Is it the same as that referred to by Jesus? (Mark xi. 30 and parallels). What was John's message?

What did Apollos do at Corinth while Paul was at Ephesus? (See I Cor. i. 12; iii. 6; xvi. 12.) Was this a cause of division? Does this account for the emphasis placed by all the Four Gospels on the inferiority of John's baptism (Mark i. 7–8 and parallels John i. 6–8, 26–34) remembering that the Gospels were written long after the Epistles?

5. From Ephesus Paul wrote to Corinth *four* letters in all:

(*a*) A letter now lost (I Cor. v. 9).

(*b*) The letter now called the First, after which Paul appears to have paid a short visit in person (I Cor. iv. 21; II Cor. xii. 14; xiii. 1).

(*c*) A third letter in stern language (II Cor. ii. 4 and 7, 8) now lost except for II Cor. x–xiii. 10.

(*d*) The letter contained in the rest of our 'Second' Epistle.

These lost Epistles raise the question of how much of Paul's thought do we really possess. Would it have changed our views of him if the lost Epistles had survived? Did Paul have a body of doctrine which he expounded or did he simply answer his correspondents on particular questions, and out of these particular cases we have to look for his general 'position'? (Refer to Deissmann's *Paul*.)

Lesson III

1. Read I Cor. i–vi.
2. Recall the circumstances. It is Paul's *second* letter. In view of the fact that four letters were written in two years and that Paul also pays a flying visit, the situation must have been serious.

The order of events seems to have been as follows:

(1) Soon after he has left them he sends a letter to remind them of their danger from immorality (I Cor. v. 9–10).
(2) Some of Chloe's household write and tell him about the unhappy divisions in Corinth (I Cor. i. 11).
(3) Paul sends Timothy to see about it (I Cor. iv. 17).
(4) He begins this letter and gets as far as the end of ch. vi.
(5) Then arrive Stephanus, Fortunatus and Achaicus (xvi. 17) from the household of Stephanus in Corinth (v. 15) and tell him of other problems vexing the little society.
(6) Paul continues this letter in answer to these further questions (chs. vi–xvi) and sends it back to Corinth with Stephanus.

3. 'Denominations' have appeared at Corinth—'Paul', 'Apollos', 'Cephas', and even a group taking exclusively the name of Christ and denying it to others (i. 12). From vv. 13–17 we gather that after conversion the converts were baptized and some had got into the habit of calling themselves after the person who had baptized them.

Do these verses give the impression that baptism is not really necessary? Then why was it done?

4. In what ways was Paul's procedure different at Corinth from what it was at Athens? Was he justified in this, despite the quarrels

that had arisen among them? The educated Athenians gave rise to one kind of problem and the uneducated Corinthian to another. Would you say that such distinctions and differences arise today? The only safe attitude is that quoted by Paul (in *v.* 31) from Jer. ix. 23 and 24 (ix. v.). This he follows up in iii. 4–8, and, with a change of metaphor, in iii. 10–23.

5. Yet there is a *Christian* wisdom. Wisdom is not all on the side of the scientists! Spiritual things have their own standards of judgement (ii. 6–16). Is Paul's statement an adequate answer to the last chapter in F. Hoyle's *The Nature of the Universe*?

6. He sums up what he has to say about their unhappy divisions by reminding them that they are *all* having to bear witness to Christ before a heathen world (compare Phil. i. 18) and he and Apollos more than any of them (iv. 6–13). Note that he associates Apollos with himself. Does this affect any conclusion you may have come to about Apollos in the preceding lesson?

7. They are still given to immorality (v. 1–8. There is one very bad case of a man taking his father's wife!) about which he had written previously (v. 9), and now he writes again (v. 11–13; vi. 9–20). The body is the instrument of the spirit. You cannot rejoice in the things of the spirit if you dishonour your body. You cannot be spiritually high-minded while physically impure.

8. Lastly (vi. 1–8) he is grieved to hear that they take their disputes before heathen judges. Is it not better to put up with annoyances among themselves than to use the law-courts?

Is this relevant today?

Points to notice:

(1) The words 'mystery' (ii. 7) and 'spectacle' (iv. 9, a stage play).

(2) The term 'the day of our Lord Jesus Christ' (i. 8; v. 5). Compare I Thess. i. 2. This means the end of the world. Is it different from the Old Testament use of the phrase in Joel i. 15; ii. 1, and Amos v. 18–20?

Lessons IV and V

[Chapters vii–xvi raise the question of how much of a document should be used in any one lesson. In other subjects selections are made on the basis of easier and harder, earlier and later, but somehow in Scripture the very principle of selection is apt to be suspect. Nevertheless there is no reason why the whole of this section should be used as lesson material. Some of it is rabbinic argument (e.g. x. 1–22) and has only an antiquarian interest for us and none at all for children. For some of it (e.g. vii. 10–13, and xi. 1–16) a full understanding requires a considerable knowledge of the position of women in Corinthian society. Yet this last has no doubt something of a present-day reference (although due to lack of historical sense!) when people get concerned about women not wearing hats in church! The question of meat offered to idols seems remote enough except that it raises the question of the 'weaker brother' which is certainly far from remote. 'Speaking with tongues' was a local phenomenon but Paul's handling of it suggests that the will of God is better known through inspired common-sense ('prophesying') than in exotic experiences.

Accordingly, in these two lessons a selection is made under various headings. They are to be dealt with strictly in their historical setting. Dogmatic questions arising out of such events as the Last Supper and the Resurrection should not be *raised as personal issues by the teacher*, although they may possibly come up in discussion. It must be remembered that the class in all probability will be composed of children from homes of various denominations and of none. In a denominational school, of course, such questions may have their place, having due regard to the age of the children concerned and their psychological maturity or immaturity.]

PROBLEMS SUBMITTED BY THE CORINTHIANS
TO ST PAUL FOR HIS RULING

(Subject-matter for two lessons, or selection to be made for one lesson)

1. In order to serve God properly is it better to be married or not?

2. Ought Christians who are married to a heathen to seek the dissolution of their marriage?

3. Ought widows to remarry?

Paul's answer to all these questions depends in every case on the fact that 'the time is shortened' (vii. 29), i.e. the return of Christ and the end of the world are imminent. (Notice again what he said to the Thessalonians, the phrase 'the day of the Lord Jesus Christ' and the word 'maranatha' (xvi. 23, R.V. margin).) If this was so, they should live the ideal life for the short time that remained. Apart from this expectation, would Paul's advice have been different?

4. Ought Christians to eat meat that has been 'offered to idols'? Read chs. viii and x. 23–33.

This is not a problem that vexes us nowadays but it raises the general question of consideration for the 'weaker brother'. How far can this argument be taken, e.g. in regard to Sunday cinemas, teetotalism, having a penny on the pools? How far should it be taken in regard to matters we believe to be *right*, e.g. going faster with reforms or new ideas than other people are willing or able to go?

5. Should women keep their hats on in church?

This was concerned with the whole status and behaviour of women in Corinth in those days, and if the question is raised at all, these conditions should be studied. But how far are you going to apply what Paul says in a very special case to the situation in our own country centuries after?

6. How should the Lord's Supper be observed?

The heathen had great orgies of eating and drinking in connexion with their religion. The Lord's Supper was not to be like that. It was a dignified symbolic meal, recalling the last days of Jesus on earth.

Read xi. 17–34, noting particularly the 'words of institution' in *vv.* 23 and 26, and refer to the parallel passages in the Synoptic Gospels.

7. Which are the best spiritual gifts to cultivate?

Evidently this was a sore point with the Corinthians as they seem to have been jealous of each other's capabilities. Read xii, xiii and xiv. 1–33, especially noting ch. xiii in Moffatt's version.

All gifts of the spirit are good and it needs all sorts in the Christian community. People must exercise the gifts they have and rejoice in others' gifts. But one gift they ought *all* to have, namely Christian love.

What do we ourselves value most as signs of the true Christian—unusual behaviour, 'speaking with tongues', rhetoric, 'orthodoxy', common-sense, poise, domestic virtues, soberness?

8. Did Christ rise from the dead, and what does it matter?

The great ch. xv in answer to this, ought to be read aloud as well as studied. It should be read to find out what Paul himself thought about the matter.

9. A personal question. Was Paul really an Apostle and what did he get out of it for himself?

Read ch. ix. He has as much right to live by the Gospel as the priest who lives by the Temple or the oxen that live by the corn which they are threshing. But as a matter of fact he has not exercised that right at all, he has paid his own way so that he can be free and beholden to nobody.

How far does his idea of being 'all things to all men' carry us?

Lesson VI

[Our first (and Paul's second) letter was sent to Corinth by the hand of Stephanus and his friends. Meanwhile Paul expected Timothy to have arrived at Corinth (I Cor. iv. 17) and he puts in a word of commendation for him (xvi. 10).

He receives bad news either through Timothy or someone else and then apparently pays Corinth a flying visit (II Cor. xii. 14 and xiii. 1) which is not recorded. He seems to have received a personal affront (II Cor. xii. 21) and so on his return he sends a third letter and gives them a very severe handling. This letter is supposed to be contained partly in II Cor. x–xiii. 10, and there are references to it in II Cor. ii. 4 and vii. 8. This letter was sent by the hand of Titus who reports the salutary effect it has (II Cor. vii. 7). Then follows the fourth letter (our Second) which is contained in II Cor. i–ix and xiii. 11–14.

It should be noted, of course, that this theory about the contents of the third letter is pure conjecture, although it is very convenient and possible. It might be added, however, that if we are to accept this theory we should *also look at I Cor. ix* which is a personal vindication and very closely akin to the argument in II Cor. x–xiii. 10. None of these re-arrangements affect the question of authorship or of date.]

Paul's third letter

Read II Cor. x–xiii. 10 and also I Cor. ix and especially in Phillips' translation which catches the personal note so well, and is almost essential for understanding these chapters.

The Corinthians seem to have had some contempt for Paul's personal appearance. (See a description of him in the *Acts of Paul and Thecla*, a document dated A.D. 160 and to be found in M. R. James' *The Apocryphal New Testament*. On p. 273 is the description: 'a man little of stature, thin-haired upon the head, crooked in the legs, of good state of body, with eyebrows joining and nose somewhat hooked, full of grace.') They do not like his letters. He therefore vindicates himself.

10. He insists that whatever they may think of him he has been duly appointed to his work by God himself. This means far more than any claims a man could possibly make for himself.

11. He then censures them for listening to those who are not preaching the true gospel, and who apparently have been making money out of it. They seem to despise Paul because he is so independent. These others can attract the crowd for Satan can disguise himself as an angel of light.

[This chapter xi is admirably rendered by Phillips who makes play in his translation as Paul does in the original with the word 'apostle'. In its literal meaning it is 'a special messenger'. The question raised by Paul is a common one even with our present churches. People tend to esteem the 'special preacher', the special evangelist, more than the person concerned with the day-to-day work of the Church. Phillips translates xi. 5–6, 'yet I cannot believe I am in the least inferior to these extra-special Special Messengers. Perhaps I am not a polished speaker, but I do know what I am talking about, and both what I am and what I say is pretty familiar to you.']

xi. 16. Yet he is not going to sit down under all this depreciation of his qualifications. He can boast as much as anybody, indeed more, if it were not that it was so silly to do it at all.

Having so much to be proud of he is glad that God gave him 'a thorn in the flesh', a physical handicap to keep him humble.

In reading this section the story of Paul in Acts should be recalled. There we have little more than a list of places visited, with a few incidents set out in full. But when and why did he receive the horrible sentence of thirty-nine lashes—five times from the Jews and three times from the Romans? We are told of one shipwreck. What of the other two? We can see from all this how little we know of Paul's life. It must have been a life of continual bitter hardship.

xii. 14. He is ready to visit them a third time, and he has no intention of being lenient with wrongdoers who should be more properly employed with examining their own shortcomings than with examining those of Paul.

A question for discussion which arises out of all this is the nature of spiritual authority. If gentleness and humility are the marks of the Christian does not this allow aggressive people to 'get away with it'? Yet if you stop them, are you not setting up yourself to be better than they are?

Lesson VII

This 'second' letter is sent out in the name of Timothy and Paul. See the references to Timothy in Acts and also the references in I Tim. i. 1; iv. 12. There was a very affectionate relationship between them.

Read II Cor. i–ix.

i. 8–11 shows the human side of Paul. The phrase in *v.* 9 'the answer of death' is translated by Phillips 'coming to the end of our tether'.

These chapters show how extraordinarily modern and mature Paul is in his attitude to life, and how primitive and childish were some of the Corinthian Christians. They were suspicious, always ready to believe the worst about anybody (hence I Cor. xiii. 6), quite sure that there was 'dirty work' going on somewhere, at one time resenting Paul's straightforwardness and at another being sure that there was some hidden meaning in what he says. They are ready to take slights. Paul had intended to visit Corinth again before going to Macedonia but because he changed his plan they at once suspected evil intentions. What *can* you do with people like that? (Refer to F. W. Faber's lectures called *Spiritual Conferences*, the chapter on 'Wounded Feelings'.)

Note how Paul always refers everything back to Christ. 'Do you think I plan with my tongue in my cheek, saying "yes" and meaning "no"?' (i. 17) and he goes on—'Jesus Christ, the Son of God, whom Silvanus, Timothy and I have preached to you, is himself no doubtful quantity. He is the divine "Yes".'

The presence of Jews as well as Greeks among the Corinthians makes relevant the words in ch. iii concerning Moses and the 'old dispensation'. The point is not easy to grasp in the A.V. or R.V. because of the phrase 'the ministration of death' but in Phillips' version it is quite clear. If the old negative religion which is now outmoded was exhibited in such splendour on Mount Sinai how much more (a favourite type of argument with Paul) should the new life-giving religion be exhibited in splendour. And yet— there is no veil on the faces of Christians who are thus required to reflect the glory of the Lord.

In what other way can men understand Christ except through the personality of those who believe in him? A famous picture by Sir William Richmond called 'A performance of the Agamemnon' shows not the stage but the audience, and you gather from the intense look on their faces what it is that they are seeing on the stage. So it is, Paul would say, with Christians.

Reference should be made to Exod. xxxiv. 29–35.

From this point Paul goes on to contrast the transitory life with the life eternal. His preaching is based not on clever ideas of his own but on solemn convictions about God. We are his agents, reconciled to him by Christ, and thus reconciling the world to him. We are God's personal representatives—that is what being a Christian minister means. It is a hard life but a joyous one.

[This metaphor of the ambassador seeking to bring together his own nation and the nation to which he is accredited, should be worked out with some care. It means much more than 'preaching'.]

From this he passes to more specific matters concerning the Corinthians. They are apparently still sore under the rebuke of his last letter. At this point we have references to Titus whose relation to Paul should be noted.

He then deals with the question of their collections of money for their less fortunate fellow-Christians, and ix. 6–end set out the principles of Christian giving.

[This might be discussed. What is the right use of money set apart for 'the Lord's use'? Is it right to spend it on specifically Church matters when people around are starving? What is the situation of, say, an African Mission Church in this regard?]

In xiii. 11 comes Paul's final word. He begs them to be grown up ('perfected') not to behave like children. And so ends this most human of all Paul's writings.

The class might now be asked to write a character sketch of Paul from material supplied in these two letters.

CHAPTER XIV

EXAMINATION QUESTIONS

In the days when a paper in Divinity was required at Oxford by every candidate for a degree in any subject whatever, an ingenious person, called Hawkins, prepared the ideal cram book. It was so complete that every possible question had been foreseen, and it was scarcely necessary to read the Bible itself. Many men were thus examined in 'Hawkins' rather than in the Gospels. One great argument therefore for the abolition of this irksome examination was that it was purely factual and required merely unrelated knowledge, in which, be it said, Mr Hawkins was a virtuoso.

It is this 'unrelatedness' which blights so many examinations, as if mere acquaintance with facts was somehow in itself a good thing. To know, for example, the names of the various stopping places on St Paul's journeys and to be able to indicate them on a map has often been assumed to be a most useful accomplishment, and some candidates have prepared for such a question by forming the initial letters into mnemonics so as to get the places in the right order. This, of course, defeats any reasonable aim in teaching the subject at all, but such questions are all too common in examinations in Scripture.

On the other hand we have equally to beware of the question that is so general that it needs no acquaintance with the Bible at all. The question, for instance, 'What is our Lord's teaching about forgiveness?' may be answered by any fairly regular churchgoer who has heard sermons on the subject and who may have paid very little attention to the Scripture lesson in school. To ask the candidate to collect as many references as possible to our Lord's teaching on forgiveness is to require the underpinning of a general knowledge with a basis of specific fact.

The tendentious question also needs to be avoided. It is said that once in a paper on Church history there appeared the question:

'Give five reasons why Martin Luther was a bad man.' Without being so blatant as that, a good many Scripture questions contain within them the expected answer. This is particularly the case when the examiner takes the line that sound doctrine is the real aim of Scripture teaching. The old 'types of Christ' provided plenty of material for tendentious questions in the Old Testament; and the doctrines of the divinity of Christ, the Trinity, and the Atonement are often worked into questions in the New Testament. There are times and places when these are legitimate, but they are not always relevant and in Council schools they may, to some people, even be objectionable.

The purpose of examination questions therefore should be to discover not only what a person knows but also the manner in which he knows it. Consequently a good examination paper ought itself to be educational. It ought to suggest lines of inquiry which are relevant even though unfamiliar, and it is therefore a form of teaching. This will naturally become more and more the case as the children grow older, but even with younger forms a good deal can be suggested along these lines. For example, it is easy to set a purely factual question such as 'Give the meanings of *Talitha cumi, Ephphatha, Eloi lama sabachthani*, and state where they occur', but there is nothing particularly significant in the knowledge that is required by the answer. The same factual basis would be equally required if we restated the question thus: 'What indications do we get in the Gospels (or, alternatively, in the Gospel of Mark) of the language spoken by Jesus?' But while the factual requirement is the same the candidate is compelled to make some use of it and not simply to repeat it.

By way of illustration of these principles the following questions are here given. Many have already been used in school, and they are offered only as suggestions of the *kind* of thing that is desirable. Not every teacher will agree in every instance with the wording and they are all capable of improvement.

THE GOSPELS

(*Age 16*)

1. What is the meaning of the word 'Gospel'? Take any one of the Four Gospels and show how it justifies the description.

2. What conclusions do you draw from the differences between Matthew's and Luke's versions of the Beatitudes?

3. Who were the Pharisees? Give some account of Jesus' attitude towards them.

4. 'The poor ye have always with you, but me ye have not always.' Give the context in which this occurs and suggest a reason why Jesus said it.

5. Why do you think Judas betrayed Jesus? Was there anything to be said on his behalf?

6. What guidance do you get from the Gospels to help you to deal with the question of Sunday cinemas and Sunday games?

7. Is it true to say that the only motive for any of the miracles recorded in the Synoptic Gospels was to help someone in need? Are there any which seem to break this rule and if so what was their purpose?

8. Collect as many references as you can to Jesus' teaching on forgiveness.

9. In the light of the later saying that 'he was tempted in all points *like as we are*', what do you consider to have been the temptations of Jesus?

10. What relationship have you noticed between the baptism of Jesus and his transfiguration? Discuss the significance of these two events.

11. 'Unto you is given the mystery of the kingdom of God: but to them that are without all things are done in parables; that seeing they may see and not perceive, and hearing they may hear and not understand; lest haply they should turn again and it should be forgiven them.'
Expound this apparent paradox.

12. Write short notes on (two or three of) the following:
The unforgivable sin, the abomination of desolation, Corban, the cursing of the fig tree, the story of Zaccheus, the Magnificat.

13. How far do you think Handel's *Messiah* is a help or a hindrance to the understanding of the Gospels?

14. Compare the attitude to miracles in the Synoptic Gospels with that in the Fourth Gospel. What does this indicate about the character of the Fourth Gospel?

(Age 12)

1. What indications are there in the Gospels of the language spoken by Jesus?

2. Take any one of the parables *except* the parables of the sower and the tares, and explain its meaning. Why, do you think, have these two been excepted?

3. Trace the connexion of Jesus with John the Baptist.

4. Give an account of the temptations of Jesus and show how he overcame them.

5. 'No man putteth new wine into old wine-skins else the wine will burst the skins and the wine perisheth and the skins; but they put new wine into fresh wine-skins.'
Explain this saying of Jesus, mentioning, if you can, the situation in which it was said.

6. Mention some of the miracles of healing done by Jesus and tell fully the story of one of them.

7. Give an account of the Last Supper. Why do you think Jesus looked upon it as so important?

8. Who were the chief enemies of Jesus? What was the reason in each case for their hostility?

9. What did Jesus teach about (*a*) riches, (*b*) keeping the Sabbath, (*c*) prayer?

10. 'The dogs under the table eat of the children's crumbs.' Who said this and what was meant by it?

OLD TESTAMENT

(Age 16)

1. In what sense does the Old Testament 'foretell Christ'?

2. In the Hebrew Bible the Books Joshua to II Kings are called the book of 'the former prophets'. What does this indicate about the Old Testament view of history?

3. Account for the similarities and the differences between the message of Amos and the message of Hosea.

4. What conclusions do you draw from the fact that the story of Hezekiah and Sennacherib appears almost word for word in Isa. xxxvi–xxxviii and II Kings xviii–xix? Mention any other examples in the Old Testament of such duplication.

5. 'The idea of copyright was unknown to the ancients.' Illustrate this from the Old Testament.

6. Trace the events that led to the Exile. How far was it inevitable?

7. The Book of Job has been called a 'dramatic narrative'. Give a short account of its structure. How far do you consider its conclusion to be satisfactory?

8. What is the meaning of 'prophecy'? Give the names of the leading Old Testament prophets and classify them in some order of your own, giving your reasons.

9. What answer would you give to a man who insisted that the story of Jonah is 'a story about a whale'?

10. What were the questions at issue between Elijah and Ahab? Were there any redeeming features in Ahab's attitude and what criticism, if any, have you to offer of Elijah?

11. Compare the 'nationalism' of Ezekiel with that of the apocalyptic writers.

12. What views have you concerning the identity of 'the suffering Servant of the Lord'?

13. Is Milton's *Samson Agonistes* a reasonable treatment of the story in Judges?

14. What do you consider to be the religious value of the book of Genesis?

15. In what way would you account for the fact that in the later part of the Old Testament period the reign of David came to be looked upon as a Golden Age?

16. What are the characteristics of the 'wisdom literature'? How far do you consider it to be religious?

17. What answer would you give to the man to whom it was a stumbling-block that 'God hardened Pharaoh's heart and drowned him because his heart was hard'?

18. How was it that the destruction of the Northern Kingdom by Assyria produced no such spiritual results as the destruction of the Southern Kingdom by Babylon?

19. 'The way of Jeroboam the son of Nebat, and in his sins wherewith he made Israel to sin.' To what does this refer and how far was it a fair judgement?

20. Was Jeremiah a patriot or not?

(Age 12)

1. Compare the call of Abraham with the call of Moses.

2. Among the people of the Old Testament with whom you are familiar who is your particular hero, and why?

3. Why did the kingdom of Israel break up after the death of Solomon? Do you think it could have been prevented?

4. What is a 'prophet'? Give an account of any two prophets showing in what ways they were alike and in what ways they differed.

5. What foreign empires were concerned in the history of Israel and what outstanding events followed from this association?

6. Why did the people of Israel desire a King? Give some account of the first King of Israel.

7. Tell the story of Elijah on Mount Carmel. Do you think it was the right thing to slay the prophets of Baal? What are your reasons?

8. What is meant by a 'miracle'? Mention some Old Testament miracles known to you and narrate *one* of them in detail.

9. 'Go and wash in Jordan seven times and thy flesh shall come again to thee and thou shalt be clean.'
Tell the story of Naaman, Elisha and Gehazi. Naaman was cured when he dipped in the Jordan. Do you think Gehazi would similarly have been cured? What are your reasons?

10. Two men recently were going along the street and passed a certain very fine house. 'That house is my Naboth's vineyard', said one to the other. What was the reference?

11. What do you think is the value of reading the Old Testament?

12. 'The Assyrian came down like a wolf on the fold.' Who was he, and what happened to him?

ACTS AND EPISTLES, ETC.

(Age 16)

1. Gandhi has often been referred to as 'a real Christian'. What would St Paul have had to say about that?

2. What is the historical background of the Epistle to the Philippians?

3. Is it true to say that every one of St Paul's Epistles was written to deal with some specific problem? Discuss the problem dealt with by any one Epistle.

4. Account for the attitude to the Roman Empire found in Acts and the Epistles compared with the attitude in Revelation.

5. State St Paul's case for immortality. Is it convincing?

6. 'Meat offered to idols.' How does St Paul deal with this example of scrupulosity? Indicate a modern problem of the same kind and discuss the possible attitude of St Paul to it.

7. From what you know of Acts and the Epistles to the Corinthians give some account of the relations between St Paul and the Church at Corinth.

8. 'Great is Diana of the Ephesians.' What indications are there in Acts and the Epistles of the existence of other religions than Christianity? Say what you know of their characteristics.

9. What was the cause of St Paul's failure at Athens? What evidence can you give to show that he had profited by it?

10. Discuss the cause of the Jew's hostility to St Paul.

11. What was the occasion of the Epistle to the Galatians and what was St Paul's attitude?

12. What light have the archaeological discoveries of the last half-century thrown upon the language and background of the New Testament?

13. 'The image of the invisible God.'

'A man gluttonous, a wine-bibber, a friend of publicans and sinners.'

Which of these statements appears first in the literature of the New Testament? What significance do you attach to your answer?

14. What is meant by an *argumentum ad hominem*? What examples are there of it in Acts and the Epistles?

15. What was St Paul's attitude to the religion of the Gentiles as exhibited in the Epistle to the Romans?

GENERAL INDEX

Grading, 23 f.

Hammurabi, 50, 169
Handel, 79
Hannah, Song of, 91
Haverfield, F. J., 162, 186
Hebrew Bible, 45
Henry, Matthew, 5 f.
Hezekiah, 97 f.
Historical method, 155–63
History, teaching of, 3, 101
History, vista of, 42
Hobbes, T., 79
Hosea, 14, 47
Hoyle, F., 112, 213
Hudibras, 164
Huxley, T. H., 17, 25 f., 33
Hwyl, 81, 139
Hybris, 98
Hymns, 112

Idolatry, 178
Ignorance, 6
Ikhnaton, 170, 181
Illustrations, 63
Inspiration, 10–13
Inspiration, verbal, 5, 12
Isaiah, 36
Ivanhoe, 90

Jacob, 43
James, M. R., 68
Jehovah, 35
Jehu, 43, 96 f.
Jericho, 153
Jeroboam I, 45, 158
Jerusalem, 154
Joad, C. E. M., 10
Joanna, 83
John, Gospel of, 39
Johnson, Dr S., 164
Jonah, 67, 99
Jordan, the, 148, 152
Joseph, 95
Josephus, 64 n.

Lamb's *Tales from Shakespeare*, 133
Lamentations, 91 f.
Land and the Book, The, 147
Langlois and Seignobos, 157
Last Supper, The, 74
Lazarus, 72 f.

Learning by heart, 106, 139
Legend, 44 f., 115
Lessing, 130
Lewis, C. S., 10, 122
Library, 194
Lincoln, A., 165
Lincolnshire Poacher, The, 83
Lindsay, A. D., 122 f.
Lowell, J. R., 13

Macbeth, 4, 96, 133
Macedonia, 78
Mackay, J. A., 77
Magnificat, 91
Maine, Sir H. S., 19
Maps, 184–7
Marston, Sir C., 59
Merchant of Venice, 108, 183
Meshalim, 81
Metaphors, 87
Micah, 128
Middlemen, teachers as, 27 f.
Miletus, 173
Millar-Burrows, 59
Milton, 94, 163, 165
Miracles, 68 ff.
Moabite Stone, 169
Moberly, Dr, 3
Models, 192
Money-changers, 66 f., 178
Moral training, 18–20
Morton, H. V., 147
Motley, J. L., 4
Murray, G., 162
Myth, 45 f., 115

Naaman, 97, 126
Nahum, 171
Nebuchadnezzar, 98, 173
Nehemiah, 98
Newman, J. H., 17
Nomenclature, 154
Nunn, Sir T. P., 24

Oesterley, W., 89, 107
Old Testament, Jesus' use of, 67 f.
Omri, 154, 158 f.
Othello, 95

Palestine, 148
Parables, 131 f.
Parallelism, 82 f.

INDEX OF SCRIPTURE REFERENCES

(BY CHAPTERS ONLY)

INDEX OF SCRIPTURE REFERENCES

For EU product safety concerns, contact us at Calle de José Abascal, 56–1°,
28003 Madrid, Spain or eugpsr@cambridge.org.

www.ingramcontent.com/pod-product-compliance
Ingram Content Group UK Ltd.
Pitfield, Milton Keynes, MK11 3LW, UK
UKHW010339140625
459647UK00010B/701